THE COLLAPSE OF NATIONALIST CHINA

When World War II ended, Chiang Kai-shek seemed at the height of his power – the leader of Nationalist China, one of the victorious Allied Powers in 1945, and with the financial backing of the US. Yet less than four years later, he lost China's civil war against the communists. Offering an insightful chronological treatment of the years 1944 to 1949, Parks Coble addresses why Chiang was unable to win the war and control hyperinflation. Using newly available archival sources, he reveals the critical weakness of Chiang's style of governing, the fundamental structural flaws in the Nationalist government, bitter personal rivalries, and Chiang's personal lack of interest in finance. This major work of revisionist scholarship will engage all those interested in the shaping of twentieth-century history.

Parks M. Coble is James L. Sellers Professor of History at the University of Nebraska–Lincoln.

THE COLLAPSE OF
NATIONALIST CHINA

How Chiang Kai-shek Lost China's Civil War

Parks M. Coble

University of Nebraska–Lincoln

CAMBRIDGE
UNIVERSITY PRESS

CAMBRIDGE
UNIVERSITY PRESS

Shaftesbury Road, Cambridge CB2 8EA, United Kingdom

One Liberty Plaza, 20th Floor, New York, NY 10006, USA

477 Williamstown Road, Port Melbourne, VIC 3207, Australia

314–321, 3rd Floor, Plot 3, Splendor Forum, Jasola District Centre,
New Delhi – 110025, India

103 Penang Road, #05–06/07, Visioncrest Commercial, Singapore 238467

Cambridge University Press is part of Cambridge University Press & Assessment,
a department of the University of Cambridge.

We share the University's mission to contribute to society through the pursuit of
education, learning and research at the highest international levels of excellence.

www.cambridge.org
Information on this title: www.cambridge.org/9781009297615

DOI: 10.1017/9781009297639

First published 2023

Printed in the United Kingdom by TJ Books Limited, Padstow Cornwall

A catalogue record for this publication is available from the British Library.

Library of Congress Cataloging-in-Publication Data
Names: Coble, Parks M., 1946- author.
Title: The collapse of Nationalist China : how Chiang Kai-Shek lost China's Civil War /
Parks Coble, University of Nebraska, Lincoln.
Description: Cambridge ; New York, NY : Cambridge University Press, 2023. | Includes
bibliographical references and index.
Identifiers: LCCN 2022057929 | ISBN 9781009297615 (hardback) | ISBN
9781009297646 (paperback) | ISBN 9781009297639 (ebook)
Subjects: LCSH: China – History – Civil War, 1945–1949. | China – Politics and
government – 1945–1949. | Chiang, Kai-shek, 1887–1975.
Classification: LCC DS777.54 .C63 2023 | DDC 951.04/2–dc23/eng/20230110
LC record available at https://lccn.loc.gov/2022057929

ISBN 978-1-009-29761-5 Hardback

Contents

Figures

Acknowledgments

I have accumulated numerous debts to individuals and institutions in the years spent researching and writing this study. None is greater than the support I have received from my home institution, the University of Nebraska–Lincoln. My colleagues in the history department have created an environment that encouraged research, and the university provided assistance throughout. I have been the James L. Sellers Professor of History since 2007, a position providing substantial research support. I am deeply grateful to the late Catherine and John Angle for their generosity. My chair is named for James L. Sellers, a distinguished historian who taught at the University of Nebraska from 1930 until 1959, through the difficult days of the Depression and World War II, and who was the father of Catherine Angle.

The archives of the Hoover Institution on War, Revolution, and Peace at Stanford University provided some of the most valuable material for this study. I thank the staff at Hoover for their assistance and support and particularly for a Visiting Research Grant for a visit in June 2016. Earlier in April 2015, I received a Visiting Research Grant for work at the Stanford University East Asian Library, awarded through Stanford's Title VI National Resource Center Grant from the Department of Education. The contents of this book were developed under grant #84.015A from the US Department of Education. However, these contents do not necessarily represent the policy of the US Department of Education, and you should not assume endorsement by the Federal Government.

I have been privileged to be an associate-in-research at the Fairbank Center at Harvard University for many years. This has allowed access to the libraries of Harvard, particularly the Harvard-Yenching Library and the Fairbank Collection at the Fung Library. I thank especially Nancy Hearst of the Fairbank Collection. Visits to Harvard also afforded the opportunity for informal discussions with scholars from around the world. It is impossible to list all who were helpful, but I would like to single out the late Ezra Vogel. Not only did he provide encouragement, but he organized important conferences, bringing together Chinese, Japanese, and Western scholars, which impacted my work.

I have been an inveterate conference-goer during my entire career, attending most regularly the Midwest Conference on Asian Affairs, the American Historical Association annual meeting, and in particular the meetings of the Association for Asian Studies (of which I am a fifty-year member). Perhaps the most significant conferences have been those with a specific research agenda with invited participants. My deepest debt of gratitude goes to Professor Wu Jingping of the Department of History at Fudan University who generously invited me to attend several such meetings in Shanghai and provided financial support for travel, which enabled me to connect with scholars and graduate students in China and internationally. Most generously, I had the opportunity to present my own research and receive the advice of Chinese colleagues.

This began in November 2013 when I presented at the "Symposium on the Soong Family and the Development of Modern China," held at Fudan University and sponsored by the Modern China Research Center of Leadership and Archival Documents at that institution, the Hoover Institution at Stanford, and the Shanghai Soong Ching-ling Research Institute, with support from the Asia Pacific Fund. In October 2014, I participated in the "Symposium on the Soong Family and the Development of Modern China," sponsored by the Modern China Research Center of Leadership and Archival Documents of Fudan University and the Shanghai Soong Ching-ling Foundation. I then presented at the conference "Bankers and Shanghai's Financial Transformation," sponsored by the Fudan University Research Center on the History of China's Finance, the Shanghai Research Institute on Financial Regulation, and the Shanghai Municipal Archives. In July of 2015, I attended the "Symposium on the Collection and Study of the Soong Family's Archives: The Soong Family and World War II," an invaluable experience that also allowed me to meet descendants of the Soong family. In August of 2015, I presented at "Shanghai Finance during the War of Resistance against Japan," a symposium sponsored by the Center for China's Financial Studies, Fudan University, and the Shanghai Institute of Financial Legislation.

In October 2016, I presented at the conference "Shanghai Finance: From the Perspective of the Interaction between Treaty Ports," jointly organized by the Fudan University Center for China's Financial History Studies and the Shanghai Institute of Financial Legislation. The following October, I presented at "The Symposium on Financial Risk Management in the Perspective of Globalization and Changes in Industry," jointly organized by the Fudan University Center for China's Financial History Studies and the Shanghai Institute of Financial Legislation. Finally, in May of 2018 I presented at a conference, "Studying in America and Modern China's Finance, Economics, and Diplomacy," at Fudan University. In addition to the Fudan conferences, I gained invaluable insights when I presented at the conference "Modern China in World Affairs: Interaction and Mutual Influence," jointly organized by the Chinese Academy of Social Sciences, Institute of Modern History, and the Historical Society for 20th Century China, held in Beijing in August 2016. I thank all the abovementioned agencies for their support in allowing me to participate in these conferences.

I gained many insights over the course of my encounters with Chinese and international scholars in China and owe debts to many more individuals than can be named here. But in addition to Professor Wu Jingping, I would like to thank the following for comments given at the above conferences: Chen Hongmin, Nancy Gao, Kubo Toru, the late Lai Chikong, Pei-tak Lee, Lin Mei-li, Liu Zhiying, Ma Linghe, Ma Zhendu, Mou Libang, Shiroyama Tomoko, Wang Chaoguang, Xiong Yuezhi, Xu Ang, Yang Tianshi, Zheng Huixin, and Zhuo Zunhong.

Over the course of the years in which I was writing this study I gained support and insights from many individuals. I would especially seek to thank Morris Bian, Sherman Cochran, Po-shek Fu, Grace Huang, Emily Hill, Kang Jin A, Elisabeth Köll, Diana Lary, Sophia Lee, Greg Lewis, Lin Man-houng, Stephen MacKinnon, Ghassan Moazzin, Brett Sheehan, and Margherita Zanasi. I also thank my editor at Cambridge University Press,

Lucy Rhymer, for her significant assistance, as well as two anonymous reviewers for the press who provided valuable feedback on this study. Emily Plater arranged permissions for the images used in the text.

This study is dedicated to the late Lloyd E. Eastman, my graduate mentor and friend who did so much to shape the field of study of Republican China before his untimely death. This study had its origins in questions raised half a century ago in classes, seminars, and discussions at the University of Illinois at Urbana–Champaign. At that time the archival sources proved insufficient to undertake this project. Yet I constantly recalled those discussions so many years ago as I wrote this study.

Introduction

O N AUGUST 15, 1945, JAPANESE EMPEROR HIROHITO BROAD-
cast a speech announcing the surrender of the Empire of Japan
to the Allied Powers. At that moment, Chiang Kai-shek (Jiang Jieshi),
leader of the Republic of China, seemed at the peak of his prestige and
power. American president Franklin Roosevelt had elevated China to the
status of one of the "Big Four" Allied Powers (Figure 0.1), although
neither Joseph Stalin of the Soviet Union nor Winston Churchill of
Great Britain favored the move. At the new United Nations organization,
China and the other Big Four Powers, joined by France, would be given
permanent membership (with a veto power) on the Security Council.
China had seemingly achieved the status of a great power and Chiang of
its supreme leader.

There were other victories. During the war, the Chiang government
had fulfilled many of the goals set by Sun Yat-sen, whose legacy Chiang
claimed. Embarrassed that a wartime ally was treated as a second-class
nation, the United States and Great Britain agreed to end the infamous
"unequal treaties." When Nationalist forces returned to coastal cities such
as Shanghai, the old foreign concessions were no more; the Chinese were
in charge. Institutions imposed on China during the heyday of Western
imperialism, such as the Maritime Customs Service, would fade from the
scene. The United States even made limited changes in the Chinese
Exclusion policy that prohibited immigration of most Chinese to
America. Facing Japanese wartime propaganda that they were fighting to
free Asia from white imperialism, President Roosevelt persuaded the
American Congress to modify US immigration policy in December 1943.
The move was largely symbolic, as the quota for new entry visas for Chinese

0.1. The Big Four Allied Leaders from World War II: Winston Churchill (Great Britain), Franklin Roosevelt (United States), Joseph Stalin (Soviet Union), and Chiang Kai-shek (China). Photo Quest/Archive Photos/Getty Images

was set at 105 annually. And though extraterritoriality was gone, American military personnel could usually operate in China without facing Chinese judicial authorities. Chinese-Americans still faced discrimination and racism in a segregated America. President Truman would not be as accommodating as Roosevelt had been to Chiang and his family.

Yet few could deny that he and his famous American-educated wife Soong Mei-ling (Song Meiling) were global stars in the postwar era. And few in August 1945 could imagine that a mere four years later, Chiang would be driven from the mainland of China to a humiliating exile on the island of Taiwan. Certainly, neither Stalin nor Truman would have believed it; and despite his optimism Mao would have been startled to know that it had occurred so quickly. The collapse of Chiang's government between 1945 and 1949 was one of the most stunning and significant events of the twentieth century.

What happened? How could a leader and a regime that seemed at the peak of its power collapse so quickly? In hindsight there were clear signs that the Chiang government was in trouble, although these were not widely known outside of the inner circle of "China hands." Observers of the Nationalist military on the scene, from General Joseph Stilwell on down, felt that its caliber and effectiveness was deteriorating. The catastrophic performance of Chiang's forces in countering the Japanese Ichigo campaign was seen by many as proof of the incompetence of his leadership. Chiang by contrast blamed that failure on the Americans, especially Stilwell, who had moved many Chinese forces into the campaign in Burma, leaving areas of China unprotected and inviting Japanese attack, in Chiang's view. After the surrender of the Japanese, Chiang had to rely on American help in transporting his troops to regain control of occupied areas. Most outsiders found the behavior of these troops and the officials who accompanied them as undercutting the legitimacy of the Nationalist government. Corruption, looting, and inefficiency led to a "botched liberation" of Japanese-held territory.

Chiang was obsessed with his communist opponents. He even had some Japanese troops or those of the puppet regimes established by the Japanese remain on duty in the occupied areas rather than permit the communists to take the surrender of the Japanese. Although several American advisers warned him about stretching his forces too thinly, he would have Nationalist troops airlifted to the northeast (the old Japanese puppet state of Manchukuo) as the Soviets withdrew. Both Americans and Soviets underestimated the Chinese communists, who had created a formidable political and military structure during the war against Japan. After careful maneuvering, they isolated many of Chiang's forces in the northeast and north and switched with lightning effectiveness from a guerrilla strategy to positional warfare. The result was a stunning collapse by Chiang's forces, which seemed to crumble totally in the last weeks of 1948.

For almost three decades after 1949, scholarship on the Civil War period was quite limited. In China, the Maoist narrative allowed for little flexibility in interpreting the communist victory. The onset of the Cultural Revolution virtually shut down academic historical inquiry in China for the last years of Mao's life. In the West (but less so in Japan), the politically charged atmosphere made work on the era problematic. The Korean War and American support for the Republic of China on Taiwan strongly favored an anticommunist narrative in the United States. Archives and research opportunities in the People's Republic were closed. A handful of classic studies of the Civil War era – many by participants in the events of the struggle – did appear, but they were few in number. All of this finally began to change with the "reform and opening" policy launched by Deng Xiaoping in 1978. The result has been a wave of new scholarly writing in China, Japan, and the West about the war against Japan and the Chinese Civil War.

In China, most of the new writing concerns the War of Resistance against Japan. A virtual avalanche of new scholarship, accompanied by an outpouring of popular writing, motion pictures, and television dramas, has dealt with the war. Why did this suddenly emerge? Perhaps the key factor is that since June 1989 the Beijing government has promoted nationalism as a key element in the appeal and legitimacy of the communist government. Much of the popular writing and dramatization of the war stresses both the cruel nature of Japanese atrocities and the heroic resistance of Chinese. This "patriotic nationalist narrative" has perhaps skewed some of the research on the war. Episodes that reflected poorly on China, such as the Ichigo campaign, were often ignored. Under Mao, writing on the war stressed only the heroic leadership of the Chairman and the Chinese Communist Party (CCP). Chiang and the Nationalists were given little credit for resisting Japan. In the new nationalist writing on the war, it became possible to celebrate Chiang's role – his trip to India or meeting with Roosevelt and Churchill in Cairo. More recently under Xi Jinping this trend has halted, and more emphasis has been placed once again on the communist role.[1]

This outpouring of new writing in China on the war against Japan has not been matched by work on the Civil War period. In part because it was a civil war, it is not so useful in promoting patriotism among young Chinese. And in China, there is little room for ideological flexibility in discussing this conflict. In the West and Japan as well, the Civil War era has not drawn as much attention as the war against Japan. Still compared to the paucity of publications in the early decades after 1949, there has been a significant increase in studies that deal with this conflict. Not surprisingly, the great majority of this scholarship has focused on the Chinese communists and the elements that led to their success. A lively debate about the causes of that success has broadened as archival access has made possible far more detailed studies of individual communist base areas. This has led to recognition that there was an enormous diversity in regional factors creating success or failure for the communist movement.

There has been less new scholarship on the Nationalists, but key works by Rana Mitter, Hans van de Ven, Diana Lary, and others have provided a much richer understanding of the collapse of Chiang's regime. One important feature of much of this writing is that many of these works have sought to reach a broader audience than just the academic world. The often-neglected military side of things has been increasingly covered, with new work by scholars such as Odd Arne Westad and Harold Tanner among others. Even familiar topics in Western scholarship such as George Marshall's ill-fated mission have gotten a new treatment in Daniel Kurtz-Phelan's recent study.[2] As a consequence, both academic and general readers now have access to a much wider range of scholarship than before.

COLLAPSE OF THE NATIONALIST CURRENCY

This study primarily revisits an old issue, inflation (later hyperinflation) in Guomindang (Nationalist) China during the war against Japan and accelerating in the Civil War period. Virtually all studies of the failure of the Nationalist government note the important role of hyperinflation in weakening the regime. The actual facts of the situation have been well known since the events themselves. In the 1950s and 1960s, classic studies by Arthur N. Young, a financial advisor to the Chiang Kai-shek government during war against Japan and Civil War years, and Chang Kia-ngau (Zhang Jia'ao), a key banker and government official, detailed the problem of inflation.[3] In November 1935, the Nationalist Government created a new currency, fabi, issued by the four government banks – the Central Bank of China, the Bank of China, the Bank of Communications, and the Agricultural Bank. When the war with Japan erupted in the summer of 1937, Chiang put up fierce resistance on the east coast before ultimately retreating to Chongqing (Chungking) and the base of "Free

China" during the long war against Japan. By October 1938, with the fall of Wuhan and Guangzhou, the Nationalists had lost the heart of their economy – the lower Yangzi and coastal areas. Tax receipts plummeted while military expenses remained high. By 1941, for instance, government expenditures topped 10 billion yuan, but revenue was only 1.3 billion yuan. Printing money covered most of the difference.[4]

But printing currency was but a short-term solution. Paper money declined in value, and prices of commodities rose along with the money supply. An index of commodity prices in Free China compiled by adviser Arthur Young used the average prices from January to June 1937 as a base of 1.0. Four-and-one-half years later when the Japanese attacked Pearl Harbor and declared war on America and Great Britain, the price index in Free China had increased by nearly twenty times (or 19.8). This was a substantial change but not one that would have been permanently crippling to the economy. Yet after China joined America and Britain as allies against Japan, the situation worsened. Japan occupied British Burma and French Indochina, isolating "Free China" from the outside world. By the end of 1943, the price index stood at 228 and in the last two years of the war accelerated, reaching 755 in December 1944, then 2,167 in June 1945, and then 2,647 in August 1945. The rise in prices accompanied the vast increase in the amount of fabi issued by the government. Using the amount of currency in circulation in June 1937 as a base of 1, the total amount was 10.75 in December 1941, 53.57 in December 1943, and 733.5 in December 1946. The actual increase was even more pronounced because the area in which it circulated (Free China) was much smaller than was the case when war erupted. The value of fabi shrank in proportion to the vast increase in notes being circulated, and the Guomindang government was greatly weakened in the process.[5]

Yet when the war ended, there was a feeling among observers such as Arthur Young that the situation could be rectified. After all, the Nationalists would regain control of the east coast, the economic heartland of their old government that had provided most of the tax revenue. Commodities had been scarce in "Free China," which was isolated from the world economy. With the reopening of ports such as Shanghai, foreign trade could revive; customs revenue might recover. It was widely assumed there would be a "peace dividend" as military activities were scaled back. Moreover, the United States had emerged from the war as the dominant economic force globally. As an ally, America would likely provide the assistance China needed to revive economically and to restore confidence in fabi. Despite wartime deprivations, China had a significant amount of foreign exchange to serve as a reserve. In February 1946, the Central Bank of China had holdings of gold, silver, and foreign exchange worth more than US$822 million.[6] So there seemed to be the prospect that in postwar China the economy might revive and the currency might be stabilized with no more than a manageable degree of inflation.

But this was not to be; the currency situation actually worsened after Japanese surrender. There would be no "peace dividend." Victory over Japan did not bring reduced military spending, as Chiang gave absolute priority to preparing for, what he saw as, the inevitable showdown with the communists. Meanwhile, after Guomindang authorities regained control of the lower Yangzi and coastal China, they were unable to revive foreign trade and the overall economy of the area. Consequently, tax receipts from the liberated region remained weak. Faced with continued high expenses and limited revenue, the Chiang government returned to the printing presses to pour out more banknotes.

AFTER JAPANESE SURRENDER

The sudden onset of peace did lead to a brief drop in prices as hoarders unloaded some of their goods, and for a few weeks commodity prices actually fell. In August 1945, prices dropped by almost one-third on average, the only real decrease during the postwar situation under Chiang. But this "peace dividend" would be very short lived. By October 1945, hyperinflation resumed with a vengeance.[7] As Frank Tamagna, then a financial advisor to the Executive Yuan, wrote "inflation hit Shanghai like a typhoon."[8]

In September 1945, the wholesale price index in Shanghai (using January to June 1937 as a base of 1) stood at almost 346. By December 1945, it was over 885; by June 1946, over 3,724; and by December of that year, 5,713. In June 1947, it had soared to 29,931 and by the end of that year, 83,796. In the next six months, price went up tenfold, with the index reaching 884,800 in June 1948. On August 21, 1948, the last day of fabi, the wholesale price index was 4,927,000. An item priced at one yuan in 1937 would now cost almost 5 million yuan![9] Newspapers carried pictures of people using wheelbarrows of currency to do daily shopping and shippers using shredded banknotes as packing material. Foreign observers noted the similarity to the situation in the ill-fated Weimar Republic of Germany. The Chiang government abandoned fabi in August of 1948 for the new gold yuan notes – which would fail with greater rapidity than fabi.[10]

The collapse of the value of the fabi in the Civil War era was not the result of setbacks on the battlefield by military forces. Major drops in its value preceded military losses by the Nationalists. By the time the collapse of Chiang's military position was imminent in late 1948, fabi was already gone. Currency collapse was a precursor of – not a result of – military failure.

But do we need to revisit this issue? In the decades since 1978, new sources and archives in China and globally have certainly increased our understanding of hyperinflation in wartime and Civil War China. In her 1996 study of inflation during the war of resistance period, Lin Meili was able to refine the figures for government spending and the deficit and provide detailed analyses of commodity prices in a variety of cities in Free and occupied China.[11] Yet the picture that emerges of relentless government deficits and inflation as the money supply increased is basically the same as that detailed in the early studies by Arthur Young and Zhang Jia'ao. So a new study will not dramatically alter the facts of what happened. This study will address instead two other questions.

First, what was the impact of the inflationary policy on the political and military situation of Guomindang China in the Civil War era? Hyperinflation was a precursor of military failure by the Guomindang, but was it a cause of that failure? One could argue that the value of the currency impacted only a minority of the people of China. Rural Chinese could avoid currency and tap into a barter economy. Many urban factory workers had contracts which adjusted their wages in tandem with the commodity price index. The Chiang government wanted to nip labor unrest in the bud to prevent the communists from capitalizing on it.[12]

Yet those most strongly impacted by hyperinflation were the military and civilian employees of the Nationalist government. For most, the actual value of their wages shrank daily during this period. Army officers, college professors, and government clerks – few could live on the actual wages received. This situation invited corruption and pilfering – an almost universally acknowledged phenomenon in the Guomindang regime in this era. The collapse of morale and effectiveness of the Nationalist military – so obvious in the Civil War – was a direct result of poor pay and corruption. Little funding trickled down to the enlisted soldiers, who were usually malnourished and ill equipped. Desertion was common.

The second – and more intriguing question – is why did this policy persist? Observing the impact of the printing-press approach to government deficits is a bit like watching a car crash in slow motion. Could nothing have been done to prevent this? One could argue that during the war against Japan when the Chiang government was trapped in interior China, isolated from the outside world and facing extinction at the hands of an external enemy, there was no other credible option. But after August 1945 with coastal China and the lower Yangzi regained, with access to world markets possible and with American support and aid likely, why did the Chiang government continue this disastrous policy? Were no other options available?

It is perhaps in answering this second question that the new archival and published material supports a much clearer portrait of the decision-making within the Chiang government. Much of this material is at the Hoover Institution Archives at Stanford University. Mostly famously, the opening of the Chiang Kai-shek diaries has upended the world of Republican studies. Scholars primarily from China have flocked to Hoover to consult these documents. Hoover also contains the T. V. Soong Papers, now fully opened; the partially opened archives of H. H. Kung; and those of many key players in the Guomindang era. Both Arthur Young and Chang Kia-ngau (Zhang Jia'ao) published classic studies about China's inflation from an insider perspective. Both published in the 1950s and 1960s after they left China. Yet ultimately both strongly opposed the new People's Republic of China so pulled their punches in criticizing the Chiang Kai-shek government. Arthur Young was a bit more forthcoming in his privately published *Cycle of Cathay: An Historical Perspective* in 1997, in which he was more candid in discussing key personnel in the financial circles of Guomindang China. But he was far more so in the unpublished material in his now fully opened archives at the Hoover Institution.[13]

This study will seek to understand the "why" of the decision-making process of the Guomindang government in its currency and financial policy as well as the impact of hyperinflation on China at large. The root of the weaknesses of fabi can be found in both its creation in 1935 and in decisions made during the war of resistance against Japan. A decided turning point in its downfall, however, occurred with the Japanese Ichigo campaign undertaken late in the war against Japan. More broadly, the new understanding afforded to us about decision-making in the Chiang government gives insight into failures in military and political areas.

FABI'S FATAL WEAKNESS

Fabi was created in November 1935 when the fiat currency replaced the silver standard. H. H. Kung (Kong Xiangxi), Madame Chiang Kai-shek's brother-in-law, served as minister of finance and directed the creation of the new currency. Fabi had been in circulation less than two years when the war with Japan erupted. The creation of this currency had been supported by both Great Britain and the United States, and it was widely accepted in China. Many nations have established institutions to regulate the money supply that are insulated to some degree from political influence. In the United States, for example, the Federal Reserve Board is supposed to make decisions about money supply without political interference. These systems do not always perform flawlessly but can help in creating public confidence in the currency. But the arrangements made for the creation of fabi in 1935 provided no real checks and balances, leaving political leaders with a free hand in setting the money supply.

Many private and even government bankers had vivid memories of the warlord era in China, when regional militarists tried to use banks as a source of revenue by having them issue unlimited currency. Chang Kia-ngau , as long-time manager of the Bank of China, had tried to insulate the bank from political control. Most famously in 1916 when he was at the Shanghai branch of the bank, he refused an order by Yuan Shikai, the leader of the Beijing government, to cease redeeming the bank's notes for silver. Because of his independence, Chang was removed as the general manager in 1935 before the fabi reform. He was replaced by T. V. Soong (Song Ziwen), Chiang Kai-shek's brother-in-law. Chang had recommended that the Central Bank of China be made a reserve bank, separated from the Ministry of Finance, and made independent so that the supply of money could be regulated without political interference. Inflation could be kept in check. But that was not to be.[14]

Although the inflationary aspect of the new currency system did not become obvious until after the war with Japan started, Chang Kia-ngau realized the direction fabi was headed even before July 7, 1937. He observed that "the Central Bank never gained independent status and no serious attempt was made to reorganize government finances." Between the creation of the currency in November 1935 and the outbreak of war in the summer of 1937, the amount of currency in circulation increased from 453 million yuan to 1,477 million yuan. "Only about half of this increase represented notes issued against silver surrendered," he noted.[15] In other words, the government had already started printing paper currency and increasing the money supply before the war started. The stage was set for wartime inflation.

The war situation created a new set of problems for fabi currency. China was in many ways a semicolonial country at the start of the conflict. The treaty ports were islands of foreign control where international banks such as the Hongkong and Shanghai Banking Corporation operated behind a curtain of extraterritoriality. The Guomindang government could not really control the actions of foreign banks in China. This became obvious when the banks began to move hard currency out of China (primarily from Shanghai) between the Marco Polo Bridge Incident of July 7, 1937, and the start of fighting in the Shanghai area on August 13, 1937. Fabi was convertible to hard currency, and the government in Nanjing was slow to adjust this policy. In the nearly five weeks from the Marco Polo Bridge Incident to the start of the battle of Shanghai, an equivalent of 423 million yuan in foreign exchange left China, most of it moved by the foreign banks.[16]

Even after the Guomindang forces retreated west, many anomalies of the treaty-port system continued. Although the Chinese portion of Shanghai was occupied, much of the International Settlement and the French Concession remained an unoccupied "solitary island" (*gudao*), a neutral area surrounded by Japanese-occupied territory. Because the conflict between China and Japan was not a declared war, many foreign institutions, such as banks, operated in the "solitary island" as if the war were not happening. Only after Pearl Harbor in December 1941 did Japan declare war on the United States and Great Britain, ending the special status for Shanghai.

KEEPING FABI CONVERTIBLE

As a matter of prestige, the Nationalist government was determined that fabi would remain convertible into foreign currencies and, for the first eight months of the conflict, tried to hold the prewar exchange rate of US$0.30 to 1 yuan. The Chiang government expended large amounts of foreign exchange to hold this rate until March 1938.[17] The foreign "isolated islands" were surrounded by territory occupied and controlled by Japan. It was widely believed that the Japanese exploited this arrangement, a view held by Chinese historian Qi Chunfeng. Japanese authorities, Qi argues, accumulated fabi in the occupied areas and then converted this to hard currency in Shanghai and Tianjin.[18] At the time, the major Chinese banking journal *Yinhang zhoubao* (Bankers' weekly) warned that Japan could devour China's foreign-exchange reserves.[19]

Eventually the situation became untenable, and on March 13, 1938, China had to impose severe limits on the purchase of foreign exchange with fabi. Even so, the foreign banks could evade many of the controls and continue to move money out of China. But key nationalist leaders including H. H. Kung, the minister of finance, felt that China had to keep some level of convertibility of fabi to curb the influence of currencies issued by the client regimes of Japan. Others argued then and later that the convertibility policy aided Japan because it provided hard currency that could be used to finance Japan's war plans.[20] They also argued that trying to maintain the financial markets in Shanghai and Tianjin during wartime simply served the needs of the imperialist powers and not those of China.[21]

But H. H. Kung remained adamant. He felt that Chongqing was in a currency war with the Japanese client regimes in Beijing and Nanjing. If fabi remained convertible, even with restrictions, people in the occupied area would continue to hold the currency, and the Japanese could not establish complete economic control.[22] If that population lost their trust in fabi and abandoned it for banknotes of the client states, a flood of the fabi notes would move back into Free China, which would spark more inflation.[23]

T. V. Soong was in Washington in December 1940 as Chiang Kai-shek's special representative. He telegraphed Chiang that he had heard rumors that Chongqing was prepared to abandon fabi in Shanghai. Chiang consulted H. H. Kung, who stated explicitly that:

> in fact, the ministry had never made statement about abandoning fabi in any city during the past several years. In view of such rumors month ago, a statement released in English language reiterated that government's policy on fabi currency had not changed and after receiving US loans, our currency reserves are stronger than ever. The public should not believe in rumors and fall into trap.[24]

Chiang did emphasize to Soong that stabilization loans from the United States and Britain would be crucial in maintaining the stability of fabi, but clearly both Kung and Chiang were committed to keeping the exchange market open in the "solitary island" in Shanghai.

In early 1941, one of American president Franklin Roosevelt's closest aides, Lauchlin Currie, had made a trip to China. Technically, this was at the request of the Chinese government, which paid for his expenses and even covered his government salary during his absence. His trip thus did not violate American neutrality in the Sino-Japanese War, at least on paper. In reality, Franklin D. Roosevelt was seeking ways to shore up China while Chiang, eager for American aid, saw Currie as having direct access to the American president. Currie did deliver a verbal message of support to Chiang from Roosevelt on his first meeting on February 8, 1941. On the convertibility issue, Currie concluded that trying to maintain the exchange market in Shanghai had many disadvantages and only one significant plus. Closing Shanghai would lead to a huge flow of fabi from occupied China into Free China, which would stimulate inflation.

He suggested to Chiang that they keep Shanghai open but develop a market for foreign exchange in Chongqing.[25]

Shortly after Currie returned to Washington, Kung wrote to him about this issue. "Throughout our four years' bitter struggle, the Chinese Government, realizing that the outcome of the struggle depends to a great extent upon the upholding of the currency structure, has exerted every effort to maintain the national currency." Kung reiterated that "the Chinese Government has never failed to support the currency to the best of its ability." Kung noted, however, that few applications for foreign exchange now came from the "isolated island" in Shanghai, presumably because they had access to the "black market."[26]

Another strong advocate of convertibility was Arthur Young, who stressed the advantages fabi had in the occupied areas. Its convertibility gave it "an outstanding advantage" in competition with currencies of client regimes.[27] In many rural areas of the occupied zone, actual control was held not by the Japanese military, which was thinly spread, but by Chinese guerrillas. Because the latter preferred to use fabi, "exports from this hinterland, even though sold through occupied ports, had to be ultimately paid in Chinese currency."[28] Young was certainly aware of reports that the policy was being exploited by the Japanese to accumulate foreign exchange but doubted the significance of this phenomenon.[29] In 1958, long after the war concluded, Young met in Tokyo with several Japanese bankers who were in China during the conflict. They believed that it was primarily Chinese bankers, not the Japanese, who converted fabi into hard currencies to get assets out of China during the period before Pearl Harbor. At that point, Young candidly admitted this was likely to be true, that Chinese bankers may have been responsible.[30]

But large government deficits and a reliance on the printing press to cover the red ink were too strong a force for the market to resist. The foreign-exchange value of the yuan, which was just over twenty-nine cents in July 1937, dropped to only six cents in December of 1940. The chief competitor for fabi in north China was the currency issued by the Wang Kemin client regime in Beijing. It expanded note issue by 450 percent from 1938 to 1941, and its currency lost value. But fabi declined more rapidly, so that by the end of 1940 its value fell below that of the Beijing issue. Arthur Young concluded that during 1941, the notes issued by the

Wang Kemin government "became the chief currency of occupied north China."[31] Chongqing had lost the currency war in north China.

The Japanese established a separate client regime in central China under Wang Jingwei, a prominent Nationalist politician who defected to Japan. His government in Nanjing was slow to set up a bank and issue currency but had done so by December 1941 when the Japanese attacked Pearl Harbor. Fabi was still widely held in the "solitary island" in Shanghai and in the occupied areas in the Yangzi Valley. But once Japan was at war with Great Britain and the United States, it quickly occupied foreign Shanghai and Tianjin. The anomaly of the "solitary islands" ended. Japanese seized most of the banks in Shanghai and declared that all fabi had to be exchanged for banknotes of the new Wang Jingwei government in Nanjing. A deadline of June 1, 1942, was set; after that date, fabi would be worthless.[32] When those living in the occupied zone surrendered their fabi notes, the Nanjing client state mandated a 2:1 ratio in favor of the Wang Jingwei government bank. For most Chinese, this meant their fabi notes lost half of their value, wiping out much of their savings and delivering a serious blow to the economy of the lower Yangzi.[33]

AFTER PEARL HARBOR

With the United States and Great Britain now fighting against Japan, the conflict became a declared war, with China joining the Allied Powers. Direct aid and supplies of military equipment could now be made to the Chiang government, and Roosevelt no longer needed to be concerned with the American neutrality laws. But in reality, China's fiscal situation actually worsened in the months after Pearl Harbor. Japanese forces overran British Burma, cutting off the last land route to Free China. Chongqing became even more isolated from the outside world. Trade was minuscule, and government deficits grew worse. Even morale declined, as many in the Nationalist government were now content to let Americans and the Allies bear the brunt of the fighting. China had fought alone for four-and-one-half years; it had endured bombardment of its cities, particularly Chongqing. Now others could bear the burden of countering Japan. The index for commodity prices in Free China using

January to June 1937 as a base of 1 had increased almost twentyfold by the attack on Pearl Harbor. By the end of 1943, it had soared to 228. But the worst was yet to come.

As weak as fabi was in 1942 and 1943, sinking rapidly in value, the situation might have been worse if the Japanese had adopted a more unified approach to eliminating fabi. But Japanese agents were divided. The North China Army, which had established the Wang Kemin government and bank in Beijing, would not fully yield to the central-China Japanese leaders who wanted the Wang Jingwei government and its banknotes to reign supreme. The result was that Japan maintained two separate currency zones in occupied China. In north China, the Wang Kemin notes were pegged to the yen; in central China, the Wang Jingwei notes were tied to the yuan. The two areas operated as separate currency zones with an exchange rate in 1943 of 100 yuan in Nanjing currency to 18 yen in Beijing currency. Complex restrictions on exchange actually inhibited trade between the two areas. Had it not been for Japanese ineptitude, the fabi might well have declined even more rapidly it did.[34]

Ultimately, wartime inflation could not be contained as long as the government continued to run up huge deficits. When China's ambassador to Great Britain Wellington Koo (Gu Weijun) visited Chongqing for a few weeks in late 1942 and early 1943, he had a frank conversation with the financial adviser Arthur Young. Dr. Young told Koo that "in his view, the only way to meet the danger was by reducing the national budget. Too many troops constituted a big and unnecessary strain on the treasury. It resulted in the withdrawal of men from production, and also in the inadequate feeding of the soldiers." The solution Young recommended was fewer soldiers. This "would not only save money but would also enable the government to feed the remaining troops better; at the same time there would be more men engaged in production in the factories and on the farms."[35] Indeed, malnutrition among the ordinary soldiers was a major weakness of Chiang's military.

But Chiang Kai-shek's approach was to increase the size of the military, never to cut back. Since he made the ultimate decisions, reduction in the size of the military was simply not going to happen. Chiang sometimes took note of the problem of inflation. In a speech in October 1942 cited by Matthew T. Combs, Chiang stated that "modern warfare is by no means merely a matter of military operations; economic affairs constitute another factor of first importance." In November 1942, Chongqing announced a program of price controls. Once that was done, Chiang seemed to have no new approaches to controlling inflation. As Combs notes, "for the rest of 1943 his diary records only attention to the economic problems but no new action to solve the crisis."[36] Price controls are very difficult to enforce, of course. Farmers and producers of manufactured goods would simply withhold their supplies from the market if they were not getting a sufficient price.

Fabi had inherent weaknesses from its inception. The money supply was subject to the political whims of the key leader – Chiang Kai-shek. But as late as 1943, one could argue that the damage had not been irreparable. Yet in what turned out to be the last months of the war, a series of disasters seemed to have set the currency on a spiral from which it could not escape. Military losses by the Nationalist government went hand in hand with the loss of value of the currency used to pay China's soldiers. Their effectiveness as fighters declined as well. The two phenomena were related.

CHAPTER 1

Ichigo and Its Aftermath

IT IS PERHAPS BOTH A BLESSING AND A CURSE THAT HISTORIANS generally know the outcome of the historical events that they are studying. In trying to understand the actions of people in the historical past, it is often difficult to recapture their thinking at a time when the future appeared so uncertain. One of the driving forces of hyperinflation is human behavior – people assume that paper currency will lose value at a rapid rate, therefore rationally, when one acquires a fiat currency such as fabi, one should immediately buy commodities that will more likely hold value. In wartime conditions in which commodities are scarce, this sets up a self-perpetuating cycle. Goods are scarce, but consumers are desperate to buy, which drives up prices and perpetuates inflation.

During the war against Japan, this phenomenon prevailed in Free China, and the rate of inflation even accelerated in 1943 and 1944. Yet in theory, this process should have reversed as signs of an Allied victory over the Axis Powers began to appear. Such a victory would be expected to improve the value of fabi. With victory, consumers might well dump commodities that they had hoarded, fearing a price decline. When hoarded goods are released on a market, prices in fact should go down. With the eastern ports recovered, foreign commodities might also enter the market, and more American aid might be expected. Yet few acted to release commodities and hold fabi even up to the final hours of the conflict. The psychology of hyperinflation continued even as the Allies moved toward victory.

Today, we know of course that the United States dropped atomic bombs on Japan on August 6 and 9, 1945, and that the Soviet Union declared war on Japan on August 8. We know that the Japanese emperor broadcast a speech announcing surrender on August 15. Yet in trying to understand the actions and feelings of historical actors in the months leading up to these events, it is important to remember that they had no such foreknowledge. Even at the beginning of 1945, few people living in "Free China" would have envisioned that the war would end a mere eight months later. Although knowledge of Germany's likely surrender and Japanese defeats in the Pacific appeared in the newspapers, most assumed that the fighting in China would drag on for many more months or even years. And given the harsh conditions under which so many lived, they probably feared that they and their families might not survive to see victory.

Why this pessimism? Although the Allied Powers seemed to be winning globally as 1945 began, the major exception was mainland Asia. As the journalist Cao Juren later recounted, in military terms the last year of the war was China's darkest hour.[1] In April 1944, Japan launched the largest military campaign of the China war. Indeed, as the Japanese military historian Hara Takeshi observed, it was "the largest military operation carried out in the history of the Japanese army."[2] Called Operation Ichigo (number one), the campaign saw the mobilization of 500,000 Japanese forces, approximately 80 percent of the China Expeditionary Army. In addition, the Japanese used 100,000 horses, 1,500 pieces of artillery, 800 tanks, and many airplanes.

Operation Ichigo was a tremendous Japanese victory. As historian Hans van de Ven noted, "Ichigo's forces slashed through Nationalist armies as if they did not exist, clearing them from the provinces of Henan, Hunan and Guangxi. By October 1944, Sichuan was the only large Chinese province still in Nationalist hands. A Chinese collapse appeared a distinct possibility."[3]

Why did Japan mount such an offensive even in the face of losses in the Pacific? Operation Ichigo had two goals. The first was to capture the American air bases in China in eastern and southeastern China that were giving the Allies air superiority in the area. Ultimately, the targets were air bases near Chengdu designed to host B-29 bombers, which could hit the home islands of Japan. The second was to secure an interior corridor to link north China, Manchukuo, and Korea with Japanese-held territory in southeast Asia. The Japanese hoped to establish a direct rail link between southeast Asia, north China, and Korea. As early as their defeat at

Guadalcanal, the Japanese military realized that it might lose control of the sea route and would need a rail link by land to get resources from its newly conquered territory in southeast Asia to northeast Asia and Japan itself.

However, as van de Ven observes, no matter what plans were made in Tokyo, field commanders of Japanese armies often went their own way in interpreting their orders, either ignoring them completely or going further than intended. General Hata Shunroku, field commander of the China Expeditionary Army, decided that that "Ichigo should go for the jugular and take Chongqing." Thus, during this campaign, "Japanese forces time and time again sought out the Nationalists' main forces with the aim of annihilating them."[4] Hata hoped to knock the Chiang government out of the war, offsetting Japanese losses elsewhere, and he nearly succeeded.

In phase one of Ichigo, the Japanese struck in Henan province, an area that had been ravaged by famine from 1942. Nationalist general Tang Enbo exacerbated the problem by continuing to levy grain taxes on the stricken areas. A massive Japanese force crossed the Yellow River in mid-April 1944 and encircled Luoyang. Chinese peasants attacked their own forces, such was the anger over the famine. By the end of May, Henan was in Japanese hands.[5] In phase two, they attacked Hunan province, invading in late May. After a chaotic and disorganized Chinese defense, the Japanese captured Changsha on June 18, 1944. Chinese forces put up a much stiffer defense at Hengyang, location of an American air base. But following intense fighting in which both sides suffered heavy losses, the Japanese prevailed on August 8. Japan's success dealt Chiang Kai-shek an enormous blow to his standing as the leader of Nationalist China.[6] As Hsiao-ting Lin has noted, "by July 1944, as a result of Japan's Operation Ichigo in China, Allied strategy in East Asia lay in ruins, draining the relationship between Chongqing and Washington."[7] In early September 1944, Japanese forces entered Guangxi province. The American air bases in Guilin, Liuzhou, and Nanning, built at great expense, would quickly fall to the Japanese. Japan moved forces north out of Vietnam in order to link up with the group in Guangxi. The Japanese captured Fuzhou with little Chinese resistance on October 5, 1944.[8]

The Guomindang losses in Guangxi were particularly painful. By September 10, 1944, when Japanese forces entered Guangxi province, China had 170,000 troops to defend northern Guangxi, but Chinese soldiers seemed unwilling to fight, and units simply fell apart. The Japanese invasion was virtually unopposed. The leaders of the Guangxi Clique, particularly General Bai Chongxi, concluded that neither Guilin nor Liuzhou could be defended successfully. The cities were torched and abandoned. Guilin was looted by departing Chinese forces before being set ablaze. The Japanese entered the gutted city on November 11, also capturing Liuzhou. Civilian losses were staggering.[9] General Zhang Fakuei and other Chinese commanders evacuated for Chongqing in October.[10]

By late November 1944, the Japanese were only sixty-two miles from Guiyang and 300 from Chongqing. There was widespread fear that, after holding out for so long, Chongqing might now be occupied.[11] Even the famed Burma Road, which the Allies were reopening at great expense in men and material, was threatened. If Guiyang fell, the road would be cut some 200 miles from Chongqing.[12] A wave of panic hit the wartime capital. United States authorities began monitoring a large increase in money leaving Chongqing for the USA in the autumn of 1944.[13]

In a letter written to his wife in America a year after these events happened, American Colonel John Hart Caughey recalled the panic. "A little over a year ago I hit this place. Boy, what a dismal spot it was then." The Japanese had taken the American airfield at Liuzhou and then advanced thirteen-and-one-half miles a day. They were only 250 miles from Chongqing where Caughey was stationed. "Although we weren't so worried about that as the fact that they were also 250 miles from Kunming. If they ever got there the whole show would be up." The Hump connection would be severed as well as the Burma Road. Thus, he recalled that "it looked as though China were on her last legs. That we were too. Yes, those were bleak days."[14]

The Japanese began to halt their offensive at that point, as they faced major shortages of material and trained men. Although Japan achieved its goals – seizure of the American air bases in China and opening a potential railway corridor from Manchukuo to Hanoi – these successes occurred too late to impact the outcome of World War II. The B-29 bombers that were to have been based in Chengdu in Sichuan were moved to the Mariana Islands. There, from bases in Saipan and Tinian, they could readily bomb the home islands of Japan, eventually with two atomic bombs. Allied forces controlled the sea and air in the western Pacific, and Japan could not complete a railway corridor in the interior of China. The major impact of the campaign was to expose the severe deterioration in the military of Chiang Kai-shek. American leaders realized that China would be of virtually no help in the final defeat of Japan. When Chiang Kai-shek demanded that Washington recall General Joseph Stilwell, the ranking American military man in China, Roosevelt concurred, but the damage to Chiang's standing was substantial.

Hans van de Ven details the tremendous blow that the Ichigo defeat had on the prestige of Chiang Kai-shek and his government, both within China and without. "In 1943, Chiang Kaishek had been riding high, having secured an end to the unequal treaties and having been feted at Cairo as a world leader." Yet after Ichigo, "internationally he had become an irrelevance. In July 1945, when Truman, Churchill and Stalin drafted the Potsdam Declaration, which demanded Japan's unconditional surrender, they did not even consult him."[15] The Allied Powers had concluded that Chiang, his government, and his army could not offer meaningful military assistance to the defeat of Japan and basically planned the Allied endgame without his strategy.

THE ECONOMIC IMPACT OF OPERATION ICHIGO

Most scholarly discussion of the Ichigo campaign relates to its impact on the global prestige of the Chiang government and the tilt in domestic power to the communists. The significant economic impact of the campaign is generally understudied. Yet Japanese success reshaped the financial landscape of Free China, greatly reducing its economic base in the final phase of the war. As Wang Qisheng wrote, "The Japanese north–south corridor cut in half the area under Nationalist rule. One-fourth of China's manufacturing base was destroyed. Revenue dropped sharply because of the loss of manufacturing and because of the Japanese occupation of grain resource areas, aggravating an already desperate financial situation."[16] Hunan had been a particularly important source of rice for the Chinese military.

Earlier, the Chiang government had relegated the land tax to the provinces, but in July 1941, Chongqing nationalized the tax and began to collect it in kind – mostly in grain. This move reflected the weakening of fabi and the move to a barter economy. Local army units were also given authority to requisition grain with remuneration generally well below market rates.[17] Ichigo slashed the availability of grain to feed Chinese soldiers. The blow to Chongqing's already-inadequate tax revenues occurred when the massive attacks by Japanese forces prohibited reduction in military outlays. The burden of feeding the Nationalist army fell increasingly on Sichuan province alone.

Government deficits worsened, and inflation accelerated. In 1943, the Guomindang government spent 58,816 million Chinese yuan, whereas revenue excluding borrowing was only 15,882 million yuan. A staggering 42,934 million yuan was covered by borrowing. In 1944, the corresponding figures were 171,690 million for expenditures, 35,609 million for revenue, and 136,081 million in deficit spending. And for 1945, the totals reached 1,215,089 million for expenditures, 150,061 million in revenue, and 1,065,028 million in deficit spending. The primary source of borrowing was simply bank credit.[18]

Even though Chinese forces did not for the most part fight effectively against the Japanese in the response to the Ichigo offensive, just the cost of mobilizing them increased government deficits. In the second half of 1944, the deficit increased at twice the rate of the previous six months. And in 1945, the deficit rose 378 percent before Japanese surrender.[19] Clearly, in the last months of the war, the government's financial standing declined seriously. John Service, then Secretary at the American Embassy in Chongqing, noted that the losses in Hunan would not only deprive Chongqing of commodities from this area but would also disrupt trade with the occupied areas. This was an important source for Chongqing and was already having an impact there. "Goods show a tendency to be withdrawn from the market for hoarding, and prices are going up."[20]

Arthur N. Young, who had a front-row seat to the crisis in Chongqing, observed that "beginning late in 1944 the price rise became definitely faster. A shock to confidence resulted from the strong Japanese drive in the second half of that year." By the spring of 1945, the rate of inflation was nearly 25 percent monthly, which in Young's view was a threshold that, once breached, indicated that China had now passed "the almost irreversible stage of hyperinflation, and to financial collapse before war's end."[21] Young even cites American commander General Albert C. Wedemeyer, who commented in February 1945 that inflation "was almost as great a threat to the U.S. Army operations in China as the Japanese."[22] Young's price index for Free China (using January to June as a base of 1), had reached 228 in December 1943. But Japanese success in the Ichigo campaign created the self-sustaining surge of hyperinflation that Young feared. The December 1944 index reached 755, the June 1945 index 2,167, and the August index 2,647. The psychology of hyperinflation gripped China even as the empire of Japan faced its final days.[23]

Chiang Kai-shek himself recognized that the loss of so many productive areas would pose a major problem for the Chongqing regime. The agricultural tax and grain levies had been collected directly and distributed to the military and to government personnel. Without the grain being requisitioned from Henan, Hunan, and Guangxi to feed the vast Nationalist military, the government would have to increase the levy in Sichuan province. Chiang anticipated that peasant unrest might increase as the burden became heavier. After the war, many of the local elites in Sichuan backed off supporting Chiang even in the face of communist success.[24]

Perhaps the most corrosive result of the campaign was to increase corruption in the military and to lower morale. As Chen Yung-fa noted, "Chiang began to overlook military involvement in smuggling and commercial activities, because he knew very well that the army suffered from insufficient military budgets." But once that process began, it was difficult to control. "While such profits could relieve the commanding officers of their financial anxiety," noted Chen, "venturing into the spheres of smuggling and commercial activities could give rise to rampant corruption."[25] In November 1944, Weng Wenhao, in a private conversation with L. K. Little, the American who served as Inspector General of the Maritime Customs, admitted that conditions in the Chinese Army were much worse than when the war started. He blamed "the rise in prices and the failure to pay troops and officers a living wage." Weng observed that the officers "can and do squeeze and are well off, but the troops are miserable."[26] This would be a portent of things to come in the Civil War era. Morale among ordinary soldiers plummeted.

The inability to adequately fund the army after the retreat to the interior meant that the government had to turn a blind eye to corruption. The officers had the authority and clout essentially to confiscate commodities in lieu of compensation in currency. As Lloyd E. Eastman noted, conscripts generally got only small servings of rice gruel, "because the officers in charged had 'squeezed' most of the rations for their own profit." To draft peasants into the army, recruiters raided villages and press-ganged recruits in forced marches to their units. Conditions were so poor that an estimated 10 percent of those conscripted died before they even reach their assigned units.[27]

Once in their assigned units, conditions were little better during the last part of the war. Corruption led to food and money allowances for the soldiers being siphoned off. As Eastman notes, meat, salt, and oil disappeared from the soldiers' diet for months at a time. Operation Ichigo revealed how drastically the fighting ability of the Nationalist forces had fallen. In the fall of 1944, General Wedemeyer, then the senior American military representative in China, realized that Nationalist forces could not fight effectively because they were too weak to march and were half-starved. "Chinese forces, poorly fed and badly treated, had little enthusiasm for combat; many deserted. Indeed, half of China's troops – over eight million men – simply disappeared and were unaccounted for during the course of the war," Eastman concludes.[28]

THE IMPACT OF HYPERINFLATION ON DAILY LIFE

The impact of hyperinflation on the military was the most serious issue. But it also created many hardships in day-to-day living. For a long time, the government refused to issue large-denomination banknotes well after value of the existing bills was completely inadequate. It feared that doing so would feed into the psychology of inflation. The 100-yuan note long remained the largest denomination even as it became practically worthless. In the summer of 1944, H. H. Kung did place an order in Britain for 100 million 500-yuan notes. A separate large order was placed in September 1944 with the American Bank Note Company. Another New York-based firm, Security Banknote Company, shipped 22 to 23 million notes a month during most of 1944.[29] People carried huge bundles of notes even for daily purchases.

Printing the notes was also expensive. This was mostly done in the United States or Great Britain, and then the notes had to be transported to China, no easy task in wartime. Because there was no land route into China until the Burma Road reopened, the notes were flown over "the Hump" from India in the final leg. The entire process was costly. The United States gave China a $500 million loan in 1942, but fully $55 million were spent on banknotes, paper, and ink.[30] In the nine months through February 1943, American authorities calculated that approximately 9 percent of the tonnage flown over the Hump into China consisted of banknotes, space that might have carried weapons or medicine. In October 1944, for instance, seventy tons of banknotes were flown over the Hump. American military authorities then recommended that the Central Bank of China use notes smaller in size (physically) to reduce the weight of the shipments.[31]

This issue continued right up until the collapse of the Guomindang government on the mainland. Ministry of Finance officials consistently resisted issuing larger-denomination bills fearing (correctly) that this would lead businesses to raise prices. In his diary entry for April 21, 1945, L. K. Little observed that on his way home at noon, someone had thrown three 1,000-yuan note bills on the street. "But nobody bothered to pick them up. They are practically valueless. One of my secretaries said that dollar bills are cheaper than toilet paper."[32] This would become worse during the Civil War. By the fall of 1947, the government was printing 300 million pieces of currency monthly.[33]

Wartime inflation had been a serious problem especially for individuals such as teachers, bureaucrats, and military officers, who had salaried incomes. But the seriousness of the problem increased dramatically in the last portion of the war. Chang Kia-ngau summarized the situation by suggesting that inflation in the war era fell into three phases. The first one was the moderate inflation of the first two years of the war in which prices rose 40 to 50 percent annually. "There followed a two year-year period, ending in late 1941, in which people began to lose confidence in their currency. Hoarding and speculation became widespread, and prices increased by 160 per cent a year." But the real crisis came after Pearl Harbor, when the average annual price increases in Free China topped more than 300 percent annually.[34] It was no wonder that residents of Free China had few reasons to be optimistic about their own personal situations or the likelihood that the war would end soon.

For those on fixed salaries, it became virtually impossible to remain honest. Survival forced many into a path of corruption. A military medical doctor stationed in Chongqing recalled how his military salary became completely inadequate, so he began a side practice in private medicine, sharing an office with a pharmacy run by two Shanghai refugees. "My practice permitted me to live fairly well without succumbing to the corruption which had become endemic to much of Chinese governmental and military officialdom as the inflation made their salaries almost worthless," he remembered. Yet he did not really condemn those who became corrupt. "How many men could remain uncorrupted when their wives and children suffered actual want and opportunity existed to succor them?" He did recall that malnutrition became a major problem in Chongqing, as inflation made it difficult for many families to obtain sufficient food.[35]

DECLINE IN THE ROLE OF BANKS

China's modern bankers had played a significant role in the economy in the first three decades of the twentieth century, particularly in the east coast treaty ports. But except for the Central Bank of China and other government banks, their role in society greatly diminished as inflation increased. The principal commodity of banks is currency, which under conditions of hyperinflation becomes virtually worthless. People preferred to hold real commodities including gold, silver, jewelry, even foodstuffs, as well as foreign exchange, to counter the growing hyperinflation. Bank deposits steadily lost value. Only the government banks, especially the Central Bank that held government funds, could garner deposits. The proportion of total bank deposits held by private banks had been 56 percent in 1932, with the remaining portion in government banks. In 1945, that had dropped to a minuscule 2 percent.[36] Taking deposits from customers had simply ceased to be a significant business practice of private banks in China by the end of the conflict.

As Chou Shun-hsin noted, "as a result of protracted inflation, the value of the capital assets of the Chinese banks, both private and government, became ridiculously low in comparison with their deposit liabilities or total assets." In the 1930s, before the war, the ratio had been in the 15 to 18 percent range for private banks, close to the American ratio. In 1946, after the war, this had dropped to less than 4 percent. "In upsetting the prewar capital–deposit relationship, the inflation seriously impaired the stability of the Chinese banking system."[37] Many of the assets that the private banks held prior to the war became virtually worthless with inflation. During the 1930s, Chinese banks had purchased a substantial quantity of government bonds, equaling almost 8 percent of their total business. In 1946, the government announced that it would liquidate all of these debts at the par value of the bonds. Since total inflation had soared 5,712-fold from 1937 to 1946, in effect this simply canceled all of these debts.[38]

So if their normal banking practices were no longer possible, how could banks survive the war – or did they? It appears that many of the bankers began to engage in speculation and black-market activities to survive the war. As Chang Kia-ngau, who had headed the Bank of China for many years, wrote in 1958, "the standards of banking had deteriorated greatly during the war, many of the small banks having taken the opportunity to abandon approved banking practices and having become deeply involved in speculation."[39] After the Japanese seized the "solitary island," a host of small new banks appeared in Shanghai, twenty-eight in 1942 alone.[40] Meanwhile in Free China, the Central Bank had set the approved rate of interest on savings deposits for commercial banks at 8.4 percent annually. Since this rate was significantly below the rate of inflation, many of the private banks apparently offered rates set on the black market, which necessitated engaging in unregulated activities.[41] China's banking industry was moving toward speculation and black-market activity in occupied and unoccupied areas.

The eight years of conflict with its currency wars and hyperinflation simply destroyed the environment in which a sound banking system could function. The heroic efforts of the major private bankers in developing a vital new sector of the economy had come to a halt. Yet to a degree, most of these institutions still existed at war's end but were not able to contribute to any great degree to postwar recovery.

MAINTAINING THE EXCHANGE RATE OF THE YUAN AND RELATIONS WITH THE UNITED STATES

In the four-and-one-half years from the outbreak of the Sino-Japanese War until Pearl Harbor, the Chiang Kai-shek government had been committed to keeping fabi convertible despite the high costs to China's foreign-currency reserves and suspicions that the Japanese garnered hard currency through the "solitary island" in foreign Shanghai. H. H. Kung, minister of finance, had been adamant in his support of this policy and was strongly back by Chiang. Both considered it a matter of national honor as well as a crucial weapon in the "currency wars" between Chongqing and the client regimes established by the Japanese. Once Chiang became set on an idea such as this, it was difficult to get him to change his mind.

After Pearl Harbor, conditions changed dramatically, as "island Shanghai" disappeared and Shanghai's many banks were under Japanese control. Even as inflation eroded the value of fabi within China, however, Kung tried to maintain a fixed rate for foreign exchange, although restrictions were placed on the process. Kung had set the rate at 18.8 yuan to 1 dollar in August 1941, although this was later adjusted to 20 yuan to 1. Other government officials, including T. V. Soong, had argued against trying to maintain a set rate, but Kung and Chiang insisted on the fixed rate.[42] From the beginning this rate had never been realistic – a sizable difference developed between the official government rate and the black-market rate. As the value of fabi eroded, the gap widened. In 1944, the market rate would reach 600 yuan to 1 American dollar; the official rate of 20 to 1 was a fantasy. Yet Chongqing insisted on using the official rate in financial dealings with the Allies, most notably the United States. The American military was constructing bases and airfields in China, including the B-29 bases in Chengdu; they agreed to compensate the Chinese government for its contribution. But

Chongqing calculated this using the official rate of exchange, and the cost was staggering. The US Army estimated in early 1944 that the costs of materials for building the air bases in China, calculated at the official exchange rate, would be eight to ten times as expensive as building them in the United States itself.[43]

China's insistence on the official exchange rate created serious tension with its major ally, the United States. General Joseph Stilwell, no fan of the Chiang Kai-shek to begin with, expressed his anger over the issue in a candid conversation in September 1943 with L. K. Little, the American who served as Inspector General of the Chinese Maritime Customs. Stilwell noted that the United States was supplying China with millions of dollars' worth of goods for free, but when the US Army wanted to buy an old truck from the Chinese in mid-September, the Chinese insisted on the official exchange rate, which priced the item at US$10,000. A new Buick had been offered at $60,000. If the situation continued, noted Stilwell, China could pay back all of its debts to American "with a bag of oranges."[44] But it was not just the top leadership that was angered by the policy. The average GI stationed there was acutely aware of the difference between the official rate and black-market rate of exchange.

Theodore White, a reporter for *Time* magazine in China, captured the feeling in his reporting. "The extortionate exchange rate was known to every American GI in China, who felt that America was being swindled in the most scandalous and blatant fashion." White felt that the Chiang government was shooting themselves in the foot with this policy, because it was alienating Americans who worked and served in China. In the long run, it would damage the United States–China alliance.[45] Arthur Young wrote that insisting on the unrealistic official exchange rate created a situation in which "it appeared that Uncle Sam was being taken for a ride."[46]

Tensions between the United States and China over the exchange-rate issue became sufficiently serious that Washington sent Ted Acheson to negotiate the conflict over the compensation for the air bases. Arriving in early 1944, he offered a rate of 100 yuan to 1 dollar, which was still above the black-market rates. Kung nonetheless rejected this rate, stating that this would undercut the value of the Chinese yuan. With negotiations at an impasse, the US Army adopted a policy of paying American military personnel in China in US dollars. If they exchanged this for local currency on the black market, the Army would simply turn a blind eye. Most GIs seemed to have taken that route. The US Army estimated its monthly expenses in China to be about $17 million, but only $6 million of that was exchanged at the official rate and $9 million on the black market.[47]

No matter how the American military personnel were compensated, the introduction of American forces in China even in limited numbers strained the economy of Free China. As Gregory Lewis noted, "the overwhelming presence of the U.S. Army, with its extraordinary demands to maintain living conditions, its food requirements, and construction of four east China airfields, greatly endangered the Nationalist economy via vastly increased U.S. dollars in circulation."[48] In an environment of shortages of food and commodities, maintaining the lifestyle of the US military certainly increased inflationary pressure. Madame Chiang Kai-shek wrote to Roosevelt on February 17, 1944, making this point when she stated, "the amount needed by the American military in China is such an astronomical figure ... that China's economy cannot withstand the strain and is imminently threatened with collapse."[49]

Kung realized that the United States and also Britain were effectively permitting their countrymen to exchange currency on the black market. Yet he privately told American ambassador Clarence E. Gauss that he did not object to the practice. By turning a blind eye, Kung could accommodate the GIs without having to publicly back down and lose face or confront Chiang on the issue.[50] Kung did agree to special arrangements for diplomats and government officials, allowing them a 50 percent increase in the exchange rate, which was still well below the market rate. But this accommodated those in the American and British embassies who wished to avoid using the black market.

Kung extended this courtesy rate to one other group of foreigners. Among those who had been most supportive of China were missionary groups who received donations from their home churches. Yet American missionaries found that the dollars sent from home bought very little in China when exchanged at the official rate. Kung, who had been educated at Oberlin College in Ohio and had close ties to the missionary community, extended the special rate to them as well. To receive the discount rate, one had to go through the official exchange channel at the Central

Bank of China. Although China gained foreign exchange through this process, it also lost foreign exchange when many foreigners went to the black market.[51]

Kung's concessions did little to ease the tension between Americans who dealt with China and the Chiang government. Obviously key officials such as General Joseph Stilwell were clearly alienated from Chiang. But equally annoyed was secretary of the treasury Henry Morgenthau, who had been an early supporter of aid to China before Pearl Harbor (Figure 1.1). He was also very close to President Roosevelt. Increasingly, Morgenthau saw Chiang Kai-shek as a problem in US–China relations. In a memorandum sent to the president on June 8, 1944, he wrote that the "difficulties of financing our military program in China began, you recall, at the Cairo Conference, where the Chinese leader requested a \$1 billion

1.1. H. H. Kung with Henry Morgenthau, American secretary of the treasury, and Elinor Morgenthau at the Bretton Woods Conference, July 1944. Bettmann/Getty Images

loan." Morgenthau had urged Roosevelt to deny the loans and noted that "the Generalissimo in January threatened that the Government of China would not make any further material contribution to the war effort, including construction of military works, unless we agree to grant the loan, or alternatively, to purchase Chinese currency at the official rate of exchange for our military expenditures." Morgenthau advised Roosevelt that the official rate for the yuan was five cents, the rate set in 1941, but that the current market rate in China was only one-half of one cent. He told Roosevelt that Chiang was bluffing and that he should deny the loan.[52]

The entire episode left a bitter taste in the mouths of many in Washington. It fed into a suspicion that that Chiang Kai-shek was more intent on fleecing America than being a partner. Some of this suspicion had developed much earlier in the months before Pearl Harbor. Roosevelt and Morgenthau wanted to shore up Chiang's government, seeing it as a potential Asian bulwark against the Axis. But Roosevelt was then hamstrung by the American neutrality laws. Chiang had sent T. V. Soong to Washington as his personal representative to arrange a loan, but Soong's aggressive tactics created resentment against him in Morgenthau. Soong demanded large and unrestricted loans from the United States, sometimes dangling the prospect of China's concluding a separate peace treaty with Japan.[53] But ultimately, decisions were made by Chiang Kai-shek himself. When Soong was negotiating for loans for the Stabilization Fund in Washington in the spring of 1941, American officials wanted to extend the loan in installments, perhaps not having full confidence in how China might use the funds. Chiang telegraphed Soong on April 17, 1941, that this was unacceptable. "It seems that US Treasury Department does not trust our government. If loan is paid by installment, China's government's domestic and international dignity will be compromised. Therefore, I ask you not to sign the loan agreement."[54] Some American officials eventually joked that Chiang Kai-shek's actual name was "cash my check."

US relations with China were obviously not entirely smooth during the war, and the exchange issue was a key reason. But another obvious factor was the relative position of the two countries. The United States was the dominant partner militarily and economically, and China had to strategize from a position of weakness. But Chiang was sensitive to China's being seen as a second-class nation by the Western Powers and could be adamant when he felt he was not being treated with dignity by the Americans. And Chiang did have one trump card: the United States wanted to counter Japanese arguments in Asia that they were freeing Asians from the burden of white imperialism. Having China as a major ally was a counter to such arguments. And since Roosevelt had created the public image of a close alliance between the United States and Free China, he did not want to damage this illusion.

After Acheson's visit produced no real solution to the basic problem, Chiang suggested that he send Kung to Washington to negotiate the issue. Kung was actually already scheduled to attend the Bretton Woods Conference, which would convene in July 1944. With the yuan continuing to fall in value, Kung negotiated a solution to the issue in September 1944. Yet the loss of many of the air bases to Japan during the Ichigo offensive, coupled with the capture of the Mariana Islands in the summer of 1944, meant that the value of using China for launching air strikes against Japan was diminished. The interest of the American military in building bases in China had passed.[55]

Arthur Young argued that the American treasury had originally been a strong advocate of the fixed rate. But Young concluded that Chiang suffered "from bad advice and blunders on both the Chinese and American sides." Both he and T. V. Soong had opposed the exchange-control policy with a fixed rate, but the system was set up "on advice by the American Treasury, and supported by Chiang – whom Kung convinced." Not only did this lead to great friction between the United States and China over costs of the US Army in China, but China also "misused American credits, which could have been used at a critical time to check inflation and thereafter."[56]

In examining the overall problem of maintaining a viable currency, the approach of printing currency was not sustainable without worsening the problem. In retrospect, the effort to maintain the convertibility of fabi for as long as was attempted followed by the policy of an unrealistic exchange rate was not a good use of resources. There probably were no good answers to the economic problems China faced in World War II, but there undoubtedly were better ones.

DISPUTE OVER THE SALE OF GOLD

The US Department of the Treasury was also unhappy with the Chongqing's government handling of the sale of gold that the United States had supplied to China. The sale was supposed to soak up fabi and thereby reduce inflation. But the Treasury representative in China, Solomon Adler, reported from China on March 11, 1945, that the Chinese government persisted in "selling gold at an absurdly uneconomic price." The government refused to change the official rate of the price of gold while the black-market price soared. Adler believed that this was "dissipating China's foreign exchange assets which she will badly need at war's end."[57] Both Chiang and Kung believed that lowering the official rate would simply stimulate speculation. But market forces continued to put pressure on the low price of gold in fabi and required action by Chongqing.[58]

When China finally raised the price of gold on March 28, the handling of this issue set of a firestorm of criticism in Chongqing and later in Washington. Word of the increase leaked out to key financial officials who purchased large quantities of the gold (an estimated 30,000 to 36,000 ounces) at the old price for a couple of days before the announcement. China's handling of the issue convinced the US Treasury that aid sent to China was not being handled wisely.[59] One rumor (unverified) was that the wife of Yu Hongjun (O. K. Yui), head of the Central Bank of China, had purchased 1,000 ounces of gold on March 25 for 20 million yuan. After the increase in price, the gold was worth 35 million yuan. The Control Yuan would investigate the incident and send a detailed report to Chiang Kai-shek. The latter apparently blocked public release of the document in part because it named too many "big names," but also because it would lead to criticism in America that China was misusing the American gold loan. That in fact was the reaction in the United States. The Western press also reported that much of the gold was traded to occupied China where it would end up in Japanese hands. Kung vigorously denied these reports.[60]

Henry Morgenthau sent a memorandum on May 8, 1945, to T. V. Soong outlining his objections to the handling of the program. He very bluntly stated that:[61]

> We believe that the Chinese Government should terminate the program of forward sales of gold. As you know, the U. S. Treasury was not consulted

when this program was initiated. In view of the difficulties of shipping gold, the limited effects of sales upon price rises in China, the public criticism of such sales and the desirability of using foreign exchange resources to achieve maximum effects, this program is ill-advised.

And Morgenthau was even more direct when he brought up issues of corruption and inside trading. "It is most unfortunate that the impression has arisen in the United States that the $200 million of U. S. dollar certificates and bonds and the gold sold in China have gone into relatively few hands with the resultant large individual profits and have failed to be of real assistance to the Chinese economy." He also urged Soong to crack down on speculators. "China should investigate and cancel sales to speculators and illicit purchasers and ensure that only bona fide purchasers will receive such gold as is available."[62]

Within the Treasury Department, criticism was even blunter. One aide to Morgenthau noted, "the Chinese did not consult us about these forward sales of gold, which were obviously imprudent under the circumstances and designed to act as a pistol to our head." A study by the department concluded that "the acquisition by China of additional foreign exchange and the sale of gold . . . by China will have no discernible effect in halting inflation."[63]

Soong reacted angrily to Morgenthau's implied threat to halt shipments of gold. In a May 9, 1945, meeting with Morgenthau at the Treasury Department, Soong basically delivered an ultimatum. "Unless the promise made by President Roosevelt and the Treasury to make gold available is fully implemented, a disastrous financial collapse in China is plainly indicated, which will inevitably be followed by a military collapse."[64] Soong's implied threat led the US to agree to supply the gold with shipments in May and June of 1945.[65] But in the confidential exchange on May 9, Morgenthau was more understanding of Soong's position. "In this room we are among friends. Certain things happened when you were not in control," Morgenthau stated. He noted that so far the scandal of the gold sales had only been circulated in the State Department and Treasury, but he feared the press might write about it. Soong admitted that there was faulty handling of the situation in the past. "The date after the price of gold was put up, I went to see the Generalissimo and told him we ought not to be ashamed to order an immediate investigation. If there is anything wrong, we ought to rectify it right away."[66]

Soong stated that when the credit was first arranged in 1943, the price of the certificates sold in China was in line with the market rate. "Later, when they stuck to the stupid rate of 20 – 1, of course the situation is different," noted Soong.[67] Morgenthau had assured Soong that the Treasury was prepared to meet its commitments to deliver the gold, but Soong was not convinced. He tried to reach America's new president Harry Truman. On May 16, 1945, Morgenthau met with Truman and then held a brief and less pleasant meeting with Soong. Soong wanted to speed up shipment of the American gold.[68]

Soong had appealed directly to secretary of state Edward Stettinius. In a memorandum of April 20, 1945, he stressed that "the continued sales of gold will be the most important single factor in blotting up large issuance of banknotes," a complete rejection of the arguments from Morgenthau. He was obviously attempting to get the State Department to pressure the Treasury. Roosevelt had promised China that US$200 million of the $500 million of American aid to China pledged in 1943 was to be in the form of gold, Soong stated, a promise "made with knowledge of the Secretary of the Treasury." Yet only US$7 million of the gold had been shipped, creating the possibility that China might default on payments to those who had purchased gold futures.[69]

Morgenthau yielded and had the gold shipped, but he did not modify his criticism of the process. In a letter of May 16, 1945, drafted after their meeting, he acknowledged that the shipments would be forthcoming, but he reminded Soong that the purpose of the financial aid was to assist the anti-inflationary program of the Chinese government, and "in my opinion the sale of gold by China has not proved effective in combating inflation, and I am doubtful that it will prove effective."[70] But in his earlier meeting with Truman, Soong had pledged that problems in the handling of gold shipments to China would be corrected. At the meeting, the American side brought up criticisms of the procedures for the sale of gold in China coming from the Chinese People's Political Council, and Morgenthau bluntly suggested that forward sales of gold be stopped. Soong again completely rejected that suggestion and stated that he had initiated an investigation in the issue.[71]

In fact, the Central Bank in Chongqing had commitments to deliver gold to different banks there on April 20, but the last shipment from America had not yet reached India. Yu Hongjun frantically cabled Xi Demou in America that he must alert H. H. Kung of the crisis. "Since this reflects [the] credit of our government I feel much concerned and distressed."[72] In what would be the final months of the war, China drew on the remaining portion of the $500 million credit of March 1942 to purchase $60 million in gold on May 22, 1945, another $60 million on June 12, and a final $60 million on July 27.[73] The Americans delivered the gold as promised, but the damage to relations between Soong and American treasury officials was already done. Yet Truman was not willing to have a public blowup with China as he was moving into Roosevelt's shoes.

In March of 1945, Arthur Young was in America seeking medical treatment but also trying to arrange for America to ship gold and consumer goods to China. Young was anticipating the recovery and opening of a port on the east coast of China and wanted to bring in goods and gold to help bring prices and inflation under control. But in a frank letter to the head of the Central Bank of China, Yu Hongjun, to whom Young directly reported, he wrote, "obtaining goods will be easier if American authorities can be satisfied that adequate provision is made in China to distribute the goods so that they will go into consumption and not into the hands of speculators or to be sold at cheap prices to those who could resell in the market at excessive profit."[74] Clearly, many American authorities had developed deep concerns about the Chinese leadership.

Morgenthau's warning that the American press would pick up on the scandal was accurate. Chiang Kai-shek's government had strictly censored news of the scandal from getting out of Chongqing when the story broke in March. But by May, the situation had changed. A May 14, 1945, broadcast by Raymond Swing revealed details of the scandal taken from the *Dagong bao* and the *Xinmin wanbao* in articles published in late March. He noted that when the four government banks were informed of the plan to raise the price of gold, "there was an immediate leak of the news and a wild scramble for profits." The *Dagong bao* noted that the gold had been supplied by the United States as a friend and ally and had been shipped in other people's planes and by their sweat and labor. "But no sooner had it got to China than it was sold in such a manner as to stimulate the black market and speculation."[75] The source of the news leak was T. V. Soong himself, who spoke with Mr. Swing and informed him of the March incidents. Why had Soong done this? Soong included the pledge that the government had made to punish anyone responsible. So perhaps he suspected that information on the scandal would get out and hoped to deflect criticism. But it is also possible that Soong sought to embarrass H. H. Kung, head of the treasury, and Yu Hongjun. As is noted later in this study, Kung and Soong developed quite a rivalry.[76]

The relationship between the United States and the Chiang government had developed a very troubling dynamic. As an ally, the United States provided financial and military aid to China, but American officials such as Morgenthau became very suspicious of how this money was used by the Chongqing government. Consequently, they began to demand strings be attached to the various loans and grants in guarantee that the money was spent in a way satisfactory to Washington. Chiang felt this was a blow to his dignity and to the position of China and stated so vigorously, sometimes through Kung or Soong. Yet this stand increased suspicion in America about the disposition of funds sent to China. This dynamic continued and worsened during the Civil War period.

In November 1943, President Roosevelt hosted representatives of forty-four countries at the White House to consider the rehabilitation of Allied countries who had suffered during the war. Eventually known as the United Nations Relief and Rehabilitation Administration (UNRRA), it would distribute billions of dollars in humanitarian aid to Allied countries after the war. The Big Four Powers would serve on a council to administer the program. The United States was the dominant sponsor, with additional funds from Britain and Canada, while China would be the largest recipient of aid. Yet from its inception, the mutual distrust of financial officials in Washington and Chongqing would set up a scenario that would fester during the Civil War period. Chiang wanted to control the use of the funds in China, making certain that none went to the communist areas. The Chinese National Relief and Rehabilitation Administration (CNRRA) was established in January 1945 to filter UNRRA aid through a Chinese political organization. Mutual distrust between the two sides hampered China's recovery and cost China support in Washington. The seeds of this tension were planted even before Japanese surrender.[77]

As the war came to a sudden end in August 1945, the Chongqing government was ill prepared to make the transition to a stable peacetime economy and currency. The military failures of the late war period and the loss of much of its already inadequate income led to a rapid acceleration of hyperinflation. And Chongqing's policies had alienated the major financial officials of the one foreign power that could have provided meaningful help. American support for Chiang would later become virtually unconditional. But this was after the communist victory of 1949 and when the right wing of the Republican Party had begun to attack President Truman as "soft on China." In the aftermath of Japanese surrender, American attention focused on Europe and occupied Japan. American financial officials had less enthusiasm for shoring up the Nationalist government's sinking currency.

CHAPTER 2

Hyperinflation and the Rivalry between
T. V. Soong and H. H. Kung

F OR TWELVE YEARS, FROM THE SUMMER OF 1937 THROUGH the end of 1949, inflation and then hyperinflation ravaged the Chinese economy. This was not the only factor that led to the ultimate defeat of Chiang Kai-shek, but it was certainly a major one. Normal economic activity could not occur under such strained conditions. In the last months of this era, news photos showed Chinese taking wheelbarrows full of cash to go shopping for everyday items. Morale among both the civilian and military components of the Chiang regime fell steadily, as did its international prestige. In April 1946, for instance, professors at three major Shanghai universities – Fudan, Jiaotong, and Tongji – went on strike, complaining that their salaries had fallen well below the average for rickshaw pullers.[1] In August 1946, a professor at Southwest United University (Lianda) in Kunming calculated that the real value of salaries of professors at the institution had fallen by 98 percent since the start of the war against Japan.[2] While salaries of government officials were increased on a regular basis during this era, Suzanne Pepper wrote, "these adjustments never corresponded to the actual rise in the cost of living and so did little to alleviate the impoverished conditions of teachers and civil servants whose real income remained in most cases insufficient to maintain their basic livelihood."[3]

Rightly or wrongly, the blame for this situation has often fallen upon T. V. Soong (Song Ziwen) and H. H. Kung (Kong Xiangxi). Together, the two men dominated key financial positions in Chiang Kai-shek's government from 1928 until 1949. Both at the time and in historical writing, they were deemed the architects of China's financial policies during the years when Chiang ruled on the mainland. After T. V. Soong joined with Chiang in 1928, for instance, he served as minister of finance and later head of the Central Bank of China until resigning in October 1933, after which he still held several positions including leader of the Bank of China from April 1935 until 1943 (Figure 2.1). In a semiofficial capacity, he established the China Development Finance Corporation (Zhongguo jianshe yin gongsi) to organize economic projects.[4] The agency put together financial packages for a variety of companies that became identified with Soong and his family. The board of directors of affiliated companies was usually headed by Soong or one of his brothers or Xi Demou, father-in-law of T. L. Soong (Song Ziliang) or Hu Yuzhang, father-in-law of T. A. Soong (Song Zi'an). The family identification was strong.[5]

Soong's activities blended into the private sector of the economy. In April 1937, for instance, T. V. became a partner and member of the board of directors of the Nanyang Brothers Tobacco Company, one of the largest Chinese-owned enterprises. During wartime, Soong played an

2.1. T. V. Soong, brother of Madame Chiang Kai-shek. Pictures from History/Universal Images Group/Getty Images

even larger role as Chiang's personal representative in Washington from mid-1940, and he served at times as minister of foreign affairs and head of the Executive Yuan. Even in that position, he focused on economic issues, as one of his major tasks was to gain financial support from America and Britain for China's war effort. He resigned as head of the Executive Yuan in March 1947 in part in response to the financial crisis and under heavy criticism within the Guomindang itself, but Soong remained active in determining Chinese financial policy until January 1949 when he departed China for the United States.[6]

H. H. Kung held a similarly impressive list of positions in the Guomindang government. He joined with Chiang in 1928 to become minister of industry and commerce and assumed control of the ministry of finance following Soong's resignation in October 1933, a position he would hold for over a decade. He traveled to Europe and America in the spring and summer of 1937 seeking foreign assistance even as war broke out. In the summer of 1944, he represented China at the Bretton Woods Conference, which established the postwar economic regime (Figure 2.2). But Kung resigned these positions in May and June of 1945 and moved to the United States in 1948.[7]

These two men thus dominated key positions in finance and banking during the Chiang era. Their prominence meant that they became linked to the spectacular failure of fabi during the twelve years of war from 1937 to 1949. Fabi itself had been created in 1935 when H. H. Kung was minister off finance, so he was identified with the policy from its inception.

Yet the high profiles of Kung and Soong were not simply a matter of their official positions in government but also because of their family connections to Chiang Kai-shek, who was also known as the Generalissimo. Authority in the Guomindang government ultimately rested with him. The actual power wielded by an individual who was in a position such as minister of industry or head of the Executive Yuan was far more dependent on his relationship to Chiang than on the office itself. Kung and Soong always carried both authority and responsibility associated with their family connections rather than just their formal positions in government at any particular moment.

2.2. H. H. Kung with John Maynard Keynes at the Bretton Woods Conference in July 1944. Bettmann/Getty Images

This was amply illustrated when Chiang sent T. V. Soong to the United States as a personal representative during the war. Arriving before Pearl Harbor and seeking to gain support, particularly financial support, from America, Soong immediately superseded the Chinese ambassador and foreign affairs staff in the United States. Officials in Washington dealt with Soong as Madame Chiang's brother, someone with a direct line to the Generalissimo. Soong thus assumed responsibility for a wide range of issues unrelated to any formal position in government.[8] A brief look at the telegrams between Chiang and Soong held at the Hoover Institution at Stanford University reveals this clearly.

During the war, most of the banknotes used in China were printed in the United States and shipped to China. When Pearl Harbor occurred, Soong was immediately concerned about the supply of notes and telegraphed Chiang on December 12, 1941, asking about the inventory. If the need for more was urgent, Soong was concerned about alternate transport routes in view of the eruption of war. On December 24, 1941, he telegraphed Chiang that he had arranged for a shipment in the Philippines to be burned as it became clear that they would fall into Japanese hands.[9] Soong's quick action on this matter occurred not because of his actual position in the Chinese government – he was not minister of finance – but because of his status as Chiang's personal representative and brother-in-law.

Even outside factors magnified Soong's role. Prior to Pearl Harbor, American secretary of state Cordell Hull was very concerned about alienating Japan and reluctant to take any action which might appear to aid China. Meanwhile, President Franklin Roosevelt habitually bypassed the Department of State, often using personal envoys or informal contacts to conduct foreign policy.

Roosevelt's approach was particularly notable during the period before Pearl Harbor. He was concerned about the fate of China and wished to help but was limited by American neutrality laws and isolationist sentiment in the US Congress. A foretaste of what was to come occurred shortly after Roosevelt's inauguration. At that point, the United States did not have diplomatic relations with the Soviet Union. Worried about potential German and Japanese aggression, Roosevelt felt that the United States should open channels to Moscow. The secretary of state Cordell Hull and much of the department's establishment remained firmly opposed to the move. Rather than challenge them directly, Roosevelt established a back channel. He turned to Henry Morgenthau, Jr., a political and personal associate from New York state whose wife was also close to Eleanor Roosevelt. Morgenthau was then governor of the Farm Credit Administration. The president had Morgenthau open discussions with a Soviet diplomat in Washington on the pretext of the sale of American agricultural products to the Soviets. These moves eventually led the State Department to get on board and diplomatic ties were established.[10] In November 1934, Roosevelt appointed Morgenthau as secretary of the treasury.

Roosevelt wanted to show some support for China as Japanese increased their pressure. The Chinese had moved off the silver standard in 1935 and issued the fabi. Roosevelt had Morgenthau receive a Chinese delegation led by the banker Chen Guangfu to discuss American purchase of Chinese silver, which would shore up the Chinese currency. Morgenthau agreed to have the Treasury purchase Chinese silver monthly for the remainder of 1936. Both Morgenthau and Roosevelt wanted to encourage China to resist Japan and acted despite reluctance from the American State Department.[11] Later, when H. H. Kung arrived on June 30, 1937, Roosevelt urged Morgenthau to show support for China to boost Chiang Kai-shek as well as Kung. On July 8, Morgenthau told Kung that the United States would purchase 62 million ounces of Chinese silver at forty-five cents an ounce. Neither man realized that the clash at the Marco Polo Bridge (Lugouqiao) the previous day would herald the start of war.[12] In both cases, Roosevelt bypassed the State Department, which advocated a more cautious approach to China.

The eruption of war between China and Japan in 1937 – though undeclared – would severely hamper Roosevelt and Morgenthau in their efforts to shore up China and skirt American neutrality laws. Nonetheless, the Treasury extended its silver-purchase agreement and allowed China to receive dollar credits against gold held in America. Roosevelt basically pushed the limits of the neutrality rules, sidestepping the State Department.[13] But Morgenthau had soured on Soong by 1944 and 1945. But when T. V. Soong first arrived in Washington as Chiang's personal representative, he found a situation where he could use personal diplomacy with Morgenthau. The latter was a supporter of China, following Roosevelt's lead. The Chinese diplomatic staff in the United States dealt with the more hostile State Department.[14] China's connections to America were thus forged through finance, highlighting the role of both Kung and Soong in the process. Since this was a foreign policy issue but handled on both the American and Chinese end by Soong and Kung as financial leaders, this increased their role. In particular, T. V. Soong learned to manipulate bureaucracies in Washington and proved invaluable for Chiang.[15] Eventually Soong's aggressive tactics would alienate many in the American government, particularly at the War Department and finally even the Treasury. But Soong fought hard for China.[16]

AMERICAN TIES

One striking feature of the political leaders who directed China's wartime finances, as well as key figures in banking and government who were often indirectly involved in financial policy, was the high proportion who had an American education. The most famous group, of course, was the Soong family, the six children of Charles Soong, who himself had graduated from Vanderbilt University in the United States (Figure 2.3). The two oldest sisters, Soong Ai-ling and Soong Ching-ling, both attended Wesleyan College in Macon, Georgia. Ai-ling married H. H. Kung (Kong Xiangxi), who attended a missionary school followed by study at North China Union College, a school near Beijing. He later graduated from Oberlin College in Ohio and received an MA in economics from Yale University. Ching-ling of course married Sun Yat-sen, leader of the Nationalist Party until his death in 1925. The youngest sister Mei-ling (Madame Chiang Kai-shek) lived in Macon as a teenager and then later graduated from Wellesley University near Boston, where she moved to be close to her brother T. V. Soong (Song Ziwen), who graduated from Harvard University. The second son, T. L. Soong (Song Ziliang), attended his father's alma mater of Vanderbilt, and the youngest, T. A. Soong (Song Zi'an), attended Harvard.[17]

Yet the circle of those with an American education was much wider. Chen Guangfu was a famous commercial banker in China who founded the Shanghai Commercial and Savings Bank. He had an extensive education in the United States, studying at Simpson College in Iowa and Ohio Wesleyan University. Following that, he received a degree in business from the Wharton School at Pennsylvania University, one of America's most prestigious business schools. Perhaps because of his American training, the Chinese government often prevailed on him to lead delegations to America. In 1936, for instance, he led a group of Chinese to Washington to try to persuade the government to modify its silver-purchase policy. In late 1938, he went back to attempt to arrange a loan based on tong oil exports, and in April 1940, to facilitate a loan based on tin exports from Yunnan. These were but the first of many trips that obviously built on his American connections.[18]

2.3. Charles Soong (Song Jiashu) with members of his family in Yokohama Japan, August 25, 1914. Back row: T. L. Soong (Song Ziliang), Charles Soong, H. H. Kung (Kong Xiangxi). Front row: T. A. Soong (Song Zi'an), Soong Ching-ling (later Madame Sun Yat-sen), Madame Soong (Ni Guizhen), and Soong Ai-ling, who would soon marry H. H. Kung. Not in Japan: T. V. Soong and Soong Mei-ling (the future Madame Chiang Kai-shek). Pictures from History/Universal Images Group/Getty Images

Yu Hongjun (O. K. Yui) began his Western-based education at St. John's in Shanghai and later studied at the University of Michigan, where he worked with the economist C. F. Remer. He served as vice-minister of finance under H. H. Kung from June 1941 to November 1944 and then later as minister of finance himself. In 1945, he also served as governor of the Central Bank of China.[19] Wu Guozhen (K. C. Wu) was not really a financial official but served in several positions, including mayor of Shanghai in the Civil War period – a job that put him at the forefront of dealing with inflation. A graduate of Qinghua University, he received an MA from Grinnell College in Iowa and then a doctorate from Princeton University in 1926.[20] Even those without formal training in the United States often had extensive experience there. Li Ming, a major private banker and founder of the Zhejiang Industrial Bank, studied at an academy in Hangzhou operated by Southern Baptist missionaries before going to Japan to study. Yet he spent much of World War II (March 1941 to 1945) living in the United States and was a member of the Chinese delegation to the Bretton Woods Conference.[21] But these individuals are only a few of those with educational training in the United States.

China's most famous diplomat during these years was V. K. Wellington Koo (Gu Weijun). Koo attended St. John's Academy in Shanghai before going to the United States and studying at Columbia University in New York. He finished his undergraduate degree in 1908, a master's degree in political science in 1909, and doctoral degree in 1912. His fluency and speaking proficiency in English was so great that as an undergraduate he won the Columbia-Cornell Debating Medal.[22] Shi Zhaoji (Alfred Sze), another diplomat who served in Washington during the war, had studied at St. John's in Shanghai before being appointed a student interpreter for the Chinese minister to the United States. While in Washington, he enrolled and graduated from Central High School and later studied at Cornell University, graduating in 1901 and receiving a MA degree in 1902. He served in Washington during the war, and after Pearl Harbor he handled procurement of weapons from America as vice-chair of the China Defense Supplies Commission.[23]

What impact did American education and training have on the relationship between Chinese and Americans regarding financial and banking policy? Perhaps the important factor was that, in negotiating with American leaders, those Chinese officials with an American education could usually converse in English without having to use an interpreter. That advantage was almost entirely one-sided, as few American leaders spoke any Chinese or had lived in China to any extent. Even in high-level talks where translations were needed, Americans often relied on those on the Chinese side who were bilingual. When Vice-President Henry Wallace visited China, for instance, T. V. Soong traveled with him during the entire visit and translated when needed.[24] Soong seemed to have preferred to use English even with Chinese officials. Wu Guozhen, who often worked with Soong, serving for a time as vice-minister of foreign affairs and who had done his graduate work in America, recalled that Soong talked to him in English. Wu's recollection was that Soong spoke Shanghai dialect but that his Mandarin was not so good.[25] One of Soong's major enemies within the Guomindang, Chen Lifu (part of the C. C. Clique with his brother Chen Guofu), put a much more negative spin on the issue. "T. V. Soong had come from abroad, possessed little knowledge of the Chinese language, and used English in his daily dealings and also in written communication," Chen wrote in memoirs published after 1949.[26]

The routine use of English among the top leadership of the ministry of finance meant that the American adviser Arthur N. Young could play a more active role than might have otherwise occurred if translations were always required. Arthur Young had served as an economic adviser in the US Department of State from 1922 to 1928, providing advice to American minister Jack MacMurray when he was negotiating an agreement on tariffs with T. V. Soong, then minister of finance in Nanjing in 1928. That encounter led Young to join a commission of financial experts to China headed by Edwin W. Kemmerer, who had been Young's graduate professor at Princeton University. When the commission's visit ended, Soong invited Young to stay on as an economic adviser to the Nationalist government, a task which lasted almost twenty years. With connections in the State Department and an Ivy League education that he shared with many of the top Chinese leaders, Young became a bridge between the United States and China. In a period when China needed American economic support, Young played a vital role.[27] The British adviser Cyril Rogers was in a similar situation. In August 1946, T. V. Soong invited him to take a leave from the Bank of England and become an adviser to Bei Zuyi at the Central Bank with the particular responsibility for aiding currency stabilization.[28]

Experience in America could be very useful when determining how to deal with American visitors and officials. Many Chinese lacking such experience often found the behavior of Americans baffling. But someone such as Soong Mei-ling or her brother T. V. Soong, with varied and lengthy exposure to American society, was in a good position to "size up" an American official. Many of the Americans concerned with Chinese affairs came from a missionary background. They were usually deeply religious, more commonly from the Midwest, and often abstained from alcohol. By contrast, those from a business or banking background were more likely to be from the coasts, less straitlaced and more likely to enjoy alcoholic beverages. T. V. Soong would frequently present a bottle of Scotch to visitors to China in the latter group, knowing that the gift would be appreciated. Later when he moved to the United States after 1949, he would often send such a gift at Christmas time.[29]

Soong Mei-ling was known to turn on the charm and virtually flirt on occasion with American envoys such as Wendell Wilkie, who was particularly impressed (Figure 2.4). Claire Chennault was also a great fan.[30] When Roosevelt sent personal envoys to China, Madame Chiang usually

2.4. Chiang Kai-shek with the Soong sisters in 1942. From the left: Madame Chiang Kai-shek (Soong Mei-ling), Madame H. H. Kung (Soong Ai-ling), Chiang Kai-shek, and Madame Sun Yat-sen (Soong Ching-ling). Bettmann/Getty Images

sat in on the meetings. Lauchlin Currie, an economist and aid to Roosevelt, made his second trip to China in the summer of 1942 (this time officially representing the United States). He had ten different meetings with Chiang Kai-shek, all attended by Madame Chiang.[31]

Finally, many of the Chinese who had studied in the United States had attended elite colleges such as Harvard or Yale for men and Radcliffe or Wellesley for women. In the prewar and wartime era, the number of people with a college education in the United States was much lower than today. To a considerable degree, top positions in government, banking, and business were dominated by those with Ivy League educations. Many Chinese with backgrounds in the same institutions could use school ties as part of the socialization with their American counterparts. There were exceptions, including prestigious liberal arts colleges like Grinnell College in Iowa, the alma mater of Wu Guozhen as well as Harry Hopkins, one of Franklin Roosevelt's closest associates and generally considered a friend of China.[32]

These connections provided Chinese officials with a major advantage when dealing with their American counterparts. Yet despite this, major conflicts developed between the two allies that led to considerable tension. Individuals such as Morgenthau, who had been considered in the China camp early on, became hostile to the Chiang government because he disagreed with Chinese policies on the exchange rate and the sale of gold by China, among other items. Ultimately, decisions were made by Chiang Kai-shek, who did not have experience in America.

Most of the American-educated Chinese officials recalled fondly their college days there and had close friendships with some of their fellow classmates. But there was certainly a dark side to studying in America. Anti-Chinese racist sentiment was widespread and had deep roots. In the late nineteenth century, "white supremacist politicians routinely used racial arguments to justify the Chinese Exclusion Act of 1882," noted Charlotte Brooks. "The racism that these Chinese encountered almost everywhere in the United States deeply shaped their ideas about ... Chinese identity in general."[33] In encounters with immigration officials, government bureaucrats, landlords, police, and others in almost any situation, ethnic Chinese would encounter racism in America. The 1924 Immigration Act, which banned Asians, made explicitly clear that the United States did not welcome Chinese. "Racial discrimination in the United States meant that full membership in the American nation remains elusive of all but white citizens," Brooks noted.[34]

In dealings with Americans in China, many who returned from sojourns in the United States were particularly sensitive to slights. This occurred even at the top levels. In 1943, Madame Chiang Kai-shek made a triumphal visit to the United States with speeches to Congress and large public gatherings. Her trip was designed to garner public support for China. Some Chinese groups in America hoped that she would raise the issue of discrimination against Chinese. She largely refused to do this because she felt that it would detract for the key purpose of trip, getting American support for China. But as Grace Huang noted, "no matter how Americanized Mme. Chiang and her siblings appeared to be, they had also been on the receiving end of discrimination during their years in the United States." In a speech that she made to a Chinese audience in Chinatown in New York, Madame Chiang noted that as girls, she and her sisters were not allowed to attend the public, white schools in Georgia. They were tutored in the home of their white host family.[35]

After World War II when extraterritoriality was gone, many Americans and British were slow to recognize the new reality. They often found Chinese officials, even those with substantial experience in America, hostile and nationalistic when they were not pliant in dealing with their more powerful allies. Close familiarity and shared goals often masked a prickly relationship.

TIES TO CHIANG: THE DOWNSIDE

T. V. Soong and H. H. Kung held much of their status in the Nationalist government because of their personal connections to Chiang Kai-shek. But close family ties to Chiang had a downside. Chiang had a ferocious temper and could be very stubborn. Perhaps the most famous example of this occurred when Zhang Xueliang, vice-commander of Chinese forces, placed Chiang under house arrest in the Xi'an Incident in December 1936. After Chiang negotiated with the Chinese Communists, Zhang released him and as a measure of good faith flew back to Nanjing. Chiang promptly had him placed under house arrest and kept him there. He remained a captive in Taiwan when Chiang died in April 1975.

Soong clashed with the volatile Chiang on occasion, often with disastrous results for Soong. When he returned from Washington in 1943, notes Chinese scholar Wu Jingping, he had a heated argument with Chiang in mid-October regarding the position of General Joseph Stilwell. Soong had worked assiduously in Washington to get Stilwell recalled, which had been in accordance with Chiang's wishes when Soong left China. But in the meantime, Chiang, perhaps influenced by Madame Chiang Kai-shek and her sister Soong Ai-ling (Madame H. H. Kung), had decided that he should retain Stilwell in part to deal with Lord Louis Mountbatten, then in charge of the newly created Southeast Asia Command. After an exchange that featured smashed teacups, a furious Chiang completely shut Soong out of government for several months. As Hsiao-ting Lin noted, Chiang labeled Soong "perverse, violent, foolish, and treacherous" in his personal diary. Soong had been handling China's relations with the United States and other countries from Washington, but now Chiang sent Kung to the Bretton Woods Conference in June 1944 even though Soong might have been a better representative.[36]

Soong's sudden fall from grace caught many foreigners who dealt with him off guard. When Lord Mountbatten visited Chongqing for five days in late October 1943, he found Soong "indisposed" and unavailable.[37] Soong's adviser, Dr. Ludwig Rajchman, telegraphed Chongqing in December 1943 trying to find out when Soong might return. But T. V. could only reply cryptically: "shall communicate with you in a few weeks. Warmest regards." He was confined to Chongqing and stripped of his political role.[38] Soong was not above trying to manipulate Americans to help his position. On November 11, 1943, he telegraphed Shi Zhaoji (Alfred Sze) in Washington requesting that he discreetly approach Harry Hopkins, Roosevelt's trusted adviser, and ask him to provide an endorsement of Soong.[39] Meanwhile, Soong was missing in action at the Cairo summit, where Chiang met with Roosevelt and Churchill. Chiang apparently was not well prepared for the meeting, perhaps in part because Soong did not assist in preparations and Chiang had to rely on working with Stilwell, which did not go smoothly.[40]

American leaders, many of whom preferred to work with Soong perhaps because he was more American in approach and personality than other Chinese officials, speculated about the source of Soong's problems. In a memo of March 7, 1944, John Service suggested that several factors led to the split between Soong and Chiang, including a personality clash, his failure to deliver sufficient American aid, his independence as foreign minister, and his failure to provide adequate help for Madame Chiang on her American visit. Service felt that his criticism of China's economic policy had alienated Soong Ai-ling and her husband H. H. Kung. Ultimately, he felt that the break was really a confrontation over control of finance and economic policy. At that point, Kung seemed to have gained the upper hand in control over government banks and government trading companies.[41]

A memorandum prepared by the Division of Chinese Affairs of the US Department of State for the secretary of state on May 11, 1944, notes that "although many stories indicating that T. V. Soong's difficulties in Chungking [Chongqing] have been occasioned by the Generalissimo's displeasure with some aspects of his work as Foreign Minister, it is believed that rivalry in the economic field between Soong and Kung accounts for Soong's difficulties." The report noted that Kung had managed to grab leadership of the board of directors of the Bank of China from Soong and that "the current attack on Soong should be regarded primarily as a move by Kung, supported by Chiang, to divest Soong of his economic influence."[42]

Of course, not all American officials were so enamored of T. V. Soong. His aggressive tactics in Washington had annoyed many in the War Department. Soong rarely like to go through "proper channels" and preferred to use personal connections. When Lauchlin Currie made his second trip to China in the summer of 1942, he alerted Chiang Kai-shek to Soong's behavior. Soong, he noted, "has resorted to bargaining and pressure which has caused estrangement of relations with the War Department. . . . For nine months Dr. Soong did not co-operate with the War Department but went in round-about ways." On the issue of defining the exact position of Stilwell, Soong had not been pleased with the attitude of the bureaucrats, so "he went to the President direct. The President made verbal promises. Subsequently I wired to the President and in his reply to me he adhered to his first reply to the Generalissimo which was worded by the War Department. This is Dr. Soong's peculiar way of approach." Currie told Chiang that Roosevelt was annoyed by Soong's behavior in this instance. "I hated to say anything on this personal matter in as much as Dr. Soong represents you. His present attitude is disadvantageous to China as well as injurious to the relationship between our countries." Currie contrasted the Chinese approach to that of the British, who worked through channels to receive Lend Lease aid and did not go directly to the President.[43] When Chiang has his big fight with Soong a few months later, he was thus aware that Soong had made enemies in Washington.

Currie gave one other example. Chiang had not been happy with the tonnage of war supplies being shipped to China. In Currie's view, the proper response would have been to approach the War Department. But Soong was a member of the Pacific War Council that met frequently, with Roosevelt attending. He brought up the matter there, forcing the President to refer it back to the War Department, which further soured relations. Finally, Currie mentioned that regarding Stilwell, Soong had only wired Chiang a summary of his exchange with the War Department, not the full text. "I would have given great assistance to T. V.," Currie noted, "but he did not wish it."[44]

Yet despite Soong's problems in Washington, by December 1944, Chiang decided he needed Soong and his connections to the American leadership. Perhaps Chiang concluded that "the squeaky wheel gets oiled." Britain could go through channels to get aid because it was America's top priority. China had to fight to receive aid, and perhaps Soong's style was to be successful in the long run. Soong was appointed acting president of the Executive Yuan. As Soong noted in a telegram from Chongqing to an assistant on February 6, 1945, "my position in government has been thoroughly consolidated and I possess more authority than ever before."[45]

Yet troubles persisted between Soong and Kung. In April 1944, John Service, then second secretary at the US embassy in Chongqing, detailed a report from a Chinese source about a heated and very personal exchange between Kung and Soong at the April 4, 1944, meeting of the Executive Yuan, which revealed Soong to have been frank to the point of rudeness in attacking Kung.[46] Foreigners were not the only ones to witness the bad feeling between the two men. Wu Guozhen served for a time as vice minister of foreign affairs. At that point, Chiang Kai-shek was head of the Executive Yuan but seldom attended, so H. H. Kung, the vice-head, presided. Soong then rarely came to the meetings but sent Wu instead. As foreign minister, Soong sent foreign policy updates to Chiang but did not include Kung.[47]

Wellington Koo attended a dinner party at the Kungs' home in Chongqing in mid-January 1943, which was being given for T. V. Soong, who was returning to the United States. When Koo raised the issue of a loan from Great Britain that he was currently negotiating, the two men immediately began bickering over the terms of the loan, the amount, and its potential use. Soong seem to belittle Kung's lack of understanding of the use of a loan in pounds sterling. Koo realized that the two men were sharply at odds and "it also [pointed up one of the reasons why] I had been experiencing difficulties in handling the negotiations."[48] The dispute between the two men impacted the work of other government officials.

Most famously, after American vice-president Henry Wallace visited China, he prepared a report for President Roosevelt and commented directly on this issue. "It was significant that T. V. Soong took no part in the discussions except as interpreter," observed the vice-president. Away from Chongqing, Wallace found him very outspoken. Soong "said that Chiang was bewildered and that there were already signs of disintegration of his authority." Wallace concluded that "Soong is greatly embittered by the treatment received from Chiang during the past half year."[49] In October 1944, John Carter Vincent of the Division of Chinese Affairs in the State Department reported that relations between Chiang Kai-shek and the then-American ambassador C. E. Gauss were not good. One key factor is that Gauss was close to T. V. Soong. The latter "is still in the 'dog house' and therefore the closeness of Gauss and 'T. V.' is not conductive to good working relations between Chiang and Gauss."[50]

Kung was more easygoing than Soong. During his time as head of the Executive Yuan, his meetings were leisurely, and he had a reputation for being somewhat chatty. Soong, by contrast, preferred short meetings and could be brusque.[51] But Chiang became angered with Kung because of widespread reports of corruption. He seems to have lost faith in Kung in 1944 – hence his removal from politics.[52] For whatever reason, Kung became widely unpopular among many factions in the Guomindang, leaving him with limited political support. Perhaps the imperious nature of the entire Soong clan alienated some, and perhaps attacking Chiang's in-laws was safer than attacking him. And there was no doubt that during his tenure as minister of finance, the collapse of the fabi had been disastrous.

The Kung children would sometimes cause embarrassment. When Rosamonde Kung planned a trip to America in the spring of 1943, she wanted to fly with her doctor and maid over the Hump to India. But such travel required priority clearance from Washington, so Kung had to cable T. V. Soong, then in Washington, to ask if he could get priority for the doctor to fly from American government officials.[53] After the end of the war, Madame Chiang Kai-shek asked General Wedemeyer and General Stratemeyer for the young Kung and her companion to get flight priority to return to the United States. T. V. Soong also made a request to General Wedemeyer. But the general had run out of patience and sent a very blunt refusal to T. V. Soong on November 26, 1945. He had, he noted, already "informed Madame Chiang that at the present time there are several thousands of Americans awaiting return to the homeland by air or ship." He stated that "if I were to give the Kung sisters, who insofar as I can learn contributed in no way to the war effort, I would be personally subject to severe criticism and rightly so. Also I believe that the Generalissimo would be subject to criticism."[54] The American general's frank words suggest that both Chinese and foreigners had strong reservations about the Kung family as well as the Soong clan.

David Kung (Kong Lingkan/kai)[55] also attracted unwanted attention on occasion. He was in Hong Kong in the months leading up to Pearl Harbor. While there, he became involved in espionage work for China. Rumors surfaced that he was engineering a plot to assassinate Wang Jingwei, who had defected from the Chongqing government. At the time, the British were maintaining a neutrality policy and did not want to antagonize the Japanese, with whom they were not at war, and were very unhappy with the young Kung. H. H. wrote to his son (in English) on October 28, 1939:[56]

I have been much concerned over what has happened in Hongkong. . . . Uncle Kai-shek and has been most concerned and Aunt May [Soong Mei-ling] has been very helpful in settling this matter for you; but they have heard all sorts of rumours through many sources including charges made by the Honkong people which were repeated to the British Ambassador. ... The British ambassador has been most friendly and frank and in every way he wished to be helpful ... There might be other people who have grudges against you and therefore want to create trouble and make it hard for you. But don't be discouraged as long as you are doing good work for a good cause ... with this goes my fondest love.

The British then expelled Kung and twenty other Chinese from Hong Kong, enraging the Kungs. After he enrolled at Harvard in 1942, the FBI did a background check but decided that he was okay. His activities in Hong Kong had taken place before Britain was at war with Japan, while it was attempting to be neutral in the Sino-Japanese conflict.[57] The younger Kung had informally served as a secretary in his father's office and while in Hong Kong had been involved in purchasing military equipment from Western countries. He was said to have made significant profits at least in the eyes of his enemies.[58]

After the war, David Kung was the frequent target of attacks by enemies of his father, both the communists and rivals within the Guomindang. Today, he would be referred to as a "princeling." Even Arthur Young, who was sympathetic to H. H. Kung, tended to lend credence to some of the charges in his private diary. On May 11, 1946, for instance he wrote "Hear DK brought 4,000 bales of cotton on speculation."[59] David Kung established the Yangzi Development Company (Yangzi jianye gongsi) at war's end. It became involved in import–export trade, with branch offices in Shanghai, Hankou, Fuzhou, Nanjing, Hong Kong, and Tianjin, as well as a partner firm in New York. It primarily imported cotton, electric machinery, medicine, and luxury goods and exported hog bristles, tea, and agricultural products.[60]

FAMILY ISSUES

The close family relationships also meant that personal disputes within the family (inevitable in virtually all families) often had a political side.[61] The younger brothers, T. L. Soong (Song Ziliang) and T. A. Soong (Song Zi'an), spent much of the war era in the United States engaged in government business. When Madame Chiang Kai-shek visited America, they were called on to assist, frequently traveling with her party.[62] Madame Chiang had serious health issues and often sought family members to be with her when receiving hospital treatment. In January 1943, for instance, Madame Chiang cabled her sister Soong Ai-ling urging her to come to the United States with T. V. Soong (who was scheduled to return) and join her in New York.[63] When in China, she often approached those in America for medicines and personal items. Madame Chiang attributed some of her skin problems to the time spent in damp air-raid shelters during the intense bombing of Chongqing earlier in the war.[64] In the spring of 1946, Madame Chiang was being treated in New York by her physician Dr. Edgar Mayer, who concluded that the newly developed drug streptomycin would be effective. At that point the US Army controlled the supply, and it was not generally available for civilians. T. L. Soong in Washington cabled T. V. Soong asking him to approach George Marshall to make the supply available for Madame Chiang.[65] Private family matters and public duties intermingled for the Soong family.

And then of course there was Soong Ching-ling (Song Qingling, Madame Sun Yat-sen), who was politically at odds with the others and particularly with Chiang Kai-shek. Her occasional pronouncements made her displeasure relatively clear. This family dynamic was legendary and a key reason that so many popular books about the family have been published both in China and in the West. But despite her political differences, she kept in touch with some of the family, particularly T. V. Soong, writing to him from time to time. She had a narrow escape from Hong Kong after the Japanese attacked in December 1941, traveling by plane with her sister Soong Ai-ling (Madame Kung) and niece Rosamonde Kung. She wrote T. V. a lengthy account of their escape and reception in Chongqing shortly after they arrived.[66] Like her sisters and Soong's wife, she also often requested Soong to procure medicines and skin ointments as well as such items as an electric toaster. And Soong would often ask whether she needed anything from America when he was returning to China.[67]

For all the rivalries among them, the Soongs were still family. Roosevelt's close aide, Lauchlin Currie, on his second trip to China in

September 1942, recalls listening to Madame Chiang's vitriolic denunciation of T. V. Soong. But then she suddenly said, "He is my brother and I love him."[68] And Meiling would often write to "my dear brother," writing in English and signing "May."[69]

And even between T. V. and H. H., there were still the family connections. When Kung was in Washington in early 1945, he spent a month convalescing and dealing with a kidney stone. He also suffered from bouts of malaria. On February 3, 1945, he wrote T. V. in China, and although he discussed some governmental issues, he specifically thanked Soong for the kindness of Soong's wife and daughter (then in the United States), who visited often and brought home cooking.[70] And both men were constantly called on to assist with Madame Chiang's travel and personal needs. On March 1, 1943, for instance, Soong cabled Kung from America that Madame Chiang wanted $50,000 transferred to her account in the National City Bank of New York. Soong requested that Kung authorize the transfer from the Central Bank of China to the Bank of China in New York.[71] These financial transactions involved the children and spouses as well. Madame Kung asked T. V. to transfer $3,000 from her account to America on September 25, 1943, when her daughter went overseas.[72]

The White House monitored this transfer of money from China. Lauchlin Currie, Roosevelt's close aide, noted that on May 12, 1943, the Bank of China had instructed the Irving Trust Company to issue a cashier's check of $100,000 to Madame Chiang, who turned it over to David Kung, who deposited it in his personal account. On May 17, another check for $61,000 was handled in the same way, and a third check for $59,000 was given to David Kung, who turned it over to his secretary. On June 10, 1943, Currie heard from Randolph Paul, who worked for Morgenthau, that the total amount transferred to Madame Chiang to that point was $800,000.[73] American authorities monitored the financial holdings of many prominent Chinese in American financial institutions. In a memorandum of September 13, 1943, Currie noted that Lin Yutang, a noted author who had published several successful books in the United States, held $46,800 in the United States as of 1940. But most of these reports were of politically connected individuals and companies. T. V. Soong's China Development Finance Corporation had increased its assets from 1940 to 1941 from $3.5 million to $5.4 million. T. L. Soong had received $403,000 from September 1941 until June of 1942. T. A. Soong's account in the Irving Trust had grown from $19,000 to $209,000 at the same time. T. L. Soong's account at the Chase Bank was $911,000 in mid-1941.[74] The banker Li Ming had told Currie that T. V. Soong probably kept funds at the Bank of Canton headquarters in San Francisco and possibly some cash at the Bank of China.[75]

In the fall of 1943, the Treasury Department monitored an increase of assets in the Irving Trust of approximately $200,000 in the account of T. A. Soong and sought to determine the source of the funds. Money was also moved from the Irving Trust to the Bank of Canton, which drew attention. The Treasury thought some of these transfers were related to David Kung and Rosamonde Kung.[76]

The Soong family kept a certain family dynamic despite disagreements. On Christmas Day 1944, T. V. Soong from Chongqing sent Merry Christmas greetings by cable to his wife and daughters in America, to his sister Madame Chiang Kai-shek, to H. H. Kung and Madame Kung, to T. L. Soong and his wife, and to the youngest brother T. A. Soong.[77] But pleasantries aside, the rivalry among the Soongs and particularly between T. V. and H. H. Kung spread across the banking and financial sectors of the Nationalist government and impacted both personnel and policy.

RIVAL NETWORKS AND FINANCIAL POLICY

The rivalry between T. V. Soong and Kung went beyond the family. Both tended to build networks in banking and finance, creating a complex web. Individuals were usually identified as either pro-Kung or pro-Soong even when circumstances required working with the other camp. Associates of either man would often report back that the other was trying to undermine him. In February of 1941, for instance, Kung associate Robert T. Huang wrote from San Francisco that "while in San Francisco and this part of America, I sense acutely that the opinion of the Chinese Community here and that of the Press are definitely against your Excellency. I cannot but feel that some people are out deliberately working on these people to poison their minds against your Excellency." And who were these people? "There are several groups working aggressively among the Chinese in this country. Doubtless, Dr. T. V. Soong is most aggressive. The others include Kwangsi [Guangxi] group and Chen Cheng and Chu Chia Hua." He concluded "where are these friends of Your Excellency's?"[78]

Implementation of financial policy sometimes got caught up in this web of connections. And often political and family connections intertwined. Bei Zuyi (Pei Tsuyee), one of the most prominent government bankers, held key positions in the Bank of China. In 1942, when Soong was in Washington, he found a position for Bei's son-in-law, Stanley Shen, with the China Defense Supplies Agency there. When Soong was posted to Washington, he relied on Bei to provide insider political summaries from China. In July 1942, he wrote to Soong about the decision to strip the Bank of China and other government banks of the right to issue banknotes and the consolidation of that power in the Central Bank of China. The decision was reached at a meeting of banking leaders presided over by Chiang Kai-shek. Bei quotes remarks by H. H. Kung that individuals should serve the interests of the government and not their individual institutions. Kung added that "one who is working in his institution may not necessarily work in the same institution after the promulgation of these regulations." In other words, the network at the Bank of China that Soong had built up over several years might be undone.[79]

In June of 1943, Bei sent Soong a confidential memo about Kung's proposal to terminate the currency stabilization agreement of 1941. Chen Guangfu and others had proposed revising the agreement, but Kung and Chiang Kai-shek seemed to favor termination. Bei suggested that Soong avoid acting on this because of Chiang's views. Kung was dispatching Arthur Young to Washington to deal with the matter.[80] After Kung gained control over the Bank of China, Bei continued to serve in the New York office but still sent confidential notes to Soong about the political and economic situation.[81]

Soong went to extraordinary lengths to keep his communications with Bei secure. In the spring of 1943, L. K. Little was in Washington when he was summoned to Chongqing to become the inspector general of the Maritime Customs Service. That venerable institution had fallen on hard times, with much of it functioning under Japanese control in the occupied zone, but a truncated version was headquartered in Chongqing.

Little would be the last inspector general and the only American to hold the post. Little was rather surprised when he received a request from T. V. Soong, then China's Minister of Foreign Affairs but residing in the United States, to carry a personal letter to China for him. In his diary, Little noted on May 17, 1943, "New York: A letter from Mr. T. V. Soong addressed to Mr. Tsu-yee Pei [Bei Zuyi], Chungking. Query: Why, having a diplomatic pouch, does the Chinese Minister of Foreign Affairs send this document through me?"[82] The answer was self-evident. Three years later in January 1946, Little, then in Shanghai, was surprised when an appointment of Carl Neprud, an American, to be Shanghai commissioner of Maritime Customs was blocked by T. V. Soong. In trying to figure out the cause of Soong's action, an associate suddenly remembered that Neprud had worked for H. H. Kung in Washington during the war. "It is pretty bad if the Soong-Kung feud is to extend itself to the foreign staff of Customs," Little concluded.[83]

Another back channel sometimes used by Soong was his wife, who, along with his daughters, spent long periods in the United States. When Soong was back in China, he would often use her as a conduit. In March 1945, when Patrick Hurley, ambassador to China, was in Washington, Soong cabled that he had sent a reply to a message from Hurley through his wife and asked Hurley to discuss the matter with her. She would forward the reply. Soong stated, "would appreciate if you would communicate with me through her as much as possible."[84]

Kung had not wanted to appoint another foreigner as inspector general, feeling it was time for the Chinese to take over. He had favored his son David Kung, but T. V. Soong had blocked this. Eventually Chiang himself decided on naming an American as inspector general "for the time being."[85] As a member of Soong's informal network, Bei remained loyal to Soong even when his actual boss was Kung. But being considered in Soong's "camp" could often result in attacks by those who wanted to get at Soong. In August 1947, for instance, Bei was indicted, which Arthur Young considered an attempt to get at T. V. himself.[86]

Another Soong loyalist from the Central Bank but based in Washington kept him apprised of Kung's activities at the Bretton Woods Conference. "I was told during the whole conference the Chinese delegation made not one proposal or recommendation.

Several of our delegates, I do not wish to mention names, brought along their wives and daughters and daughters in law to the Conference." The shared opinion was that Kung simply was not an effective representative for China at this critical meeting. The report also noted that "reports here is that K [Kung] has bought a house and does not look as if he will return to China in the foreseeable future. American officials and newspapermen have been asking the question: Why is it that every member of K's family is now abroad?"[87]

In fact, China was not well represented at Bretton Woods. H. H. Kung's reputation had been tainted by the gold scandal, and it was widely assumed he would be out of power soon. He also faced medical issues that needed to be treated. And as the Chinese delegation arrived, the Japanese Ichigo campaign was sweeping though China, overrunning American air bases. It was not an auspicious time to be representing the Chiang government. Ironically, one of the most effective members of the delegation, Ji Chaoding, was a communist spy.

Ji had arrived in the United States in 1924, a graduate of Tsinghua University, and enrolled at the University of Chicago. Eventually, he received doctorate from Columbia University and published an influential book, *Key Economic Areas in Chinese History*. But during those years, Ji also joined the American communist movement and later established ties with the Chinese Communist Party. During the war years, he connected with H. H. Kung because of native place ties. Ji, who was fluent in English, assisted Kung in negotiations with the Americans over the exchange rate to settle US military debts in China. Finally, for Bretton Woods, Ji accompanied H. H. Kung to the United States as his secretary. The C. C. Clique warned Kung that Ji was a communist, but when asked, Ji replied to Kung, "Uncle, I have followed you for so many years, you know all about me. . . . Do I look like a communist to you?" Kung was convinced the accusations were false.[88] Ironically therefore, the communists likely had better information on the actions of the Chinese delegation at Bretton Woods than T. V. Soong, then acting head of the Executive Yuan.

When Kung left the government, Ji was able to keep a research position at the Central Bank of China because he had good ties with Yu Hongjun, the new minister of finance. But despite his lengthy international experience and contacts, Ji was not invited to be part of the delegation to the United Nations Conference in San Francisco. This was not done because he was suspected of being a communist, but because the delegation was headed by T. V. Soong, and Ji was clearly a Kung man.[89] Ji stayed on in China after 1949 and was welcomed in the new government.

The ramifications of the Soong–Kung rivalry were serious. Kung was quite pliant to Chiang's demands and willing to advance sums to him without accounting for their use. Kung was doubtless aware that there was little backing for this currency, which would lead to inflation, but nonetheless he obeyed Chiang's bidding. Soong had grave doubts about running up large deficits and printing money. He despaired of attempts to keep the exchange rate of the yuan at unrealistic levels. But after his confrontation with Chiang had left him temporarily out of power, he became more accommodating of Chiang's demands. Such was his ambition that he was not willing to confront Chiang over the massive deficits covered by printing currency and risk Kung grabbing Soong's position. Thus neither Kung nor Soong stood up to Chiang and would continue to deliver increasingly worthless sums of money to pay for the military. Hyperinflation would consequently accelerate.

POLEMICAL ATTACKS ON SOONG AND KUNG

Soong and Kung bore a heavy political cost for their very public identification with the financial policy of the Guomindang and their high-profile financial activity. Soong was often attacked by others within the Guomindang itself, including Chen Lifu and Sun Ke. The party was highly factionalized, and groups jockeyed for power.[90] But despite attacks from with the Guomindang, the really severe criticism of Kung and Soong came from outside. The Chinese Communist Party and the political left in general targeted both Kung and Soong for intense personal criticism, labeling them corrupt "bureaucratic capitalists." The most famous of the writings was Chen Boda's polemic on China's four great families (Chiang, Soong, Kung, and Chen), who were accused of a wide assortment of social and economic crimes.[91] This line continued throughout the Maoist era with works such as Chen's "The People's Public Enemy, Chiang Kai-shek."[92] Even more than Chiang, Soong, and

Kung were attacked for their supposed personal wealth. This campaign was not confined to China but promulgated globally. Leftist groups in the West published polemics such as "How Chinese Officials Amass Millions," which detailed corrupt practice linked to Guomindang authorities.[93] These views became widespread in the West, reflected in the writings of many journalists and in public opinion.

American Arthur Young, financial adviser to the Chiang government and an admirer of T. V. Soong, still admitted that "when he left office in 1947, observers stated that his withdrawal was widely welcomed. He was blamed, though not justly, for most of the mess that had come about."[94] President Harry Truman recalled in his memoirs his reluctance in May 1945 to release $200 million in gold to China, even though Congress has authorized the expenditure in January 1942. Truman had Secretary of Treasury Morgenthau convey to China Truman's feeling that the way in which the sale was conducted "and subsequent public criticism of them in China are not conducive to achieve the purposes for which American financial aid was given."[95] He felt that corruption was undercutting the effectiveness of American aid. This attitude came to define the Truman administration's relations with Chiang at least until the outbreak of the Korean War.[96] This portrait of Soong and Kung as corrupt "bureaucratic capitalists" persisted long after they faded from power.

In China, however, there has been a gradual change in this historical image in recent years. An avalanche of historical writing about key leaders of the Republican period has appeared in China, much of it aimed at a general (rather than just academic) audience. Within this new writing, more nuanced portrayals of many leaders of the Guomindang period began to appear, particularly of Chiang Kai-shek. In contrast to the total villain depicted in Chen Boda's "Public Enemy Chiang Kai-shek," some aspects of his rule are painted in a more positive light, particularly his wartime military leadership, his visit to India, and his role as one of the "Big Four" Allied leaders. The change has not been as dramatic in writing on Kung and Soong. A 1995 biography of Kung published in Wuhan still went by the title *Da caifa Kong Xiangxi zhuan* (The big tycoon H. H. Kung).[97] And popular histories of the whole clan such as Chen Feng's *Sida jiazu miwen* (Secrets of the four great families) published in 2008 still follow the framework of the late 1940s. Yet these new studies in content offer a more subtle portrait of the men, as compared with Chen Boda, mixed in with gossip and pictures.[98]

The most significant change in the portrayal of Guomindang figures in China has been in academic publishing that utilizes newly available archival material. Most famously, the unveiling of the Chiang Kai-shek diaries at the Hoover Institution at Stanford University has produced an enormous body of Chinese writing. For T. V. Soong, it has been the joint publication of many documents from his archives at the Hoover Institution in bilingual editions by Fudan University in conjunction with the Hoover Institution that has been key. In addition to the reprint and translation of the archival material, the two institutions have sponsored academic conferences and published proceedings that have added a great deal to our understanding of Soong and his role in modern Chinese history. Although much of this has focused on Soong, volumes such as *Zhongguo renwu de zai yanjiu yu zai pingjie* (The restudy and revaluation on the Republic of China leadership), edited by Professor Wu Jingping, contain new scholarship on many key figures. Unfortunately, there have yet been far fewer new archival sources available on Kung, but perhaps this will change in the future.[99]

Ironically, these new archival materials have produced little fresh scholarship in the West. For various reasons, few new academic publications on either Soong or Kung have appeared, and relatively little yet on Chiang himself despite the availability of the diaries. Popular writing on the Chiang and Soong families continues to appear but is still under the shadow of the historiography of the 1940s. Unfortunately, the most widely read popular history written in English in the last few decades concerning the Soong family was Sterling Seagrave's *The Soong Dynasty*, published in 1985 by Harper and Row, a major commercial publisher. Subsequently a paperback edition and "Books of Tape" edition appeared. Widely read and circulated, this book is still readily available today. Seagrave gives an extraordinarily negative view of the Soong clan, depicting them as virtually a criminal gang, stealing billions from the Chinese people.[100]

Two more recent popular accounts have focused on Madame Chiang Kai-shek. Laura Tyson Li's *Madame Chiang Kai-shek: China's*

Eternal First Lady was published in 2006. Although Li is a journalist and the book appeared through a commercial not academic publisher, the author used a wide range of archival sources, including material from the Butler Library at Columbia University, collections at Cornell, Harvard, the Hoover Archives at Stanford, the Truman Library, and the Wellesley College Archives. Interviews and archival sources included numerous friends and contacts of Madame Chiang in America and China. Containing relatively little on T. V. Soong and H. H. Kung himself (much more on his family), the book offered a nuanced and largely sympathetic portrait of Madame Chiang.[101] Just three years later, Hannah Pakula published the massive (almost 800 pages) biography *The Last Empress: Madame Chiang Kai-shek and the Birth of Modern China*. Like Li, Pakula used a commercial press and cited many personal letters from Madame Chiang's American friends, which allow for an inside look at Soong Mei-ling. Nonetheless, much more than Li, Pakula was willing to include a great deal of "gossip history" in the text.[102]

The most recent addition to this literature is Jung Chang's *Big Sister, Little Sister, Red Sister: Three Women at the Heart of Twentieth-Century China*, published in 2019 by Alfred A. Knopf, a collective biography of the three Soong sisters. A well-known popular writer on modern China, she is known for her strong opinions, seeing the Empress Dowager Cixi as the key force for modernizing reforms in the late Qing and willing to believe any negative account of Sun Yat-sen. Jung Chang rarely engages with or acknowledges academic writing that does not support her ideas. Determined to portray Sun Yat-sen in a bad light, she tends to praise the warlords, dismissing their conflicts as minor. "The fighting was sporadic and small-scale, and most outbursts lasted no more than a few days." But missing in her bibliography are works such as Edward McCord's *The Power of the Gun: The Emergence of Modern Chinese Warlordism*, which might offer a different view.[103] Her book is really a biography of the Soong family from Charlie Soong until the death of Soong Mei-ling in 2003. For Jung Chang, the leader of the sisters was the eldest, Soong Ai-ling, married to H. H. Kung. In her telling, not only did Soong Mei-ling look up to her but after 1927 Ai-ling "would exercise a bigger influence than anyone else on the Generalissimo."[104]

The three books mentioned above are a testament to the enduring interest in the saga of the Soong sisters, a story that combines family struggle with national history. Yet the men of the Soong clan, including H. H. Kung, attract little attention, and almost none regarding their economic policies.

NEW PERSPECTIVES ON SOONG AND KUNG

The opening of new archival sources and the voluminous publications in China have yet to make a significant impact on Western scholarly writing on T. V. Soong and H. H. Kung. Yet such an effort is clearly needed, and not simply because of the new sources. The entire historical era looks very different today when viewed from the perspective of the twenty-first century rather than the 1940s; it is time to break out of the earlier framework. When the CCP attacked "bureaucratic capitalism" in the 1940s, communist writers assumed capitalism and market activity themselves were evil. Private business activity, whether conducted by those connected to the government or by international firms, was universally condemned by communist writers. Today, with the Chinese economy booming, private and semiprivate business activity plays a key role, as does the investment of global capital, and capitalist-style business activity is far more acceptable in China. In 2001, then-Chinese leader Jiang Zemin even invited entrepreneurs to join the Chinese Communist Party. "Entrepreneurs and technical personnel employed by scientific and technical enterprises of the nonpublic sector, managerial and technical staff employed by foreign-funded enterprises, the self-employed, private entrepreneurs . . . have contributed to the development of productive forces . . . in a socialist society." These private entrepreneurs should be eligible for membership in the party itself, Jiang concluded.[105]

From this new perspective, the careers of Soong and Kung might be interpreted quite differently. In looking back at T. V. Soong's China Development Finance Corporation (CDFC), for instance, a first reaction might not be that it was evil simply because it was capitalistic, but rather how little it accomplished. Founded in 1935 at a time when the effects of the global depression meant that little foreign capital was available, the few projects underway in the summer of 1937 were largely destroyed by the Japanese. Some that were completed ended up benefiting the Japanese. The CDFC put together financing with French help to build a railway from Vietnam to Nanning in Guangxi province, only to have it captured by the Japanese shortly after completion.[106]

The CDFC had built a major high-rise building in Shanghai, but this was used by the Japanese after Pearl Harbor. Late in the war, the Japanese removed radiators and piping from the building. After Japanese surrender, the US Army commandeered the building for its use. Eventually, the US Consulate in Shanghai leased much of the space in the building, and the CDFC continued with a small staff.[107] The failure of CDFC projects contrasts sharply with today's China and its high-speed railways, gleaming skyscrapers, and modern airports. A study of the CDFC done today actually reminds us of the high cost of the Japanese invasion. Even the issue of corruption itself looks different today. The major anticorruption campaign launched by current leader Xi Jinping suggests that this is an endemic problem not confined to any one historical era.

The time is thus right for Western scholars to reevaluate the careers of T. V. Soong and H. H. Kung. Should they have been blamed for wartime inflation? In retrospect, the problem appears unavoidable and beyond the power of either man to control. Early in the conflict, the Chiang government lost control of its main tax sources on the east coast while military expenses remained high. Even at the time, many observers recognized that in fact neither Soong nor Kung could really control this process. Theodore White, who covered China during the war years for *Time* magazine, noted that Kung had to bow to Chiang Kai-shek's wishes when he demanded funds for his military. Kung complied and had the money printed. "To run China on any sound economic basis required basic political decisions that only Chiang Kai-shek could make," White concluded, and Chiang was not inclined the make them.[108] But if Kung and Soong could not really solve the fundamental economic problems of China, there is still much room for debate about specific policies that they supported at different points during the war.

RESIGNATION OF H. H. KUNG

Chongqing's financial and economic failures claimed one victim before the war's end with H. H. Kung's resignation from government positions. Kung seemed to have been the scapegoat for the financial disaster that befell wartime China, and his reputation declined long before his resignation. When Lauchlin Currie made his first trip to China before Pearl Harbor, he was funded by the Chinese government and took a leave of absence from his job at the White House. This was done in large measure to comply with American neutrality policy. Because of this relationship, Currie's exit interview with Chiang on February 25, 1941, with Hollington Tong translating, included some rather blunt advice about Chinese officials. But this was delivered not as a representative of Washington, but as a paid adviser to the Chinese government.[109] And Currie was blunt.

He was particularly critical of Kung. "I feel that Dr. Kung has been too long on the job . . . and is referred to again and again as representing the Old China. Moreover, he is not trusted and ugly stories concerning him have gained wide credence." Currie even suggested that "he has not, as far as I have been able to discover, any able men in his Ministry." He recognized that "Dr. Kung is loyal to the Generalissimo and accommodating. However, new eras demand new men."[110] In a confidential report made to Roosevelt following his return to the White House, Currie elaborated on what he considered the incompetence in Kung's Ministry of Finance. "Large-lump sum payments are made to the military and the Minister of Finance had no idea how they are spent. . . . I did not meet one person whom I considered competent in the whole Ministry of Finance."[111]

Currie was also rather perceptive about T. V. Soong. He thought him "able and aggressive. I also believed him to be self-willed and probably unable to successfully subordinate himself. I do not think, therefore, that he could get along for any length of time with the Generalissimo." Thus in February 1941, Currie instinctively realized that Chiang would have a personality clash with Soong.[112] In his report to Chiang, Currie pushed as an alternative the banker Chen Guangfu, who had already led missions to Washington and was seemingly well liked by people in the Treasury Department. "He has a reputation for honestly and incorruptibility. He is outside of politics and is well known to have no personal ambitions." Currie was even sensitive to the politics of the situation. Chen, he noted, "is an old friend of Kung's so the transition could be made without too much loss of face on Kung's part." Currie concluded that "his appointment would be a symbol of a new era ... and would convince opinion both at home and abroad that the National Government really intended to put its financial house in order." Currie felt that Chiang was appreciative of his report, but of course he stuck with Kung for another three years. Still, Chiang was aware of certain misgivings in America about Kung even at that point.[113]

AMERICAN DOLLAR BOND ISSUE SCANDAL

Eventually the persistent reports over corruption led Chiang to remove Kung. It was a scandal related to the American Dollar Bond issue that broke the camel's back. This had its origin in the period after Pearl Harbor, when both the United States and Great Britain wanted to provide visible support for China even as their actual ability to get supplies to China fell with British Burma. Both advanced loans to Chongqing; America provided a credit of US$500 million and Britain 50 million pounds. There was considerable discussion about how best to use this money, but Chinese authorities decided to issue US$200 million in American dollar bonds and gold sales. Purchasers in China would buy the bonds with fabi at the official exchange rate and would be paid in dollars when the bonds were redeemed following victory over Japan. The idea was that the bonds would absorb excess fabi and curb inflation. Gold purchases would do likewise. The American Dollar Bonds were issued on March 24, 1942.[114]

American advisers initially thought the scheme would work, but they made incorrect assumptions about how the plan would be implemented. First, they assumed that wealthy Chinese would be under some pressure to buy the bonds, so hoarders would be forced to sell much of their merchandise for fabi to buy the bonds. With commodities being released on the market, the rise of prices could be stemmed. They also assumed the bonds would be sold in a short period of time. Neither of these scenarios was realized. No pressure seemed to have been applied, so after eight months only 10 percent of the bonds had been sold. Although in theory they were a good deal, the public seemed very dubious about whether the bonds would be paid at maturity. Most took their chances by hanging on to commodities, trusting the return would be greater than on the bond issue. Sales remained slow even as the black-market rate for fabi rose far beyond the official rate of 20 yuan to 1 dollar, making the actual cost for Chinese purchasers much more reasonable. At the end of December 1943, the black-market rate almost reached 84; by the end of June 1944 nearly 192. Following the Ichigo debacle, the black market soared reaching 600 yuan to 1 dollar in December 1944, yet the official rate remained at 20 to 1.[115]

In early October 1943, Kung sent a secret memo to Chiang Kai-shek requesting that sales of the bonds be terminated. Subscription was closed on October 15, 1943. An official of the Central Bank, Guo Jinkun, announced that all the bonds had been sold. The actual figure was about half; Kung ordered all of the banks to stop sales and return unsold bonds to Chongqing. Secretly, it appeared that insiders had then purchased the remaining bonds at the official rate of 20 to 1 but of course using currency acquired at the black-market rate. Word of the windfall spread among the inner circles, especially in the Legislative Yuan. Charges appeared that Kung had made profits of over US$3 million in the process.[116] Others said to benefit were all of the Soongs, underground leader Du Yuesheng, banker Chen Guangfu, military leaders Wei Daoming and Long Yun, and many more.[117] Morgenthau told Roosevelt of the charges and stated that the $200 million in aid for the program had made little difference in stopping inflation.[118]

This widespread criticism of Kung apparently led Chiang to lose confidence in him. By May of 1944, the British minister in Chongqing reported to London that there was a great deal of ferment in Chinese politics. "We think position of Chiang Kai-shek is still sound but public dislike of H. H. Kung and his associates gives him a good weight to carry. On the whole, we think a slow deterioration must be noted on the political side."[119] One source of the criticism appeared to be T. V. Soong himself. He sent a telegram to Guomindang elder Li Shizeng in June 1944 attacking the financial policies of Kung.[120]

Chiang came to perceive Kung as a liability rather than an asset to the Chongqing government. Attacks on Kung came not only from groups like the communists but also those within the Guomindang. American diplomatic personnel in China became seriously concerned by reports that several Guomindang military commanders were plotting to kidnap Chiang (possibly in Kunming on his return from the Cairo Conference) and force him to rid the government of individuals they deemed corrupt, notably H. H. Kung and He Yingqin. The US ambassador informed the secretary of state on February 3, 1944, that one of the demands was that Kung be removed and shot.[121]

Meanwhile, an American source, the leftist journal *Amerasia*, noted that the *Dagong bao* had published an article sharply critical of Kung in early 1945, claiming that he had spent the previous ten years as minister of finance "building up his personal fortune at the expense of government duties, and for having a large bank balance" in the United States. Since the newspaper was subject to Guomindang censorship, this article could not have appeared unless prominent factions in the government had permitted the attack on Kung. "Their publication suggests that the political prestige of Dr. Kung ... has reached a new low." The journal believed that officials associated with the Political Study Clique were behind the attacks.[122]

In September 1944 when the People's Political Council met, H. H. Kung was still in the United States, in part for medical treatment. The vice-minister of finance, his close associate Yu Hongjun, was subjected to vigorous rounds of questions and criticism. Questions involved the Kung family's business operations, the management of the Central Bank, the buying and selling of gold, and in particular the issue of the American Dollar Bonds. As the British representative in Chongqing commented, "the Council was really after Dr. Kung's blood."[123] British reports concluded that Kung "is not over-scrupulous in his methods and has retained the favor of Chiang Kai-shek (in spite of the general distrust and hostility of the people) owing to his ability to produce funds when required for military purposes."[124]

Chiang was sufficiently concerned with the Dollar Bond question to commission a confidential investigation. As Zheng Huixin notes in his study of the issue, Chiang concluded that a substantial portion of the bond issue had in fact been purchased (presumably by insiders) after the official close of sales on October 15, 1943. Ultimately, Chiang realized that Kung was responsible and sent several telegrams to him in America. Kung did not want to admit this, and Chiang was loathe to make the issue too public for fear of giving potential enemies within the Guomindang, not to mention the Chinese Communists, an issue with which to attack him.[125] Yu formally replaced Kung as minister of finance in late November 1944, but this did little to stem the criticism. Kung remained vice-president of the Executive Yuan and head of the Central Bank of China. Even after he lost these two positions in the spring of 1945, Chiang appointed him head of the board of directors of the Bank of China to "save face."[126]

With the Japanese success in the Ichigo campaign, the Chiang government and its military were humiliated and subject to criticism overseas as well as at home. Chiang reacted by giving the appearance that ministers in his government who faced heavy criticism from Allied leaders would be removed. General He Yingqin, for instance, was removed as minister of war but given a new and significant command. Chen Lifu, widely viewed as reactionary, was removed as minister of education, although he was given a substantial position within the party. The final blow was to H. H. Kung. In December 1944, Chiang brought T. V. Soong back to power as acting president of the Executive Yuan. Kung, the vice-president, had apparently wanted the position but was leaving for the United States. Losing favor at home, Kung remained in America until July 1945, first for the Bretton Woods Conference and negotiations in Washington, and then for medical treatment, according to the official statement of the government.[127]

When Kung did return on July 8, 1945, there were rumors that he would be given a post with the four government banks, but that did not happen. He resigned all remaining positions, with Soong taking over control of the government banks and Yu Hongjun, then minister of finance, the Central Bank. The British authorities in China, in their official summary of events of July 1945 for the Foreign Office in London, noted that "Dr. Kung is obviously unpopular among the general public and has been held to blame in some quarters for the present financial crisis." The report included a quote from the *Dagong bao* of

July 12 that clearly attacked Kung, as it had earlier. "Who allowed our finances to get into this mess? Who allowed inflation to reach this stage? Who allowed prices to soar to the present level? Who openly maintained that there was no objection to public servants engaging in business?" The paper concluded that "we cannot allow this sort of man to deal with China's financial policy."[128] So why did Kung return? The British speculated that Chiang might have summoned him as a counter to T. V. Soong and to "warn Dr. Soong of the vulnerability of over-playing his hand here." Chiang apparently appreciated Soong's abilities in dealing with the West but remained somewhat suspicious and jealous of his status, as Lauchlin Currie had predicted.[129]

When Kung did return, he met with Chiang on July 14, 1945. Unsatisfied with Kung's responses on the bond question, Chiang requested a detailed list of who had actually bought and sold the bonds. In addition to the full accounting, he wanted to know if purchases had been made through the black market. Almost simultaneously, T. V. Soong returned to China from his talks with Stalin and met with Chiang on July 18 and 19.[130]

Following Kung's return, Fu Sinian and others in the People's Consultative Congress demanded an investigation into the American Dollar Bond scandal. Chiang discussed the matter with Chen Bulei, who simply asked Chiang how much he wished the public to know about Kung's behavior – it would reflect on the family. Chiang received the investigative report on the matter from the Central Bank on July 16 and discussed this with Kung. The following day, Chiang learned that Fu Sinian and twenty-one others in the congress had started procedures for the impeachment of Kung, greatly distressing Chiang. Fu, a distinguished scholar at Academia Sinica, had long been a critic of Kung and had sent a number of private memos to Chiang about Kung's corruption. Lower-ranking officials in the treasury began to secretly supply Fu with proof of Kung's malfeasance. Kung defended himself by claiming again that it was difficult to learn the names of all those who had purchased the bonds. On July 21, Kung sent a new report on the issue to Chiang justifying his behavior in handling the bonds, but his answers seemed evasive. This angered Chiang, who assigned several people to make discreet inquiries into the bond issue. Yet ultimately Chiang followed Chen's advice and was not able to face the problem in a public way.[131]

A separate scandal enveloping the Ministry of Finance in the spring of 1945 involved questions surrounding the sale of gold supplied by the United States. The charge was that certain officials took advantage of advance knowledge of the government's decision to raise the official price of gold from 20,000 yuan per ounce to 35,000 by buying immediately before the new policy. This was still well below the then-black-market rate of roughly 50,000. Soong returned from the United States, where he had been at the United Nations conference in San Francisco, and he pledged to purge the ministry of these officials. He then obtained the resignation of several individuals. Yet the subtext for this was that Soong was attempting to purge officials who were close to H. H. Kung as he attempted to consolidate his control.[132]

It is perhaps understandable why a man who had been minister of finance for ten years would bear the brunt of criticism for China's difficult financial situation. But what of the charges of corruption and mismanagement? Arthur Young worked with Kung for many years and personally liked him. In his memoirs, he glossed over the issue of corruption and its relationship to Kung's resignation but concluded that it was Kung's "misfortune to face wartime problems for which there was no really good solution. Not understanding some issues, he adopted and persisted with policies bound to fail. This ... brought about his retirement after more than ten years in charge of the finances."[133]

Chinese scholars have weighed in on the issue in recent writings. Based on his reading of the Chiang Kai-shek diaries, Wang Chaoguang concluded that Chiang was often unhappy with Kung, feeling that he was too active in looking after private interests without regard for public opinion. Chiang became concerned about the management of the American loan, which reportedly had been mishandled.[134] Wu Jingping also raised several key points. Ultimately, Chiang felt that Soong was more effective in dealing with Washington than Kung. Beginning in March 1944, he began giving more and more diplomatic tasks to Soong, and Kung's position eroded. Chiang thus removed him from the Central Bank of China in July 1945.[135]

Zheng Huixin and Yang Tianshi both noted that Chiang's discovery that Kung was culpable in the American Dollar Bond issue scandal deeply troubled Chiang, even disrupting his sleep. His diary contains several references to his distress over the issue. Following Kung's final report to Chiang, he was dismissed from his remaining posts at the Central Bank on July 24, 1945. But Chiang was unwilling to go too public in discussing this issue, because he wanted to prevent family disharmony from being used by his enemies. Ultimately, he protected Kung and instead dismissed lower officials at the Central Bank and Ministry of Finance. Lu Xian and Guo Jinkun were made scapegoats. Chiang blocked newspapers from printing the charges made by Fu Sinian, determined to limit the damage from this incident. After the Japanese surrender in August, Chiang decided to wrap up his own investigation into the matter. He wanted nothing to undermine the Guomindang government as he confronted the Chinese Communists.[136]

CHAPTER 3

Sudden Surrender and Botched Liberation

I N THE WEEKS BEFORE THE UNITED STATES DROPPED ATOMIC
bombs on Japan on August 6 and 9, 1945, and the Soviet Union
entered the war on August 8, Japan had been withdrawing from several
occupied areas in China and consolidating its hold in a few areas in
anticipation of an American/Allied landing on the east coast of China.
Chinese officials in Chongqing as well as many in the Allied camp
assumed that such a landing would occur, resulting in several months
of additional fighting before Japan's final defeat. Chinese leaders therefore believed that they would have ample time to regain control of the
occupied areas as part of the military campaign assisted by the United
States.

A British intelligence report on China for June 1945 stated, "the war
news from the China theatre during the month continued to be encouraging and optimism about 'an early return to the coast' became more
widespread." And while a July 1945 report realized that China's economic and fiscal problems were severe, relief appeared to be on the
horizon. "It cannot therefore be said that the political and economic
situation of Free China has shown any improvement. There continues
to be the hope that the opening of a port will have an almost immediate
effect upon the economic position."[1] Americans in the field anticipated
the coastal landing and were preparing for it well into the summer of
1945. Clayton Mishler, attached to SACO, recorded in May 1945 that
the Americans anticipated landing near Xiamen in the immediate
future. He trained what would be his final groups of Chinese to assist
in the last weeks of June.[2] The swift end of the war caught all these
groups off guard.

Among those anticipating an Allied landing on the southeast coast of China was Arthur Young, who served as an economic adviser to the Chinese government.[3] In what turned out to be the final months of the war against Japan, Young was worried about the accelerating pace of inflation, yet felt that China might turn things around after victory. China's wartime inflation had been severe but perhaps unavoidable. The Guomindang government lost control of the eastern part of China, which had been the foundation of its revenue. The retreat to the interior, especially after the fall of Burma, left "Free China" almost completely cut off from the outside world with very little trade. The plunge in revenue coupled with crippling military expenditures led the government to cover the deficit by printing money, leading to the inflationary spiral.

In 1941, for instance, government expenditures were over 10 billion yuan, but revenue was just 1.3 billion, leaving a deficit of 8.7 billion yuan covered primarily by printing banknotes. As the value of these notes diminished, the government increased the issue, and the deficit soared to over 38 billion in 1943 and 1.1 trillion yuan in 1945.[4] The total value of fabi notes in circulation increased from 1,407 million in June 1937 to 336,485 million in May 1945. Those figures understated the increase, because in June 1937, fabi was used throughout much of China, whereas in May 1945, it was only used in "Free China," not in the occupied areas. In total during the war, the official banks extended advances of 1,261,921 million to the government. The price of average commodities in urban areas had increased from a base of 1 in June 1937 to 2,168 in May 1945.[5]

But Young felt that, after peace, the government might curb military expenditures while regaining control of its revenue base in eastern China. Like many observers based in China, however, Young did not anticipate the war ending as early as it did. He assumed that an Allied landing on the east coast would be a necessary step before any invasion of Japan itself. In a letter to the then-minister of finance Yu Hongjun on March 15, 1945, Young expressed concern that the rate of inflation in Chongqing had accelerated in the weeks since the Ichigo offensive. "I trust that a landing on the coast of China would not be too long delayed. A landing would probably do more than any other single thing to strengthen confidence and curb inflation."[6]

Young believed that, after an Allied landing, one or more of the eastern ports would become open for trade. Despite the opening of the

Burma Road (officially named the Stilwell Road) and the increased tonnage carried over the Hump, China's imports from the outside world were very restricted, far less than what was needed. Young assumed that the opening of ports would vastly increase the flow of goods into China. This was critical because it could break the psychology of hyper-inflation. With money losing value rapidly, people spent fabi almost as soon as they got it, preferring to hold commodities. This pattern led to hoarding of goods, causing scarcity and further escalating prices. Once China had an open eastern port, he hoped that people would suddenly divest themselves of hoarded goods, fearing that prices would drop.

Young also anticipated that the United Nations Relief and Rehabilitation Administration (UNRRA) would be providing relief commodities that would help drive down prices once they could be imported. The government could also raise funds by selling Japanese enterprises and those of collaborators.[7] Finally, at that point China still had considerable reserves in gold and foreign currencies. So a bit of optimism that China could turn the corner once peace began was not out of line.

Once the threat of hyperinflation was brought under control, regular economic activity could revive. One factor that Young often emphasized in his reports to the Chinese government was that the huge increase in the amount of fabi in circulation more than evaporated if that figure was adjusted for inflation. The amount of fabi in circulation had increased exponentially during the war, even as the area of circulation shrank. For instance, in June 1937, the total value of fabi in circulation was 1.4 billion yuan; in May 1945, it was almost 336.5 billion. However, if one adjusted for inflation, the latter figure decreased to only 155 million in equivalent yuan of June 1937.[8] This trend is partially explained by the smaller geographic area that used fabi in 1945, since much of eastern and northern China were still using the currencies issued by puppet governments. But Young basically argued that China's real money supply had shrunk drastically and that people needed confidence in the use of currency for recovery to occur. He noted:

> A characteristic of acute inflation is that the total value of a country's currency is grossly inadequate for the needs of the people. China's pre-war currency of all kinds excluding Manchuria was around C$2 billion equivalent at the pre-

war exchange to about US$700 million. The C$462 billion outstanding July 31, 1945, at the exchange of US$ notes of 2880 to 1 was worth only US$160 million. This situation explains the many complaints about the shortage of money, but the shortage can be relieved only momentarily by printing more money.[9]

The unanticipated Japanese surrender meant that the Guomindang forces were in no position swiftly to regain control of the occupied areas of eastern China. Japanese soldiers remained in place in many areas, still in possession of their weapons, and the Nationalists were in no hurry to round up puppets before they gained control. Lacking adequate transportation, Chongqing had to rely on American forces and airplanes to assist them in "liberating" the coastal areas.[10] All of this contributed to the chaos of the postsurrender period and slowed the recovery of normal economic activity. The *Dagong bao*, in an editorial on November 28, 1945, complained that over three months after the victory, these chaotic conditions persisted in much of China.[11]

There was no China landing; no gradual increase of imports that would have strengthened the fabi and led to an orderly replacement of puppet currencies in the east. In much of eastern China, the currencies that had been issued by Japanese client regimes in Nanjing (for central China) and Beijing (for northern China) were still in use. Yet Young remained hopeful. In a confidential memo of September 6, 1945, he wrote, "the stabilization of a depreciating currency in a free market need not be technically difficult or costly provided confidence can be restored, which depends largely upon definite ending of inflationary issues." China simply had to stop printing money to cover government deficits, curb expenditures (mostly military), and restore the tax base.[12] Unfortunately, the government would pursue virtually none of the policies that Young advocated.

NO PEACE DIVIDEND; INFLATION QUICKLY RESUMES

Even without an Allied landing on China's coast, the end of the war did bring a brief drop in commodity prices. For a few weeks after Japanese surrender, this appeared possible, as hoarders unloaded their stashes and prices fell. As Chou Shun-hsin commented, "anticipation of the resumption of international trade and the flow of fresh supplies from coastal provinces into interior China resulted not only in a reduction in the buying pressure on the market; but in a large-scale dishoarding of commodities by speculators."[13] For a few weeks, commodity prices fell. In August 1945, prices dropped by almost one-third on average, the only real decline during the war and postwar situation under the Chiang Kai-shek government. The price for cotton textiles, items which could be easily hoarded, dropped 40–50 percent in August, as people sold. Even the price of gold took a sudden, if brief, drop. But by October 1945, hyperinflation resumed with a vengeance.[14]

As Frank Tamagna, then a financial advisor to the Executive Yuan, wrote in an unpublished report on money and banking in October 1946, "after short-lived deflationary pressure, following the elimination of the Central Reserve currency in the autumn of 1946, the outlays of funds by the National Government, the spending of American forces and the inflow of funds from the interior resulted in an inflationary spiral." The result, he concluded, was that "inflation hit Shanghai like a typhoon."[15] The Chinese Maritime Customs Service estimated that the monthly cost of subsistence living in Shanghai increased 245 percent from October 1, 1945, to November 5.[16] In January 1946, the price index in Shanghai stood at over 1,600 (with January to June of 1937 as a base of 1). A year later, the price index there was at 8,177, and in January 1948, at 140,743. In July of 1948, it reached a stunning 2,877,000 before the government adopted its ill-fated gold yuan reform.[17]

For government officials and those in the middle class, joy at the end of the war was tempered by financial woes. Economist He Lian (Franklin L. Ho) wanted to return to Nankai University at war's end. He had been working for the government during the war. But he recalled that "ten years of government service under conditions of hyperinflation had bankrupted me; I was literally 'broke.' My wife even had to sell some of our possessions." Therefore, he began to seek out employment in the financial field, joining the Jincheng Banking Corporation.[18]

Why did inflation resume so quickly? Fundamentally wartime inflation had been caused by heavy military expenses but declining and inadequate revenue. The Guomindang government failed to resolve either of these issues so that government deficits continued, and the printing presses churned out currency whose value began to rapidly decrease.

Anticipating conflict with the communists, Chiang Kai-shek did not demobilize troops but kept the military on active war footing. The major cause of the deficits thus remained. Government expenses increased by 3.2 times in 1946, and revenue sources only covered 37 percent of expenses. Victory had brought not a new era in Chinese finances but an acceleration of old problems.[19] As the *Wenhui bao* noted in an editorial of April 3, 1946:[20]

> During the past eight years of war of resistance, our Government relied solely on the issuance of paper currency to defray military expenditures. .... After the victory, if the Government had actually had the welfare of the country and the people at heart, it should have lost no time in reducing the Army and curtailing military expenditures, thereby deflating the currency. But, exactly on the contrary... instead of reducing the Army, has expanded it.

Ultimately financial officials such as H. H. Kung and T. V. Soong could not alter Chiang's decision to use a military approach to deal with the communists. Although many of his American advisers, military and civilian, urged him to reduce the size of his military and modernize that which remained, Chiang was unwilling to do so. Chiang still had the old mentality that the number of your soldiers was the basis of your political power – a throwback to the warlord years. He also rejected advice that he limit the role of his military in Manchuria because it would be too exposed. Forces of the Soviet Union had taken control after it entered the conflict on July 8, 1945. Recovering Manchuria had become a rallying cry during the war. Chiang decided to go with the maximum military plan, printing money to cover bills and dooming the currency to fail. Many of the key financial leaders of the government realized very early in the postwar period that Chiang was not willing to contain military spending.

Arthur Young wrote in his personal diary on May 8, 1946, "the Generalissimo recently raised the army budget by a handwritten order from 90 to 170 billion monthly. That is dictatorship!"[21] The pattern begun under H. H. Kung as minister of finance continued. Chiang demanded the money, and the treasury supplied it with little accounting for its use. China would print money; hyperinflation would continue. There was no "peace dividend."

Young's private diary has not been published but kept at the Hoover Institution Archives. As a supporter of the Guomindang government, Young was more guarded in his published comments on the leadership. But he acknowledged in the diary that:[22]

> It is a great pity for China that [Chiang] does not understand finance and will still take action without consulting those who do. He feels that those who predicted financial collapse before are wrong and that it will not happen. He got the country through eight years of war, and now wants his own way with spending and finance.

Chiang decided that he wanted ninety divisions, which Young felt would bust the economy in 1947 unless there was a change. China desperately needed to repair its railroad system, but the railways faced a 47-million-yuan deficit during the first half of 1946. Yet Chiang ordered the railway administration to undertake the building of new lines that served his military campaigns, so that restoring commercial functions took a back seat.[23]

There is substantial evidence that much of the enormous military budget was simply wasted. The Office of Intelligence Research of the United States Department of State issued a detailed report on China's budget for 1946, made in the summer of 1947. The report noted that "the unusually large volume of expenditures attributed to the military in 1946 (CN\$ 4 trillion) is difficult to account for on the basis of reasonable assumptions regarding the pay and supply requirements for a Nationalist army of less than 4 million men." Although the report only provided crude estimates, it suggested that 2.5 trillion would have been sufficient, leaving a gap of 1.5 trillion. Where did the money go? "It seems probable that the major portion of this balance can be explained only in terms of incompetent administrative controls over military expenditures resulting in corruption on a large scale."[24]

The report cited two key problems. First was the lack of control over military expenditures. Branch offices of the Central Bank of China "in areas dominated by military commanders consequently are forced to issue currency to the military on a more or less uncontrolled basis." These outlays, which were outside of the regular budget process, were estimated to have accounted for half of the military expenses. Much of this likely went for speculative purchases by military officers. The second was that "rice counts" for troops were "substantially higher than actual head counts." A traditional problem in China, this meant that money was appropriated for a large number of soldiers who did not actually exist and whose officers confiscated these salaries, often paid in rice. The report suggested that, based on salaries, China's army had more than 5 million men, but some intelligence sources suggested the actual number of troops was fewer than 3 million. So military expenditures were enormous and yet poorly managed.[25]

The report also noted the failure to revive revenue streams that which had been crucial to the Nanjing government prior to the war – customs revenue, consolidated consumption taxes, and the salt tax. Customs revenue had been the single largest source of revenue in prewar China, 30 percent of receipts in 1936–1937. But in 1946, the customs collections were only 20 percent of prewar yields. The report suggested that the severe decline of foreign trade and the elimination of customs taxes on exports were the causes. It also attributed some of the decline "to a deterioration in customs administrative standards."[26] As Philip Thai noted in his study of smuggling, "corruption became especially problematic in the postwar years." Because salaries of the inspectors fell far behind inflation, "corruption was also a survival strategy for frontline employees."[27] How could officials resist bribery when their wages had drastically declined in value?

Consolidated taxes on commodities such as tobacco, sugar, wheat flour, beverages, and cotton yarn were another important prewar revenue source. Revenue in this category was down 30 percent from prewar levels in 1946. The report attributed this to "disorganization in productive and commercial activity during 1946." Receipts from the salt tax, a major source of revenue before the war, were estimated to have declined 70 percent in 1946. The report found several likely causes. The government taxed based on the official prices of salt rather than the black-market rate, which meant financial yields were much lower than they might have been. Finally, "revenue leakages and salt smuggling" probably exceeded prewar levels.[28]

The land tax had been a key component of the government's income during the war. Earlier, this had been allocated to provincial governments, but in 1941, the national government (then in Chongqing) took control and converted the tax from cash to in kind, primarily payments in grain. After the war, the national government returned administration to the local level and reduced its share to only 30 percent. Grain receipts therefore played a much less significant role in providing revenue. Receipts from north China were increasingly uncollectible because of the military situation.[29] In sum, military expenses continued to mushroom, while revenues sources were generally less productive than prewar. The government was unable to regenerate income in the liberated areas of eastern China, while the ability to tap older sources of revenue likewise declined.

BOTCHED LIBERATION AFTER JAPANESE SURRENDER

When Nationalist personnel – military and civilian – made their way back to the occupied areas in the days after Japanese surrender, they universally made a negative impression. As Diana Lary observed, "to many in Shanghai, the GMD takeover felt more like the onslaught of a plague of locusts than a liberation. ... Within a short time, so many houses, businesses, cars and private possessions had been lost by the locals to the incomers from Chongqing that there was widespread disillusion [*sic*] and anger." Locals began to use a play on words, Lary notes. *Jieshou* (takeover 接收) was replaced by the homophone *jieshou* (plunder 劫收). She noted that the Guomindang made no exception for the big capitalists who might seem like allies. "They were squeezed just as hard as less wealthy people."[30]

This impression was almost universal among Chinese and foreigners alike. F. H. Burch was a banker with the Hongkong and Shanghai Banking Corporation. During the war, he had been interned in the Longhua concentration camp along with his colleague A. S. Adamson. With liberation, they left the camp to try to take possession of the bank headquarters on the Bund only to find the Japanese still maintaining law and order and an official of the Yokohama Specie Bank on site. But when interviewed a few years after the war, what angered Burch was not that his former captors were still in charge, but rather the behavior of the Nationalist operatives when they returned. He recalled, "the Japanese kept law and order until the 'vultures' as we called them, the Chungking [Chongqing] crowd ... took the Japanese surrender."[31] And Arthur Young reflected, "what happened in the early months of the war set the pattern for what lay ahead. ... The Nationalists badly mishandled the takeover."[32]

The report by the British embassy in Chongqing to London for September 1945 observed "The enthusiasm of victory which marked the first few days of the month has given way to the aftermath of disillusionment." Despite censorship, the report continued, "disappointment at the lack of enthusiasm with which the relieving armies were received by their compatriots (in Nanking in particular) and the activities of carpet baggers in the most important liberated centres, has found expression in the press."[33]

One hope for the postwar economy was that domestic commerce and foreign trade could be revived and once again provide income for the Guomindang government. In theory, this should have occurred, but in reality, the economy began to stall. War damage to railways, roads, shipyards, and other facilities could not easily be replaced or repaired. But government leaders also had great difficulty managing the newly liberated areas. Chiang Kai-shek had been forced to abandon much of east China early in the war, so most officials who fled to Chongqing had been gone for more than seven years. But the east coast they left had been the old treaty-port China. Many sections of key cities such as Shanghai, Tianjin, and Qingdao had been under de facto foreign control. Public services such as electric-power generation, harbor management, police, and so on had been dominated by foreigners, most of whom enjoyed the privilege of extraterritoriality.

All of this had disappeared during the war. On May 20, 1943, Britain and the United States ratified agreements that ended the unequal treaties and extraterritoriality; foreigners were now subject to Chinese law. This also marked the termination of foreign entities such as the Shanghai Municipal Council.[34] And many foreigners were simply gone. The Japanese had been the largest group of foreigners in China, and they were to be repatriated. Most Allied nationals had either fled the coast or ended up in concentration camps. Many died; others were physically and psychologically scarred. Even if they were able and willing to resume their former roles, Chinese officials seemed unenthusiastic about their continued presence. Chinese authorities stated that few foreigners would be given their old jobs back and that China would not provide pensions promised by the Shanghai Municipal Council. Many former foreign employees found themselves in financial straits after being released from Japanese camps. But the era of foreign imperialism was over. The hated unequal treaties were gone, and China was to be free of the foreign control.[35]

The returning Guomindang government could not thus simply "restore" its early control of the coastal cities, because they had never exercised full sovereignty. Thus, reopening ports, repairing railroads, creating an effective police force, and many other tasks needed to provide sound urban government were often new tasks to be undertaken under chaotic conditions. It is not surprising that this proved to be daunting.

British diplomat Sir Horace Seymour traveled to Shanghai from Chongqing in October 1945 and reported back to London that "there is practically no shipping in the port, the municipal authorities have no money, and the public utilities are working at such a heavy loss that they obviously cannot be carried on on the present basis." He met with T. V. Soong and raised the issue that British ships from Hong Kong could not get permission to bring in goods into Chinese ports. "It seems difficult to believe that there should be any question in Chinese minds about the desirability of getting overseas trade going again at the earliest possible moment. In fact there seems to be considerable hesitation about doing this."[36]

During the war, the Guomindang government had severely limited exports so that commodities would not leave "free China" for the occupied areas. But these restrictions continued well after the war. When the President Lines managed to get a ship to Shanghai, it found that even in late November it was impossible to take cargo because the wartime restrictions had still not been lifted.[37] In a memorandum of October 18, 1945, Arthur Young urged the government to take action to increase trade. Limitations on exports should be lifted, and for imports, the government should provide a list of commodities that could be freely imported without restriction. These were commodities that would assist in economic recovery for which foreign exchange would be provided. The government might prohibit the importation of certain luxury, non-essential commodities. But the regulations should be clear.[38]

But management problems at the port of Shanghai persisted. The *China Weekly Review* in an editorial "Shanghai Port of Chaos" published almost a year after Japanese surrender noted "the chaotic mess that is the Shanghai port today may well cause the city to lose its chance of becoming the greatest export and import center of Asia." The biggest problem was theft. Official reports from the Maritime Customs Agency admitted that approximately one-third of all imports were stolen after being unloaded at the port.[39]

FLEECING "COLLABORATORS," SEIZING ENEMY PROPERTY

Many Chinese capitalists had remained in the occupied area during the war. Some had stayed in Shanghai during the period from July 1937 until December 1941 when the "isolated island" offered some neutrality and then became trapped there after Pearl Harbor. In many cases, the Japanese confiscated their property, and they endured grim conditions during the Pacific War period. But when Guomindang officials "liberated" the occupation areas, they often considered these individuals to have collaborated with the Japanese.

Some of the capitalists had hedged their bets during the war and were able to evade censure. Zhou Zuomin was one of the most important of the private bankers in the prewar period, the founder of the Jincheng Bank. During the war, Zhou had stayed in Shanghai and Hong Kong. He was placed under house arrest in Hong Kong by the Japanese after Pearl Harbor and then was returned to Shanghai. He had chances to leave the occupied zone for Chongqing but refused to do so. Moreover, he frequently visited with Zhou Fohai, a key official in the Wang Jingwei client regime, during the war. Zhou Zuomin also allowed branches of the

Jincheng Bank to operate in the occupied zones (as well as in Free China). But during the war, Zhou was also shrewd enough to avoid publicly joining puppet organizations in Shanghai. After the war ended, he quickly set out to mend ties to Chongqing, meeting with individuals such as Yu Hongjun, Wu Tiecheng, and Green Gang leader Du Yuesheng.[40]

Ultimately Zhou decided that only a personal meeting with Chiang Kai-shek himself could stifle the odor of collaboration with the Japanese. Zhou arranged a personal conference with Chiang in Chongqing on January 12, 1946. The forty-five-minute meeting with Chiang was devoted to a discussion of the economic situation. In his diary, he described Chiang as cheerful and exuberant in the meeting and that he saw him out of the room. Reports of the event gave the public the impression that he was cleared of the charges of collaboration even though that issue was seemingly not discussed. Before returning to Shanghai, Zhou made the rounds, having lunch with H. H. Kung on January 15 and dinner with T. V. Soong that evening.[41] But most capitalists lacked Zhou's extensive political contacts and could not easily escape the charge of collaboration. And even Zhou could not fully dispel the taint of his wartime activities. In his diary, he recalls incidents in the press where he was attacked and even labeled *hanjian* (traitor to the Chinese). He mentioned a letter sent to the supplement of the *Wenhui bao* entitled "What kind of person is Zhou Zuomin?" and a similar attack in the *Xinmin bao*. The diary entries suggest he was very sensitive to these attacks.[42]

Businesses that the Japanese held at the time of surrender were seized, with little effort to return them to their previous Chinese owners. In theory, both Chinese and foreign businessmen could petition to regain control of property seized by the Japanese. If the Japanese had invested in new equipment after they took the facility, that was to be the property of the Chinese government. The reality was that a great deal of the property ended up in the hands of the government and its officials. The rule of "first come, first served" seemed to be the guiding principle in seizing the property of those deemed collaborators.[43] Chongqing set up an Enemy and Puppet Properties Supervision Bureau (Diwei ye waili ju) that was charged with taking over and operating businesses which had been confiscated. T. V. Soong, then head of the Executive Yuan, directed the establishment of the office along with the minister of finance. But as the *Dagong bao* noted December 3, 1945, pilfering from confiscated properties was rampant, particularly from warehouses.[44] These were technically sealed because they contained enemy property but were not completely secure. An unintended problem was a severe shortage of warehouse space in Shanghai in the months after Japanese surrender. A considerable number of warehouses had been damaged or destroyed in the war, and since the government was slow to clear those holding enemy property, ships arriving in Shanghai had difficulty finding a facility into which to unload their cargo.[45]

As the *China Weekly Review* noted nearly two years after surrender, "the victorious Nationalist Army and the incoming civil officials had been fighting for years with their back to the wall. They suffered from inadequate food, clothing shortages." The consequence was, the journal concluded, that they "took this [Shanghai], their own city, as a victorious army would take an enemy city. Shanghai became a prize of war, a source of loot and booty."[46] Guomindang officials began to extort money from individuals under threat of labeling them "collaborators."

It was not always clear who might be behind some of the extortion. The Rong family textile and flour-milling enterprises had been among the most important in China before the war. The family had ambitious plans for postwar China although beset by internal disunity. But one of the senior family members, Rong Desheng, had remained in Shanghai during the war and had some dealings with the Japanese. He was afraid of being labeled a collaborator following Japanese surrender. Yet when he was seized on April 20, 1946, the culprits seemed to be criminal kidnappers. When the family paid a reported US$500,000, he was released on May 28. Yet this was but the most-high profile of many such cases.[47] Lack of clarity about those responsible for holding "collaborators" created real anxiety among the Shanghai business community.

One reason for the chaos was the overlapping agencies that dealt with punishing *hanjian* (traitors) and seizing their property. As Yun Xia notes in her study of the treatment of traitors, "Chiang deliberately created multiple layers of power in his administration and played one faction against the other so no single individual or clique would threaten his central authority."[48] In this case, two secret intelligence agencies were bitter rivals. The Juntong (Bureau of Investigation and Statistics under the Military Affairs Commission) was led by Dai Li, the notorious spymaster who worked closely with the US Navy. Its rival was the Zhongtong (Bureau of Investigation and Statistics of the Party Central Office), which was part of the C.C. Clique of Chen Guofu and Chen Lifu. After the Japanese surrender, the two groups competed to arrest the greatest number of *hanjian*. Business leaders who had cooperated with the Japanese were particularly targeted because they generally had financial assets that could be seized. Many who had remained in the occupied area claimed to have been secretly working with Chinese intelligence during the war. But Juntong would particularly target those who has cooperated with the Zhongtong.[49]

Not long after the war against Japan ended, Chiang Kai-shek seems to have turned against Dai Li, feeling that he was becoming too powerful. Chiang planned a conference of seven intelligence chiefs in the spring of 1946 to sort out the functions of each group. When Dai Li saw that three of the names were his archrivals, he became convinced that the meeting would lead to Juntong being dissolved. Before the issues could be resolved, Dai Li was killed in a plane crash on March 17, 1946, effectively removing Juntong as a competitor. Meanwhile, Chiang had selected one of Dai's rivals, Xuan Tiewu, affiliated with the Zhongtong, as head of the Shanghai police, which gave him the authority to arrest *hanjian*.[50]

In theory, the government provided regulations and due process for the confiscation of property of those deemed to have collaborated with the Japanese. On November 23, 1945, it issued "Regulations on Handling Traitors Cases" (Chuli hanjian anjian tiaoli) that specified ten kinds of collaborators whose property would be confiscated. Additional guidelines were issued in December and again in the following spring. Guidelines specified court guidance for property taken by the Alien Property Administration.[51]

Despite the various regulations, in the chaos of the postwar situation rules were often ignored. As Feng Bing and Wang Qian point out, the embezzling of traitors' property was the norm, as were cases of property being concealed and evading confiscation. Property was often confiscated by key military leaders or government officials, which "undoubtedly made the work of handling traitors' properties all the more difficult." The major villas of collaborators were among the most visible targets. Liang Hongzhi's home was occupied by Guomindang general Bai Chongxi and Chen Gongbo's villa by the family of T. V. Soong. But most of the property that was simply seized was taken by officials at a much lower level who took advantage of the chaos of the postwar situation.[52]

As Yun Xia concludes, "laws against hanjian . . . created new channels for government corruption, embezzlement, and nepotism. The public grew increasingly bitter while watching those with political privileges receiving the lion's share of the wealth and possessions of hanjian."[53] The *Dagong bao* ran an angry editorial on September 9, 1946, the first anniversary of Japan's formal surrender:[54]

> The taking over of enemy properties in China has been regarded by some people as an opportunity to amass a fortune. These people have occupied foreign style houses, grabbed automobiles, sealed warehouses and sent gold bars to other parts of the country. Everything which could be removed or hidden or which could make people get rich quick and enjoy life was quickly taken over. One the other hand . . . foodstuffs stored in warehouses were allowed to mold, and large numbers of trucks and steamers were allowed to rust.

Some of the collaborators had managed to get property and money out to Hong Kong where it could be deposited in foreign banks. "Hong Kong has become a paradise for those wanted by the Chinese government . . . from where they could find a better place to escape due punishment."[55] Finally, because of the large number of cases involved, trials and processing of traitors proceeded very slowly. In theory, the property of these individuals was to be sealed until after a guilty verdict. But because of long delays, the property had often been looted or pilfered by the time the case was settled.[56]

TRASHING THE WANG JINGWEI CURRENCY

When the war ended, there were still three major, separate currency regimes in China in the occupied areas. In central China where the writ of the old Wang Jingwei government had held sway, the currency was the

Central Reserve Notes, as they were usually labeled in English. In north China, the banking system established by the Wang Kemin puppet government had issued the Federal Reserve Notes, while in the northeast, the Bank of Manchukuo's currency was dominant. Interestingly, the Japanese never unified the currencies, which were subject to exchange control between areas. Prices of commodities varied dramatically across the different currency areas.[57] The government wanted to retire these currencies as soon as possible, replacing them with fabi, but this was easier said than done. Setting an exchange rate was the first order of business.[58]

The government decreed a minimal exchange rate for notes of the old Wang Jingwei regime at 200 yuan in the Wang currency to only 1 yuan in fabi. This move wiped out the savings of most of the people who had survived the years of occupation and alienated them from the Guomindang. Few felt that they had really been "liberated" by the returning troops. The impoverishment of the population of east China meant that few could purchase manufactured goods, making an economic revival difficult.[59] Arthur Young had advised the government to adopt a more lenient exchange rate, noting that actual prices in the two currencies made 30 to 1 a more realistic ratio. When the government did not heed his advice, "holders who had only puppet money, mostly loyal Chinese, suffered greatly," he observed.[60] Scholar Diana Lary calls the action, "one of the most damaging decisions that the GMD made in the immediate post-war period. ... With a single executive order, thousands of innocent people under the puppet government became bankrupt overnight. ... Bank balances melted away."[61]

Ironically, the low exchange rate for the Wang notes was one of the factors that triggered the revival of inflation. People were given four months to convert the Wang Jingwei notes to fabi. Since they were so undervalued, most rushed to buy goods with the old notes while they could still be used. The resulting rush started prices on an upward spiral.[62]

The punitive exchange rate for puppet currency also opened the door for an army of carpetbaggers to arrive from "Free China." With the Wang Jingwei currency suddenly nearly worthless, demand for fabi in the formerly occupied areas increased quickly. Officials from Sichuan brought large quantities of fabi with them and went on a buying spree in the newly "liberated" areas.[63] One official in Chongqing, Mi Qingyun, who worked in grain management, recalled the aftermath of Japanese surrender. On August 20, 1945, another official arranged for them to fly to Shanghai, where the sudden increase in the value of fabi relative to the local currency made it advantageous to purchase commodities such as gold. In addition, many hoarders in the occupied area unloaded commodities to acquire fabi. Realizing that the situation would not last long, Mi and his friend arrived by air to take advantage. At first, they were able to make a substantial profit in purchasing gold in the local market, but Mi noted that prices adjusted within ten days. The thriving black market in gold was centered on Hankou Road in Shanghai. Meanwhile the locals in Shanghai suffered, and it was difficult for businesses to recover from the war.[64]

The overvaluation of fabi versus the Wang Jingwei currency meant that commodities in the lower Yangzi area were relatively cheap for those arriving from Chongqing. The buying frenzy by those coming from the interior in part helped set off a new round of inflation. The famous department stores on Nanjing Road in Shanghai were cleaned out of commodities by the incoming officials. The "peace dividend" had been very short-lived.[65]

The other currencies used in Japanese-controlled areas fared a little better. In northeast China (formerly Manchukuo), the government decreed an exchange ratio of 1 Manchukuo yuan to 13 Nationalist yuan. This was a relatively fair exchange rate based on commodity prices and similar to the market rates for currency.[66] The exchange rate for the old currency used by the Wang Kemin government in Beijing was announced in November and was set at 1 yuan fabi to 5 of the Wang Kemin currency. This approximated the black-market rate so was much less of a burden for those who had lived in the occupied area.[67] These areas would be contested with the communists, so the cautious exchange policy may have reflected those concerns.

THE FOREIGN EXCHANGE RATE AND ITS ECONOMIC CONSEQUENCES

In the final months of the war, the Chinese government had persisted in maintaining an artificially high exchange rate for the yuan against both the dollar and the pound sterling. The yuan continued to weaken in the black market, but the government refused to adjust the rate. Chiang Kai-shek seemed to feel that lowering the rate would be a blow to China's prestige. Meanwhile, British officials in China noted that the Chinese had eased up on wartime restrictions on foreign trade in October 1945 but felt that there was little hope of a revival of foreign trade "until shipping is available and able freely to enter Chinese ports and until a new and realistic exchange rate has been fixed."[68]

The Chinese government had stated that it was eager to have foreign business resume activity in China, although it would no longer be protected by extraterritoriality. But the official exchange rate made it difficult for foreign firms to invest. In a statement of October 16, 1945, the Foreign Bankers Association in Shanghai noted "foreign companies and firms in China are anxious to resume their former activities ... but they lack the local currency funds necessary to rehabilitate themselves and they cannot afford to sell their foreign currency funds at the Chinese Government's official rates." And the foreign banks could only sell at the official rates, not the market rates.[69] Most businesses who exported did so by smuggling goods out and then selling the foreign exchange on the black market. Arthur Young advised Bei Zuyi, head of the Central Bank, in a conversation of December 13, 1945, that China should simply abandon the idea of trying to manage currency exchange at a fixed rate. His argument was that fixing the rate was very difficult, the costs of covering the foreign exchange would be too high, and that frankly it would not be well administered. But Bei did not have the final say in this policy, of course.[70] Chiang seems to have become entrenched on the idea of holding the foreign exchange value of fabi as a matter of national pride.

T. V. Soong as head of the Executive Yuan managed to launch a reform program in early 1946. The government adjusted the official rate to a level of US$1 to 2,020 yuan in February 1946, abandoning the pretense of the $1 to 20 yuan. This temporarily eased some of the problems, although the rate would be raised on August 19 to $1 to 3,350 yuan.[71] The government reopened the foreign exchange market and on March 8, 1946, resumed sales of gold, hoping that this would help stabilize the value of fabi. But too many tried to purchase gold, so the government suspended the sales on April 29. Many bankers and business-men felt that the government had not really issued a clear statement on

its foreign-exchange policy. With so much uncertainty about the ration-
ale behind decisions on the rate of exchange, some felt it was difficult for
the government to stabilize the currency.[72]

At that point, all foreign-exchange transactions had to be handled
through the Central Bank of China at the fixed rate. Twenty-two banks
were listed as "appointed banks" who could deal with foreign exchange
by going through the Central Bank. The government also issued a list of
approved imports for which foreign exchange would be provided.
A second list included items for which a special permit was needed to
receive the foreign exchange. And finally, some items were listed as
nonessential and could not be imported. In theory, these regulations
gave the government some control over foreign trade. To order products
from overseas, merchants had to deposit funds in yuan at the Central
Bank before foreign exchange could be arranged and goods ordered
from abroad.[73]

That rate of 2,020 yuan to $1 had been roughly comparable to the
black-market rate, but that rate increased an average of 25 percent
monthly, which meant that the official rate was quickly overvalued. This
triggered the adjustment in August to 3,350 yuan per dollar.[74] As Arthur
Young remembered, "It was not long until we met the expected difficulties
from overvaluation . . . The printing presses spewed out a flood of money,
and reserves were sold too cheaply. Reserves . . . dwindled alarmingly."[75] By
late September 1946, the black-market rate for American dollars reach
almost 4,400 yuan for $1. The local press reported that there was over
US$100 million in American banknotes being hoarded in China, primarily
by wealthy Chinese who had lost faith in fabi and had the means to acquire
US currency.[76]

The exchange-rate policy had a major impact on China's difficulty in
recovering from the war. Almost a year after surrender in late June 1946,
the *Dagong bao*, one of China's best newspapers, ran a lengthy analysis of
what it considered to be an industrial crisis in China. It noted that two
sectors of the industrial economy were suffering the most. Industries such
as drugs, paper, cement, and tobacco that faced foreign competition
suffered because imports were cheaper in the Chinese market and limited
the growth of Chinese firms. The second was industries that relied on
foreign sales such as silk, knitting, and handkerchief production, whose

products were more expensive when sold overseas. By contrast, cotton textiles relied on cheap, imported American raw cotton and thus found their costs reduced.[77]

In another editorial on April 29, 1946, the *Dagong bao* noted that the situation had not improved. "More than eight months have elapsed since the conclusion of the war and five months have passed since sea traffic was re-opened. But China's foreign trade has been shrouded by an atmosphere of pessimism." The paper blamed the greatly overvalued yuan relative to the dollar "so import trade is in a very favorable position and export trade is in a very unfavorable position." The paper also criticized the government for relying solely on the United States for trade. Developing an export market in Southeast Asia was critical.[78]

Not long after, on May 14, 1946, the *Xinwen bao* ran an editorial "Save the Export Trade!" The editorial put direct blame for the crisis in exports on the government, whose exchange-rate policy priced China's exports out of foreign markets. "If our exports cannot establish a good standing in the new, postwar world market, who can guarantee that Japan will not re-expand her export trade after a certain period of time? Who can guarantee that India will not take Japan's place?"[79] These sentiments were echoed by a *Shenbao* editorial of June 4, 1946. "Since V-J Day the European and American shipping companies have resumed operations and large numbers of ships have called at this port [Shanghai] but due to the high commodity prices prevailing in this city the amount of exports has been small, so that most of these ships have left port without any cargo." By contrast, the imported goods were quite cheap when sold in Chinese currency. "We depend upon foreign countries not only for the supply of cotton and wheat, but also for oranges, aerated water, candies, cigarettes and even the soap bubbles with which children play. Yet our exports are almost nil."[80]

Statistics verified this journalistic account. According to an analysis done of the Shanghai trade for the first six months of 1946, Shanghai's total volume of trade was 380 billion yuan, which was US$190 million at the official exchange rate. Of this total, 347 billion yuan were imports and only 34.8 billion exports. In other words, imports were ten times the amount of exports. China's foreign-exchange reserves were thus being drained in the process. Almost half of the total was for cotton and cotton products, with gasoline and other fuels being second. Chemical and medicines were next, followed by cars and trucks. As for exports, raw silk, bristles, leather goods, and knitted cotton goods led the way. Only a negligible amount of tea was being exported. The official statistics underestimated the trade deficit because some products were smuggled into China without legal clearance.[81] Arthur Young predicted that China would run out of foreign-exchange reserves if it continued current policies.

China adopted a more widespread program of control of trade in November 1946, designed primarily to restrict imports. Import permits were required for all items, and many items were prohibited entirely. The latter included luxuries, toys, and so on that were deemed nonessential. Other items that were legal to import faced quota restrictions. Raw materials and capital goods were given priority for importation. The regulations required equal treatment for government and private enterprises. The new regulations were designed to eliminate the black market in US dollars, since all imports would have to have a government license and foreign exchange arranged through the Central Bank of China. The black-market rate had been almost 50 percent higher than the official rate.[82]

But altering the situation was not easy. Importers needed to demonstrate that they had foreign funds available to receive an import license. But since most could not obtain them legally, they attempted to acquire such funds on the black market, which drove up the rate. So, the licensing system did not rein in the gap between the official and black-market rates of exchange. The government attempted to only grant licenses when the foreign exchange had been obtained legitimately, but this was difficult. In January 1947, the black-market rate for American dollars was nearly two- and-one-half times the official rate.[83]

One important effect of the failure of China to revive trade was the loss of customs revenue. A confidential study of the Chinese national budget done by the US State Department in July 1947 looked at the drastic shortage of revenue by the Chinese government. It noted that the yield from customs duties in 1946 in comparative terms was only 20 percent of the prewar level. "This failure of customs revenue to recover to the prewar level" was largely due to factors such as "foreign trade subject to duty during 1946 was sharply reduced from the prewar level in terms of both value and quantity." A reduction in trade meant a reduction in tariff revenue. Additionally, imports for government agencies were generally exempted from tariffs.[84]

SHIPPING AND TRANSPORTATION PROBLEMS

Foreign-exchange difficulties and government regulations were not the only factors that inhibited a recovery of trade. Transportation woes plagued China. Prior to the war with Japan, foreign shipping companies had played a major role in China. Under the unequal treaties, foreign ships were allowed to ply the interior rivers of China carrying freight and passengers. Britain had been especially dominant. In 1937, 42.4 percent of China's domestic shipping and 36.5 of her international shipping had been carried by British vessels.[85] Foreign gunboats could also enter the interior waters to "protect their interests," hence the famous gunboat diplomacy. Decades earlier, the Chinese had tried to counter by establishing the China Merchants Steam Navigation Company but with limited success.

Foreign intrusion into the interior of China under those conditions had rankled Chinese nationalists from Sun Yat-sen to most of the postwar leadership of the Guomindang Party. Restricting foreign commercial and military ships in interior areas had been a long-standing goal. When the new Nanjing government began negotiating with the foreign powers to end or modify the unequal treaties, top priority went to the issues of tariff autonomy and terminating extraterritoriality, but the issue of shipping rights was not far behind. In August of 1929, the Guomindang's Central Political Council decided to add recovery of China's shipping rights to the treaty revision effort. The Shanghai Shipping Association (Shanghai hangye gonghui) headed by Yu Xiaqing conducted propaganda on the issue, demanding that the government do more to get foreign ships out of Chinese domestic waters. Although Nanjing had made limited progress on the issue before the war, it was of deep concern to many within the Guomindang.[86]

With the unequal treaties terminated during the war, Chinese leaders across the board favored prohibiting the ships of foreign companies from entering interior rivers. This was, in fact, the policy of many nations, including the United States. America allowed foreign ships to trade at select international ports but did not extend the right of domestic trade, a policy that China seemed prepared to adopt at war's end.[87]

While it is understandable why Chinese would favor ending foreign privilege in shipping, the hard reality was that China was desperately short of water transport at the conclusion of the war. A great deal of shipping had been destroyed, railways were still not fully restored, and China lacked a usable highway system for the most part. The Office of Intelligence Coordination and Liaison of the Department of State of the United States undertook a confidential assessment of Chinese merchant shipping in July 1946. The report noted that in 1935 vessels involved in shipping in China that were over 100 gross tons in size totaled 6.6 million gross tons. Chinese ships were only about half of the total of the inland and coastal trade, the rest were foreign. But during the war, much of this was sunk. "China in these years lost most of its merchant fleet by seizure or sinking. When the war ended in the summer of 1945 the Chinese merchant fleet was reduced to about 90,000 to 100,000 gross tons of river craft, including vessels retaken from the Japanese." The China Merchants Steam Navigation Company lost virtually all its shipping during the war.

Compounding the difficulties, less than one-fifth of the railway mileage in China outside of Manchuria was in service in the summer of 1946. With the ban on foreign shipping in interior rivers, the report concluded, China desperately needed 1.0 million gross tons of river and coastal vessels. The report concluded that China lacked any ship-building industry and could not develop one in the short run. Most commercial ships would have to be purchased from the United States.[88] A similar report done in 1948 by the Chinese Ministry of Communications concluded that China lost 86 percent of its shipping vessels during the war.[89]

Late in the war era, the Chinese government began to plan for a revival of shipping and designated the China Merchants Steam Navigation Company as the key agency for government investment. The Ministry of Communications developed a five-year plan that highlighted growth of the company. At the time, the company had a very limited number of river vessels in the Sichuan area. An immediate source of vessels was those seized from the Japanese. In October 1945, the minister of communications Yu Feipeng telegraphed T. V. Soong requesting all boats confiscated from enemy shipping companies. Chinese authorities confiscated eleven steamers from the Japanese Toa kaiun kaisha (East Asia Navigation Company) and gave these to the China Merchants Navigation Company.[90] But in fact Japan had lost a great deal of its commercial shipping to Allied submarines and surface ships. Ultimately, the only solution was to purchase foreign ships, primarily from the United States, with some coming from Canada. Soong announced in March 1946 that purchases from America were underway.

Soong did try to diversify his sources. In early 1946, he worked to arrange purchase of five Danish ships and two Swedish ships through the China Purchasing Agency in London. These would have gone to the China Merchants Company.[91] But despite these efforts, many of the purchase attempts fell through because of complications in the negotiations or questions about the quality of the vessels. These problems delayed Soong's attempt to establish domestic and foreign shipping under Chinese control.[92]

The China Merchants Steam Navigation Company did manage a significant revival in the postwar period. At the end of 1945, it had 366 ships, and by June of 1948, it reached a peak of 490. Nearly 74 percent of these ships by tonnage were purchased overseas; less than 20 percent had been confiscated from Japanese companies, and only 6.3 percent of the total tonnage remained from the Yangzi fleet in Sichuan. One major shift in the shipping industry was the move toward government control. In 1935, only 11 percent of total tonnage of Chinese shipping was held by the government; the figure for June 1948 was 44 percent, with the China Merchants Steam Navigation Company the dominant player. Private shipping was still the majority, but many of these companies were small firms with small ships. The largest of the private companies was Lu Zuofu's Minsheng Shipping Company, which held 7.6 percent of all tonnage. With the Guomindang government backing the China Merchants Navigation Company, Lu turned to Canadian funding with some assistance from the Jincheng Bank. A major problem for all shipping companies was that the government used their boats to ship supplies and troops during the civil war but was slow to compensate the firms.[93]

Despite this modest revival of Chinese shipping after the war, transportation problems inhibited the revival of commerce. The textile mills of Shanghai, Tianjin, and Qingdao had to rely on imported cotton as the domestic supply could not reach the cities. Transportation difficulties and communist control of cotton-growing areas prevented raw cotton from getting to the cities. Before the war, China's textile industry had used 2.5 million bales of domestically grown cotton. After the war only 500,000–800,000 bales were estimated to be available. Before the war, China had imported about 300,000 bales of cotton, but from the end of July 1945 until early 1946, 1,250,000 had already been imported. This was a significant strain on China's balance of payments issue, so getting more domestic cotton in production and to market was essential.[94]

The issue of foreign ships in the interior flared up almost immediately over relief shipments that were arriving under the auspices of UNRRA. These were distributed in China by its domestic counterpart, CNRRA. In August 1946, the US Department of Agriculture, the only source supplying UNRRA with wheat, expressed reluctance to provide the monthly quota of 50,000–60,000 tons because CNRRA had not been able to ship earlier supplies to famine areas in the interior.[95] CNRRA had proposed an exception to the shipping rule so that British ships could carry relief supplies directly to famine areas. Arthur Young noted that when CNRRA proposed this, there was strong objection from Nationalist leaders and domestic shipping firms. The dispute, he noted, had significantly delayed getting relief supplies to inland locales that desperately needed them.[96] Soong agreed, and British ships were given permission to bring the relief supplies to inland ports until July 15, 1946. The Chinese Shipping Companies Guild in Shanghai protested this action, stating that Britain was using delivery of emergency aid as a pretext to regain the right of interior navigation.[97]

Shipping was not the only issue that led to problems between UNRRA and its Chinese counterpart CNRRA. In a Senate inquiry held in Washington, DC in July 1946, UNRRA reported that they had curtailed some exports to China because of problems with CNRRA. Specifically, they found that the agency lacked funding and began selling relief goods for cash on the open market, and they used relief goods to pay laborers. Flour meant for relief of famine areas was being dumped and sold for profit on the black market, as was fertilizer. Meanwhile, owners of wharfs in Shanghai were refusing to give space for unloading relief supplies because CNRRA was not paying its bills. The report stated that thirty ships carrying relief supplies were anchored at Wusong without adequate berthing space in Shanghai. Fiorello LaGuardia, the director-general of UNRRA, stated to the Senate Committee that he had no choice but to curtail relief shipments and that he had directly contacted Chiang Kai-shek on May 29 to resolve the situation. Meanwhile, 300 UNRRA officials wrote directly to LaGuardia in July 1946 noting improper handling of supplies, pilfering, and profiteering with China supplies.[98]

UNRRA had been created in November 1943 to aid areas that had been occupied by the Axis Powers. The China program was the largest single program, and 72 percent of the funding came from the United States. From the outset, UNRRA was designed for the relief of civilian populations in war-torn areas. Reports that UNRRA cotton was used to produce military items led to the China office issuing a circular directive to cotton mills in Shanghai in August 1946. Relief cotton could only be used to produce cloth for civilian use, not for uniforms for Chiang's military. A similar directive was issued to Tianjin mills. But this issue did not go away. Reports in the summer of 1947 suggested that UNRRA vehicles and rolling stock were being used for the transportation of military supplies and soldiers. Nonetheless, pressure from LaGuardia and the US Congress seems to have resolved some of the disputes between UNRRA and CNRRA. By mid-August 1946, for instance, additional wharf space become available in Shanghai.[99]

The UNRRA program had made its first deliveries to Shanghai in November 1945, and the program was largely completed by November 1947 with nearly 518 million dollars' worth of supplies delivered. A study done in the immediate aftermath acknowledged some of the problems. "Early congestion in the ports, paucity of transportation facilities within China, and the chronic shortage of local currency with which to operate provided almost insuperable obstacles to effective distribution." The report also was candid about issues between UNRRA and CNRRA. "Relations between CNRRA and the China Office of UNRRA were, in the early period of active operations, marred by disagreement, inefficiency, and the piling up of UNRRA supplies in the ports without adequate organization, transportation facilities, or funds for distribution."[100] The problems were simply yet another area of friction between the United States and China in the aftermath of World War II, which plagued economic relations in particular.

Arthur Young tried to find ways to increase China's exports, which were so minimal compared with imports. He felt an increase in Chinese shipping was crucial. In a letter sent to T. V. Soong, then head of the Executive Yuan, on July 1, 1946, Young noted that many of China's exports such as wood oil, bristles, and hides and skins, were produced in the interior. Many egg products needed immediate refrigeration. If these had to be shipped to Shanghai on domestic shipping and then transferred to oceangoing vessels, this would increase the cost. Allowing foreign ships to take on cargo along the Yangzi River and at other interior ports would help boost China's exports, especially since there was a significant shortage of river shipping. Also, Tianjin exporters could not ship to Shanghai but had to ship directly overseas, which inhibited economic recovery, in Young's view. Although he realized this was politically sensitive, Young felt that the most urgent matter was to increase exports to strengthen the yuan and to revive the economy.[101]

In this case, the Supreme National Defense Council decided in early June 1946 that four Yangzi ports – Nanjing, Wuhu, Jiujiang, and Hankou – would be reopened for foreign shipping for one year. Once again, Chinese shipping leaders objected to this policy.[102] An editorial in the *Shang bao* on June 13, 1946, criticized the new policy, stating that many of the imports were luxury goods that China did not need, wasting valuable foreign exchange. Further, "after the opening of the four river ports, the dumping of cheap goods will be made even easier, due to the fact that foreign steamers can sail to the inland ports."[103] But foreign observers felt trade was still stifled. The Hongkong and Shanghai Bank reopened its branch in Hankou in 1946, but the manager observed that "we were doing no business at all." Their big bank building on the Hankou Bund was no longer needed; most was rented out. The manager reported that "there was virtually no shipping, there was nothing, the only ships that were moving up and down the river were tank landing craft which were carrying the UNRRA supplies to starving Chinese in the interior."[104]

T. V. Soong was also approached in February 1946 to allow American shipping of cotton to Qingdao and Tianjin from Shanghai. A shortage of raw materials was stifling the textile industry in those cities, but the only available cargo shipping was American coal ships that carried coal to Shanghai but were empty on the return trip north. The Chinese Textile Industries Group wrote Soong on February 9, 1946, supporting this request, noting that the shortage of raw material in Qingdao and Tianjin threatened to shut down textile production. Permission of the Executive Yuan was required for this, which Soong apparently granted in this case.[105] Still, Frank Tamagna, in a draft report for the Executive Yuan written in October 1946, observed that "economic conditions in Northern China in the summer of 1946 may be described as stagnant." He attributed this to the shortages of raw materials and coal caused by the lack of transportation. "This state of affairs affected particularly foreign businesses, which were reduced to almost a complete standstill." He observed the primary causes: "the high costs and inadequacy of Chinese shipping, the restrictions imposed upon shipping and the complications involved in foreign-exchange financing were the chief obstacles to import and export trades."[106]

Shipping was not the only transportation issue. Despite wartime conditions, aviation grew in importance during the war. Indeed, flying over the Hump became the key link with the outside world. During the conflict, China had relied on American ties. The China National Aviation Corporation (CNAC) had been established as a partnership with Pan-American airways, which held 45 percent of the ownership. Beginning as early as November 1943, Kung began to entertain proposals for postwar aviation. Although he recognized that China would need foreign capital, there was strong feeling that China must protect its sovereignty and maintain control over its domestic airlines. In January 1944 Kung received a confidential report that in postwar China, foreign ownership in domestic Chinese airlines should be limited to 20 to 25 percent of the stock and that contracts with foreign firms should give the Chinese government the right to purchase the foreign shares at a fair price at any time during the contract. In addition, China should diversify its foreign partners. TWA, an American airline, had made an offer to train pilots for China as a first step to get an entrée into the China market and break Pan-American's monopoly. John Keswick of Jardine's had written

Kung in December 1943 about a postwar partnership between China and Britain for international routes.[107]

W. L. Bond, vice-president and ranking American partner in CNAC, recognized that China would like to limit foreign ownership of Chinese domestic airlines while benefiting from foreign capital and technology. He noted that the United States provided that any American domestic airline wishing to carry airmail had to be at least 75 percent American-owned. He thought a similar limit might be suitable for postwar China. In addition, he understood that the Chinese government might wish to have the provision that it could buy out foreign partners if it so chose. Overall, Bond was very optimistic of the future of Chinese aviation in the postwar era.[108] One concern was that Stalin was pressing China for joint development of aviation links through northwest China to the Soviet Union. When the war ended suddenly, the future organization of postwar Chinese aviation was still unclear. But the importance of aviation – a vital lifeline during the war – would not change. The slowness in restoring shipping and the rehabilitation of China's railways guaranteed that the reliance on air transport would be undiminished.

A DIFFICULT BEGINNING

When the war ended in the late summer of 1945, the feeling of euphoria in China was short-lived. The prospect of a looming civil war was perhaps the key factor. But the failure to stabilize the currency and restart foreign trade played a vital role in the despair. The psychology of hyperinflation continued. Industrialists found holding raw materials and finished products more profitable than manufacturing. As a US State Department intelligence report noted, under conditions of hyperinflation, "industrial production was frequently a bad gamble for low stakes. Many private manufacturers preferred to hold material inventories for the almost inevitable appreciation in their market values rather than to accept the risk of converting those inventories into finished goods the prices of which might not cover the mounting costs of production."[109]

A series of bad policy decisions by the government and inept administration undermined the takeover of the formerly occupied areas. Rapacious behavior by officials arriving from Sichuan and a disastrous exchange policy for the old currency of the occupied area created an atmosphere that undercut both demand for products and a feeling of security in business investment. Proud of its achievement in fulfilling Sun Yat-sen's goal of ending the unequal treaties, Chinese officials began to exclude foreigners from China's economy, which made recovery of transportation especially difficult. Guomindang policies alienated Chiang's American partners, particularly in the Treasury Department. Could the government salvage the peace? Events in 1946 would be decisive.

CHAPTER 4

1946

Failure to Revive the Economy in the Aftermath of War

DR. ARTHUR N. YOUNG HAD SERVED AS A FINANCIAL ADVISER to the government of China for seventeen years. In the late summer of 1946, however, Young decided to resign and return to America in part to seek medical treatment for several health issues, including malaria. Young assumed this would end his China adventure, but in fact he would return for a time in 1947 and worked for China in the United States. But another reason for his departure from China was his deep pessimism about the financial situation and his assessment that neither Chiang Kai-shek nor other officials would change a course which he saw as disastrous. Only a few months earlier as the war seemed to be heading toward an Allied victory over Japan, he had been more optimistic. But the botched liberation of coastal areas, the difficulties of revival of trade and commerce, and the quick onset of hyperinflation suddenly changed his perception.

Young was not the only foreigner working for the Chinese government to become quickly disillusioned. L. K. Little, inspector general of the Chinese Maritime Customs, wrote in his diary on September 19, 1946, "I am very discouraged, after one year of China's 'rehabilitation.' I realize there is unrest all over the world and that no country is escaping problems and trouble, but China's mishandling of her great opportunity is so easily avoidable and so unnecessary that it is most saddening." A few days later, he added the observation that "the feeling of hopelessness and frustration among the honest Chinese is one of the most tragic and disturbing features of the present day."[1]

Arthur Young wrote a farewell memorandum to Chiang Kai-shek on August 31, 1946 in which he was brutally frank about the situation.

"The financial situation in China is basically unsound. ... The violent phase of inflation – in which prices multiply several-fold in a month – is postponed only by heavy use of reserves of foreign exchange, gold, and enemy property." Those reserves, he argued, were fast being depleted. To maintain the stability of the fabi at a rate of 2,020 yuan to US$1, which had been set on March 4, 1946, China spent US$40 million a month in June and July of 1946. China's foreign reserves would be gone by the end of 1947 if nothing were done. "Drastic curtailment of expenditures, especially military, and firm rebuilding of revenues to restore equilibrium is the fundamental policy needed before the situation gets completely out of hand."[2]

It is doubtful that Young held out much hope that any of his policy suggestions would carry the day; earlier warnings had largely fallen on deaf ears. But his prediction of financial collapse proved accurate. Estimated price indexes for China based on the prewar average of January to June 1937 as a base of 1 show a price index in January 1946 of 1,827. The following January in 1947, it reached 7,550. By June 1947, 24,830, and by December 1947, 103,400. By July 1948, when the government abandoned fabi for the ill-fated gold yuan, the index reached an astounding 2,877,000.[3] By autumn 1947, the government was printing 300 million pieces of currency monthly.[4] Small denominations of yuan were so worthless that in Hong Kong they were shredded and used for stuffing in packing crates.[5] The financial collapse that Young had predicted was realized.

Attempts to implement price controls repeatedly failed, as almost universally happened in cases of hyperinflation. In the spring of 1946, the price of rice in Shanghai began to accelerate. Shanghai mayor Wu Guozhen had mandated a fixed price for rice sales. As a result, the supply began to drop as farmers were unwilling to sell rice to Shanghai buyers at the set price.[6] China was simply too big and too chaotic at the time for the Guomindang government to impose fixed prices.

Young had hoped that China could turn things around with victory over Japan. But little went as Young wished. The abrupt end of the war provided no transition period for imported goods to enter the market before China faced the problem of eliminating the puppet currencies. In Young's view, the Guomindang government had mishandled the conversion of the currency of the Wang Jingwei regime, greatly undervaluing the banknotes. This had impoverished the population of the lower Yangzi, alienating them as well. It also reduced the ability of the easterners to purchase goods, stifling the revival of the economy and restricting the recovery of tax revenue. Most critically, however, was Chiang's decision to focus on the military. There would be no disarmament after the war against Japan; Chiang was gearing up to fight the communists.

Sensing that the chance to stabilize the currency was being lost forever, Young sent a confidential memo on April 3, 1946, to Bei Zuyi, general manager of the Central Bank of China, for whom Young directly worked. Bei apparently shared the contents of this memo with Chiang Kai-shek. In it, Young outlined what he thought were the key steps that had to be implemented to stabilize the currency. The failure of Chiang and the Guomindang leadership to implement any of these in part triggered his resignation and the final memo of August 1946. The key item was that China must expedite troop disbandment "and stop expansion of military, air, and naval projects except those immediately needed for maintaining internal order and national defense." China should also "suspend expansion of Government economic enterprises and limit public works to those necessary for rehabilitation and those whose internal costs can be covered by non-inflationary means." The government should "gradually reduce by sales, the number of Government enterprises and restore and encourage private ownership and management both Chinese and foreign."[7]

The above steps were aimed at reducing government spending to eliminate the need for deficits. But Young also felt China had to restore a revenue stream that had largely been lost when the Guomindang retreated from the coast under the Japanese onslaught. "Reduce current Central Bank advances by actively developing non-inflationary revenue from the sale of imported consumer goods . . . the sale of domestic goods and property that is under government control; and the sale of gold, silver, and foreign exchange."[8] Young argued that following these steps could restore confidence in the financial system and curb inflation. Yet the writing was already on the wall; the massive expenditure of foreign exchange in June and July 1946 revealed clearly that none of the measures he recommended were being followed.

There were a few bright spots. Some sectors of the industrial economy such as cotton textiles recovered, quickly reaching prewar levels.[9] But Young felt that this recovery could not be sustained without stabilizing the currency and improving transportation. He had strong reservations about the large role that government was coming to play in the economy. And he felt that China was squandering its foreign-exchange reserves both by an unrealistic exchange rate and by too many expensive and ill-advised projects that increased government spending and reliance on foreign imports.

LIMITING GOVERNMENT ENTERPRISES AND PROJECTS

One reason for Young's pessimism in the early months of 1946 was that he had become increasingly disillusioned with the Nationalist leadership, particularly T. V. Soong. Young felt that China had very limited foreign-exchange reserves and should be cautious in using them. Purchases should be directly related to rehabilitating the infrastructure and economy as frugally as possible to restore economic activity. Young felt that Soong had become overly enthusiastic and was not being careful in picking his projects. In an entry in his confidential diary of January 23, 1946, Young noted that "T. V. is spending a lot for ships, etc. sending telegrams from all over the country, and apparently has no systematic record. The Central Bank does not know the whole picture, nor the Ministry of Finance or anyone." Careless budgeting was not a luxury China could afford. "Payments might be credited against funds due from U.S. for army costs in China but not arranged."[10] He reiterated this point in late March. "The Government still is spending recklessly and pumping out money, which is beyond Central Bank control." Leadership was the problem, he admitted. "T. V. [Soong] is not holding a tight rein, but has become more of a politician. O. K. [Yu Hongjun] is not strong enough to hold back."[11]

Young was also dismayed as some Americans pushed China into investments and deals that he thought wasteful of foreign exchange. Perhaps the most egregious in his view was the American effort to get China to purchase a great deal of surplus US military equipment that was left in the Western Pacific. Young felt that much of this – including large trucks – would not be useful in China and would be a waste of foreign exchange. The costs of the deal, which was pushed through, was an estimated US$240–$300 million.[12] General George Marshall, who had arrived in China to negotiate a coalition government between the Guomindang and the communists, had pushed this because he thought the American property could help stabilize prices and control inflation.[13]

The Chinese Supply Commission, a Chinese agency in Washington, arranged lines of credit with the US Export-Import Bank of Washington to purchase capital equipment in the United States for railway materials, power plant facilities, coal-mining equipment, old ships, and other materials, designed to help revive China's economy. For instance, the line of credit for purchase of coal-mining equipment was US $1.5 million.[14] Had China entered a period of economic stability, these advances would have been very helpful in recovering from the war. But in the circumstances in 1946, they increased debt, while China was unable to get mining moving under existing conditions.

The continued division between T. V. Soong and H. H. Kung plagued China in Young's view. Soong had presented his plan to Chiang Kai-shek, who had not objected. But Young felt that Chiang would consult H. H. Kung, who would oppose the plans because they came from Soong. Thus, Chiang would have "divided consul [*sic*] and this is unfortunate for China." In addition, Soong did not support or cooperate with the minister of finance Yu Hongjun, whose position was therefore undercut.[15] Young recalled an awkward meeting with Yu in Soong's outer office in January 1946. Soong had sent for Yu to discuss a financial plan that Young had not shared with Yu. When asked why, Young had to admit that Soong had asked him not to discuss it. "I am much embarrassed by T. V.'s needlessly keeping O. K. (Yu) out," Young confessed.[16]

JAPANESE REPARATIONS

One area from which both Arthur Young and most Chinese financial leaders had hoped for revenue was in reparations from Japan. Yet this proved problematic. Confiscation of Japanese resources such as shipping was not very successful because so much had been lost in the war. Most of the industrial plant in Manchuria had been seized by the Soviet Union. One minor success occurred with the rehabilitation of the silk industry in China, which had been devastated by the war. Much of the machinery in filatures was seized for scrap by the Japanese and the market for silk in the West disappeared with the war. Mulberry acreage had dropped by 40–60 percent compared to prewar. Filature silk production in 1946 would be less than one-third the prewar output, although handicraft production had actually increased and ameliorated the decline.[17]

T. V. Soong sought to have 5 million grams of silkworm eggs delivered from occupied Japan. General Wedemeyer, commander of the US forces in China, sent repeated messages to General Douglas MacArthur, Supreme Commander Allied Powers, Tokyo, regarding this matter. In January 1946 after some delay, US Army headquarters finally agreed that 150,000 sheets of silkworm eggs of 5 grams each would be shipped from Japan. China also sought a substantial number of mulberry seedlings to provide food for the silkworms. The initial shipment had only a modest impact on Chinese production. Problems developed with the Occupation authorities over the quantity and terms of the shipments, so the process was terminated in 1947. In both the Chinese press and statements by Chinese government officials, there was substantial criticism of US authorities in Japan for their failure to provide additional Japanese silk supplies as war reparations. This became another irritant in US–China relations.[18]

THE ROLE OF PRIVATE BUSINESS: STATE ENTERPRISES FAVORED OVER PRIVATE

In the immediate aftermath of Japanese surrender, the Guomindang government and its officials greatly increased their control of business enterprises. Much of this occurred when government authorities confiscated properties and firms owned by the Japanese or by Chinese labeled as collaborators. Chongqing set up an Enemy and Public Properties Supervision Bureau (Diweiye chuli ju), which was charged with taking over and operating businesses that had been confiscated. T. V. Soong, then head of the Executive Yuan, directed the establishment of the office along with the minister of finance. But as the *Dagong bao* noted

December 3, 1945, pilfering from confiscated properties was rampant, particularly from warehouses.[19] Nonetheless, private business had clearly taken a back seat to government firms in the aftermath of war.

The private businesses that did reopen after Japanese surrender often faced difficulties getting access to capital. Private banks had played a significant role in prewar China in providing liquidity to private industrialists but were greatly weakened by the war and did not recover their earlier position. Wartime conditions led to an increase in the dominance of the government banks. In 1932, about 56 percent of total banking deposits were in the hands of private banks in China. In 1945, this figure fell to less than 2 percent, while the Central Bank alone held 71 percent. Government banks financed primarily government deficits and the enterprises controlled by government-connected individuals and agencies. Private banks, which had been the main supplier of business loans, had few resources. The lack of access to bank loans thus hampered the recovery of private industry.[20]

When economist He Lian (Franklin L. Ho) left government service in 1946 and joined the Jincheng Banking Corporation, he first made a study of the private bank's business operations. He urged the banking management to broaden their activities from banking into subsidiary activities in trade and industry. The opportunities in banking itself were just too limited for a private bank. "I was of the opinion that under present conditions in the country, the prospect for development of commercial banking was limited. When an economy is inflated, few people are inclined to make deposits, and few banks inclined to make loans of money which, in all probability, would be valueless when paid back." Most money was deposited in government banks, not commercial banks. "I was of the opinion that commercial banks would do best to use their accumulated assets for productive purposes outside of banking per se." He advised the Jincheng Bank to continue to diversity its other business interests such as its holdings in the Yongli Chemical Industry and Minsheng Industrial Corporation of Lu Zuofu.[21]

Zhou Zuomin, the founder of the Jincheng Bank, who employed He Lian, seems to have followed that strategy. Although dogged by rumors that he had collaborated with the Japanese during the war, Zhou had partially dispelled these when he met personally with Chiang Kai-shek in

January 1946 in Chongqing. Following that encounter, Zhou would engage in a series of meetings with various businessmen and bankers in an effort to revive the Jincheng Bank. Before leaving Sichuan, he met with Lu Zuofu, whose Minsheng Company was a leading private shipping firm. Throughout the spring of 1946, Zhou visited with many banking and business leaders particularly in Shanghai, as well as government officials such as Yu Hongjun and Chen Lifu.[22] But the traditional business practices of prewar private banks such as Jincheng could not work in the postwar, high-inflation world.

Arthur Young felt that given greater freedom to operate, private enterprises would speed up economic growth, and he was frustrated with the unwillingness of the government leaders to give up control of enterprises. Young wanted to increase tax revenues to curb the deficit, but he felt that the government firms were not contributing very much to this goal. Many government enterprises were rather a failure. As the United Nations Relief and Rehabilitation Administration (UNRRA) office noted in its report of January 1947, the Chinese state controlled a significant number of businesses, and the profits from these could have been a significant source of revenue. Yet the report noted that in the previous fiscal year, only 2 percent of revenue came from these profits, which covered a minuscule 0.7 percent of government expenditures. Clearly the government-run enterprises were not successful in that regard.[23]

Because the government-connected businesses were not providing much tax revenue for the government, Young had hoped that private business and banking could be revived so as to provide a source of revenue. But this was slow to happen. Government-connected firms had several advantages unavailable to the private sector. A secret US government report noted privileges which accrued to government firms:[24]

Plants owned by the government or by ostensibly private interests with strong government connections ... possessed a number of competitive advantages. The nature of these advantages varied from plant to plant, but most government plants have received some or all of the following forms of financial assistance: [1] direct subsidies; [2] tax exemptions; [3] low interest on loans from government banks; [4] opportunity to purchase fuel and materials from other government enterprises at prices below market; [5] access to government-rationed rice for use as part of wage payments; [6] favorable government contracts for the purchase of output; and [7] advanced payments for output and moratoria on payment for materials, with resultant opportunities to invest surplus funds in profitable speculative ventures.

Under these conditions, government firms began to increase their hold on China's economy as the sector of private manufacturing shrunk.

LIMITING FOREIGNERS AND FOREIGN FIRMS

Prewar China had been a semicolonial country with many foreigners enjoying extraterritoriality and foreign firms dominating the treaty ports. With an end to their privileges, many foreign companies found it difficult to restart their businesses. Chinese government enterprises were privileged over both Chinese and foreign private firms. As noted earlier, the unrealistic exchange rate, the limitations on conversions of foreign exchange, and bureaucratic obstacles all hindered private foreign firms. As China began to draft a new company law, leaders in the Executive Yuan favored a policy approach that would allow foreign firms to have an active role in the economy. The Legislative Yuan, however, tended to be opposed to foreigners. The economist Ma Yinchu was the leader of the antiforeign faction.[25] After the end of extraterritoriality, Chinese authorities required foreign companies to register with the Chinese government and comply with its regulations. But many foreign firms felt that the regulations were cumbersome and unclear and that they would be fleeced by Chinese authorities.[26]

These issues came to the fore when the United States and China signed a new treaty of commerce in November 1946. The result of months of negotiations, the treaty appeared to be one of equality, but much of the press, especially the liberal and leftist press, was skeptical. The *Dagong bao* in an editorial of November 6, 1946, noted, "a perusal of it gives one the impression that it is truly equal in form. However, since China and the United States are entirely different in national strength,

the advantages or disadvantages of the treaty to one nation will be different from those to another." The newspaper was very suspicious that the
treaty was heavily weighted toward the United States. The terms of the
treaty opened both countries up for businesses to establish themselves in
the other country and to engage in trade. But the paper felt that this
would greatly benefit American business, which could take advantage of
the China market, while Chinese firms would lack the strength to do so in
America.[27]

The editorial also noted the glaring inequality in terms of immigration. The United States continued to restrict Chinese entry, and many
states barred Chinese from owning property, yet the treaty gave
Americans the right to travel freely in China and purchase property.
Extraterritoriality might be gone, but the editorial writer suspected that
Americans in China would get better treatment than Chinese in America,
where discrimination would continue. The treaty provided for equality in
navigation but, the paper noted, "since China does not have a single
ocean-going steamer, the result will be that only one of the contracting
parties will receive 'most favored nation treatment.'"[28]

Key leaders of the Legislative Yuan feared that, because American firms
were much stronger than Chinese, they would dominate the Chinese
economy. Meanwhile, American firms lobbied the State Department to
pressure China to open its economy to foreign business. When George
Marshall went to China on his year-long mission, he was asked to press
Chiang Kai-shek on the matter. Although Chiang was eager to accommodate Marshall, the latter was primarily focused on military and political
matters not economic. The final treaty satisfied neither group – American
businessmen with interest in China nor the members of the Legislative
Yuan. The Shanghai American Chamber of Commerce opposed ratifica-
tion of the treaty on the ground that it violated the Open Door Policy.[29]

Many leftist writers, including those affiliated with the Chinese
Communist Party, supported limits on imports. They argued that the
United States was taking advantage of its dominance in East Asia in the
wake of Japanese surrender and dumping American products in China.
They maintained that the Chiang policy was to allow America to "indus-
trialize America and agriculturalize China." This became a dominant
theme in communist rhetoric.[30] Two areas where the competition

between enterprises controlled by the Guomindang government and its officials and by private firms – Chinese and foreign – was especially strong were textiles and electric power production.

TEXTILES

When the war ended, the textile industry was in terrible shape, with most mills producing very little in the last months of the war. In her study of the Shanghai textile industry, Wang Ju noted that in early 1945 only 5.9 percent of spindles and 8.1 percent of looms in Chinese-owned mills were actually operating. Shortages of power, capital, and raw material were severe. Yet Wang argues that textile production revived quickly in 1946. Demand for textiles was intense because of wartime shortages. Raw cotton was available from overseas, mostly America but also India and Brazil. Half of China's imports in 1946 was raw cotton. Most importantly, one of the major constraints on production by Chinese mills in the prewar era – the competition from Japanese mills – was now gone. Japanese competition was also removed in overseas markets in Southeast Asia, opening the door for Chinese sales.[31]

Government-connected ventures had the upper hand in the postwar era; they had a much easier time of getting access to bank loans. T. V. Soong established the China Textiles Development Company (Zhongguo fangzhi jianshe gongsi), which took over mills confiscated from the Japanese, on November 26, 1945. Although many of the private textile magnates called on Soong to sell the mills to the private sector or transfer ownership to Chinese industrialists who had lost equipment in the war, Soong rejected this approach. On January 22, 1946, he held a press conference in Shanghai and stated that private businesses lacked the capital to revive the industry, so the government would retain control these mills for the foreseeable future.[32] Of the 5.4 million textile spindles in mills in China in September 1945, this new company held about 2.1 million.[33] It began operating textile mills in Shanghai, Tianjin, Qingdao, and even in the northeast and became the key player in the textile industry. In 1947, it had thirty-eight mills in China, seventeen in Shanghai alone. The government provided capital and access to raw materials.[34] The manager of the company was Shu Yunchang, who had close ties to Soong. The government mills also benefited from the confiscated Japanese equipment, which was generally superior to that in Chinese mills.[35]

He Lian (Franklin Ho), an economist with Nankai University and an adviser with the Ministry of Economic Affairs before working with the Jincheng Bank, recommended to the government that it sell most light industry, including textiles, to private entrepreneurs. Government enterprises, he argued, should be limited to heavy industries such as steel and mining. Professor He noted that his suggestions were not well received by government officials. "I feared that government ownership and operation of textile mills might lead to bureaucratic capitalism. ... Although the textile mills would initially be controlled by the government, the inducement to manipulate them would be too great." In his memoirs, He Lian noted that the officials who favored government rather than private control of the textile mills saw it as a great source of income for the government. So T. V. Soong's plan moved forward.[36]

But private industrialists were not entirely devoid of resources. Many, like the Rong family, had extensive experience in textiles and widespread networks. Total production by both private and government mills increased, and the production of cotton yarn by Chinese mills surpassed the level of 1936 by the beginning of 1947. Private textile mills also began to generate profits; they tended to be more profitable than state-owned mills because they were not burdened by so many political factors. Wang Ju labels these months as a "golden age" of the textile industry in Shanghai, although this came to an end in late 1947.

Christian Henriot in his study of Shanghai industries in the civil war era also notes that textiles initially did well. In the last months of the war, because of the lack of power to operate mills, most factories were idle. But "in the immediate postwar period, Shanghai industries recovered promptly ... with textiles moving ahead of all other sectors." And textiles were by far the dominant sector of industrial production, employing over 62 percent of all industrial workers.[37] But this boom faded. "The process was unsustainable under conditions of high and then hyperinflation. On the opposite, hyperinflation killed the momentum."[38]

Foreign businessmen in textiles did not fare as well. Many felt that they were being shut out of the supply of cotton. They felt that imports were difficult to get, and their mills were at the back of the queue.[39] Complaints from American businesses were sufficiently strong that the US Export-Import Bank, which was supplying a credit of US$33 million for China to purchase American cotton, specifically asked the Chinese government what percentage of the cotton was going to government-connected mills. Arthur Young answered with a memo of December 11, 1947, stating that the China Textiles Development Company and two other mills owned by the Bank of China received about 40 percent of the total cotton allotment and had gotten no special financial credit to purchase it.[40] But writing several months earlier in his private diary, he acknowledged that the US Export-Import Bank had "made a condition that the loan be made available in equal terms to private and government mills in China. Previously the Government favored Government mills." [41] Whatever the truth of the situation, private businessmen felt stymied. On June 24, 1946, the *Dagong bao* noted that almost a year after Japanese surrender, private industry had still not really recovered. The foreign-exchange policy of the government inhibited recovery, while the government made few loans available to private industry.[42]

One group of textile mills that did not fare well were those which had relocated to Free China early in the war against Japan. As the Chiang government retreated inland, ultimately moving the capital to Chongqing in Sichuan province, the government had announced an effort to move factories from eastern areas to the interior. Because of chaotic conditions in the early days, few were successfully moved from the coastal cities such as Shanghai. But when the Guomindang government evacuated Wuhan in October 1938, a much better result was achieved. After arriving in Free China, these factories had a mixed record of success. Lack of electricity, skilled workers, and Japanese bombing plagued most. But demand for cotton textiles was high, so many of the mills were profitable, even under difficult conditions.[43]

When the war abruptly ended, many of these factories had great difficulty reversing the process. Moving back to their original home often proved difficult, particularly if they were not part of a large network like the Rong Brothers group. Much of their equipment was in poor shape, transportation was very difficult, government help minimal, and competition from the better-funded government mills sharp. With the exodus of most of the wartime leadership from the interior to their prewar homes in eastern China, the interior found itself once again overlooked by the government.

The Yudahua Business group had been one the largest textile groups in China on the eve of the war. Unusually, its mills were centered in interior cities, their largest in Wuhan. That mill migrated to Sichuan in 1938, taking its spindles with it. After a profitable stretch during the war, the company was faced with returning to Wuhan. At war's end, management decided not to move that equipment back east, deeming it out of date and not worth the expense of the trip. Even during the war they began to order equipment from Britain, to be delivered when possible. Forty thousand spindles and over 500 looms were on order in 1946. But European production lagged and demand for equipment in India was high. Consequently, the Wuhan factory did not reopen until September 1948 and had only 12,000 spindles in operation when the communists arrived.[44]

The company's other properties fared no better. A mill at Shijiazhuang had been captured by the Japanese early in the war. Much of its equipment had been lost to frequent scrap-metal drives by the occupiers. In the civil war, the mill ran into the same delays in ordering equipment and was unable to get any allocated from Japanese-owned mills. Those had all been claimed by the government. Production was only about 40 percent of the prewar level. A couple of small mills in the interior had been established in isolated areas to escape Japanese bombing as well as government regulations from Chongqing. Yudahua thus missed out on the "golden age" of the textile recovery immediately after the war with Japan.[45] Many of these industrialists were bitter because they felt that they had sacrificed in relocating to help the war effort. But the government seemed to have forgotten their sacrifice and kept the best mills for itself.

The silk industry had a long history in China, although in the modern era it was dwarfed by cotton textiles. Japanese confiscation of filatures for scrap and the collapse of global demand had drastically curtailed silk production in China. Shortly after the end of the war, the government established the China Silk Corporation, which was the equivalent of the government cotton textile group. It was given control over the silk market, setting prices for cocoons. One of the jobs of the silk company was to take possession of silkworm eggs and mulberry seedlings sent from Japan as part of the reparations and barter agreement arranged though the American Occupation forces there. This effort was not very successful, as farmers exhibited little interest in restoring silk production because of low prices and demand for the cocoons. An American intelligence report suggested that only 20 percent of the Japanese eggs and 16 percent of the seedlings actually reached farmers. The corporation set the purchase price for silk cocoons in the spring of 1946 at a fixed rate of 120,000–160,000 yuan per picul. The cost of producing the cocoons by the farmer was estimated by roughly at 168,000 yuan per picul. As a consequence, interest in silk production by the farmers was low.[46]

Ultimately, weak demand overseas, particularly in the United States, inhibited a recovery of the silk industry in China. To get the silk filatures to operate, the China Silk Corporation set the price for finished silk at a price high enough that producers could earn some profit. Unfortunately, this price was about 30 percent higher than the market value of the silk in the US at the official exchange rate, so the corporation ended up by October 1946 with about 10,000 bales of silk held in warehouses. Revival of the silk industry proved elusive.[47] In contrast to the cotton textile industry in which the government controlled nearly half of all mills, the government only owned about 5 percent of the silk filatures. Its involvement was in providing subsidies to produce silk cocoons and in January 1947 providing weaving mills with raw silk. In effect, the government subsidized production so that Chinese silk would not be priced out of the American market.[48]

ELECTRIC POWER

One of the major problems facing industry in China was the shortage of electricity needed to power China's factories. Shanghai, still the industrial center of China, experienced a shortage of electric power after the war that limited industrial production. The Shanghai Power Company was a legacy of the old treaty port system, and Chinese officials made no secret of their desire to create a new, modern Chinese-operated plant. But meanwhile, the existing plant operated well below capacity because of the difficulty of obtaining coal and the inability to replace equipment damaged by the Japanese and American bombing. On the eve of the war with Japan, the plant produced approximately 19 million kilowatt hours weekly. At war's end, production was only 2 million. Damaged equipment was about 40 percent of the total for the plant, and the company borrowed US$3 million in America to purchase replacement parts. But the manager, Paul Hopkins, who had been interned by the Japanese during the war, could not get around foreign-exchange restrictions to buy replacement parts and faced a worldwide shortage of electric power-generating equipment in the aftermath of the war. Eventually, the company was able to repair some of the equipment. Of the estimated 119,000 kilowatts of generating equipment destroyed, 46,000 kilowatts was repaired by 1947.[49]

The shortage of generating equipment limited the revival of textile production in Shanghai. In April of 1946, the usage of electric power by cotton mills in Shanghai was just over 15 million kilowatts. By June, this had increased to almost 19 million. But this was still well below the average monthly usage of 1940, which was 35,685,000. The industrial output index for cotton mills in Shanghai followed this trend closely. With the average production in 1940 as a base of 100, output in April 1946 was only 42.53, for May 45.23, and for June 53.15.[50] The inability of the power plant to replace equipment destroyed in the war limited the economic recovery of Shanghai.

The desire to have Chinese-owned and operated electric power plants is understandable, but in the chaotic conditions of postwar Shanghai, the net result was that the power shortage persisted and shadowed the recovery of industrial production.[51] T. V. Soong had visited the plant in October of 1945 but concluded that they did not have the personnel to operate it. The company needed government permission to raise rates, which was crucial in an environment of rapid inflation. Paul Hopkins persuaded T. V. Soong to grant permission in December 1945 and again in April 1946. But the increase in rates did not keep up with inflation, and the company continued to lose money.[52]

In early April 1946, Arthur Young noted in his diary that the Shanghai Power Company was had lost 3 billion yuan since the end of the war.

Fundamentally, Young suspected that Soong wanted to set up government-owned power plants and therefore provided only limited support to the Shanghai Power Company. "Why not encourage private Chinese and foreign capital?" Young felt that the National Resources Commission was also planning its own plant and was blocking Shanghai Power from importing new generators. He felt this was a poor strategy because China did not have the foreign exchange to buy equipment for the new plan nor the technicians to operate it.[53]

The foreign-owned utilities encountered problems of labor unrest in the last quarter of 1945. Foreign managers of the plants felt that the government was fueling worker grievances and promoting antiforeign sentiment in an attempt to get the foreign owners to turn over the enterprises to the government. The Shanghai Power Company had faced considerable labor unrest in the lead up to Chinese New Year in 1946. Although American diplomatic sources suspected that Guomindang officials were encouraging the labor unrest, they concluded that the Guomindang had become deeply concerned that the communists were infiltrating the labor movement. The government then pressed for the labor activists to compromise with the company, and the police told the workers to return to the plant. Among labor's grievances was the difference in pay scale between foreign and Chinese workers; the latter demanded equal pay for equal work. The union also wanted to monitor and approve dismissal of workers by management.[54]

Major strikes hit the French-owned Tramway, Light and Power Company in Shanghai and in the British-run tramways in Shanghai in January 1946 before Chinese New Year. Labor representatives sought a large bonus to counter the rise in the cost of living.[55]

Government policies also forced a French-owned power plant in Tianjin into bankruptcy. Prices charged for power were set by authorities, but costs of fuel escalated rapidly. A US State Department intelligence report concluded that the government essentially wanted to confiscate the plant. "Such a company can conceivably be indirectly confiscated in China without compensation to the owners."[56] Most employees came with an automatic wage increase tied to the cost of living, but the index ran about a month behind for most workers. The reality of China in 1946 to 1947 was that the monthly delay could be critical. Strikes became common at department stores, cinemas, and restaurants. Many Western businessmen believed that they were being deliberately targeted by the government;[57] rightly or wrongly, they perceived labor unrest to be a secret government attempt to force them out of China.

Although foreign businessmen had become very suspicious of the motives of the Chiang government, evidence suggests that the key reason the government was more attentive to the demands of labor was fear of the movement becoming totally controlled by the communists. Suzanne Pepper contrasts the government's "uncompromising attitude toward the students," with its "more flexible posture vis-à-vis labor. While continuing its effort to weaken and subdue the labor movement, the Government also attempted to pacify workers by acknowledging the legitimacy of their principal demands," hence the willingness of Guomindang authorities to index wages for industrial workers to the cost-of-living index.[58]

Soong did press ahead with government plans to improve power production. In July 1946, China received a credit of US$8.8 million to purchase ten auxiliary power plants in the United States through the Chinese Supply Commission.[59] But getting new equipment to China and up and operating entailed a substantial delay, during which time the power crisis continued. Soong also pushed plans for the Yangzi Power Company, a subsidiary of the China Development Finance Corporation (CDFC), to expand its operations in Nanjing, Wuxi, and the lower Yangzi area. In July 1947, the company submitted a detailed proposal to the Export-Import Bank in Washington for the acquisition of US$15 million credit for the period 1947–1952. The CDFC held almost 44 percent of the stock in the power company; the Ministry of Economic Affairs 30 percent, and the Bank of China 10 percent, with the remainder among other banks.[60]

At the time of the new proposal, the Yangzi Power Company operated two plants, one serving the Nanjing area and the other supplying power to Wuxi and Changzhou. Of the power they generated, 70 percent went to industrial consumers, particularly the textile mills in the area. The 1947 plan outlined an ambitious program of expansion, but getting the new equipment delivered to China was clearly a problem. The report estimated a four-to-five-year period from the placing of the order for equipment in America until the machinery was operating. An order for a 50,000-kilowatt generator placed with General Electric was scheduled to be shipped in March 1950. This was the earliest available date because of production issues in the United States.[61]

HEAVY INDUSTRY AND THE NATIONAL RESOURCES COMMISSION

Although consumer goods such as textiles were often controlled by T. V. Soong and his agencies, much of the heavy industry and mining was now under the dominance of the National Resources Commission (NRC) under Weng Wenhao. Until 1938, the NRC had been under the Military Affairs Council, but in 1938, it was moved to the Ministry of Economics and began to focus on developing heavy industry in wartime. In 1946, it was placed directly under the Executive Yuan. The later years of the war against Japan had been challenging for the agency, but with Japanese surrender, new opportunities arose. It seized control of many of the factories and mines in the east-coast areas, while liquidating mines and factories in the interior. Many of the confiscated industrial plants and mines had been developed by the Japanese. The NRC thus gained control of much of the heavy industry and mining resources. It took over 107 units in the formerly occupied areas including Taiwan. By the spring of 1947, it had 220,000 workers in its factories and mines and 32,000 other employees.[62]

In late May 1946, the government established the China Petroleum Company, to be headquartered in Shanghai with Weng as general manager. The company was to consolidate existing operations in Gansu, Sichuan, Taiwan, the northeast, and a refining plant in Shanghai. The plan was to take the oil pipeline that had been developed for wartime use connecting China and India and move it to Gansu. Oil from the Gansu fields would be transported to the coastal region for refining.[63]

THE END OF 1946: HAD CHINA REACHED A TIPPING POINT?

It is difficult to determine, but it is likely that the financial situation reached a tipping point by the end of 1946. The government was neither going to raise more revenue nor curb military spending.

Many of China's wealthy now focused on acquiring foreign exchange (one way or another) and getting their capital out of China. The process obviously became a vicious circle that just spiraled out of control. Once the psychology of hyperinflation set in, the cycle was all but impossible to escape. Regular accounting practices, calculating return on investment, and getting bank loans all because problematic. It was not "business as usual."

CHAPTER 5

1947

Speeding toward Disaster

A SECRET INTELLIGENCE REPORT DONE BY THE OFFICE OF Intelligence Research of the US Department of State in March 1947 was very pessimistic about the economic situation in China. As some American advisers had earlier warned, Chiang's insistence on recovering northeast China strained Nationalist resources. "Territory in North China and Manchuria brought under the sphere of the National Government has required heavy administration costs without commensurate tax revenues." The logistical lines for Chiang's strategy were stretched out and expensive to maintain. "The cost to the government of fighting an offensive civil war appears to be greater than the cost of fighting a defensive war against the Japanese." The consequence of these circumstances was economic disaster. "Prospects for 1947 indicate that the requirements of the government for support of its military operations will continue to grow; that the government will have to finance a larger proportion of its expenditures through note issue; and that the deflationary inflow of resources from abroad will be reduced." Under these conditions, the report concluded, "continued currency depreciation at an accelerated rate appears to be inevitable, and currency collapse in 1947 seems likely."[1] The report proved correct.

Prices in Shanghai, the report noted, had increased 700 percent during the previous year to reach a level 7,500 times that of the prewar level. This was nearly twice the rate of the increase in note issue during that year. Public confidence in the currency was low so people rushed to purchase commodities as soon as possible, driving up prices. Clearly inflationary psychology was increasing its hold on the Chinese population.[2] F. C. B. Black, who worked for the Hongkong and Shanghai Banking

Corporation, recalled that "nobody put money in the Bank. As soon as ever they had money, they rushed out and bought something." A shipment of oil arrived once a month in Shanghai, but once sold the company could not hold the cash because it would steadily lose value. "They would do things like buying silver bars ... which was illegal ... anything to avoid holding cash. So they didn't put it in the bank, they got rid of it."[3]

A report of late December 1947 showed that advances from the Central Bank accounted for 67 percent of government revenue in the first eleven months of the year. Everything else – taxes, profits from government enterprises, and sale of public assets – accounted for only 33 percent.[4] The crisis had begun early in 1947 and seemed to deepen during the year as the rate of inflation began accelerating. The departure of General George Marshall from China in January 1947 was a clear signal that the United States was not going to bring a halt to the civil war in China, which would (and did) escalate. Meanwhile L. K. Little, inspector general of the Chinese Maritime Customs Service, wrote in his diary for January 1, 1947, "I have never entered a New Year with so little confidence in the future of the Customs Service or of China as today."[5]

The open-market price for gold and US dollars increased 30 percent in January 1947 and 50 percent in the first two weeks of February. The press referred to this as the "gold rush." Rumors had circulated in mid-December 1946 that the Central Bank had taken half of its gold bars out of the Chase Bank, but even this could not keep up with demand. On February 1, 1947, the black-market rate for the US dollar was 7,800 yuan, and by February 8 it had already risen to 11,500. The government raised the exchange rate to 12,000 yuan to US$1 but once again failed to keep up with the market.[6] On February 3, the Central Bank quit throwing gold bars onto the market to support the yuan, indicating that it no longer had sufficient gold to continue sales. By February 11, panic hit the market, and the US$ reached 16,000 yuan on February 11 (Figure 5.1). In less than a week, the price of virtually everything had increased from 50 to 100 percent.[7] The government had for a long time refused to issue larger denomination banknotes, fearing it would spike inflation, but finally relented and issued a 10,000-yuan note in early 1947, and then a 100,000-yuan note in December 1947.[8]

5.1. Hyperinflation begins. January 1, 1947: The girl is holding up a US$10 bill and the Chinese equivalent in fabi notes at the black-market rate. Things would soon get much worse. Underwood Archives/Archive Photos/Getty Images

NEW CONTROL POLICIES IN EARLY 1947

Faced with this crisis, the government mandated a series of wage and price controls in January and February of 1947 in an effort to stem the tide. Labeled the "emergency economic measures," they highlighted the severe nature of the situation. Wages were to be frozen at January levels, and in return the government was to maintain fixed prices on essential goods and supply government workers with the commodities if the market failed to do so. But in the chaotic conditions of early 1947, this was almost an impossible task. Efforts to freeze prices in the past, including during the war against the Japanese, had usually failed because they led to hoarding of commodities, which increased shortages. As Odd Arne Westad noted, Chiang's government "had neither the economic strength nor the political will to follow through on these policies."[9]

One by one, the policies announced as part of the reform package fell away. The government initially announced a policy of providing subsidies for exports and surcharges on imports to preserve foreign exchange. But this move unsettled the market and brought strong objections from the United States and Britain. After ten days, China abandoned that policy and announced new ones, a process which suggested an inability to sustain a reform program.

Other measures were announced but were slow to be implemented. The government pledged to enforce strictly the collection of various taxes such as the income tax. Shares in government-controlled enterprises were to be sold to the public to bring in revenue, except for those needed for national defense or public health. But little seemed to be done to implement these over the next few months. Had the companies been sold off, the contribution to government coffers would have been a one-shot deal. The government pledged to implement mandated price controls of commodities in certain areas.[10]

The most significant changes announced in February 1947 concerned foreign currency and the gold market. The government suddenly prohibited the use and circulation of foreign currency such as US dollars. In orders issued by the National Defense Council, all Chinese citizens who held foreign assets had to register these with the Central Bank of China. The requirement extended not only to currency but to other items such as stocks, insurance policies, and bonds. Any sale or transfer of foreign assets required permission from the Central Bank of China.[11]

In response to the "gold rush" that had sent the gold market into a wild acceleration, the buying and selling of gold was likewise banned in the February emergency regulations. This reversed long-standing policies in which the government had sold gold to the public to absorb fabi. Some supported the new policy. The *Shenbao* noted on February 12, 1947, that "inasmuch as China is not a gold-producing country, the sale of gold bars is tantamount to wasting foreign exchange." Even if the government could hold the price to 4 million yuan per bar, "it is quite doubtful whether the general price level would drop in sympathy with the price of gold."[12] Some officials, including Shanghai mayor Wu Guozhen, worried that the new policies might fuel the increase in commodity prices. Because few wanted to hold fabi, idle money that had been held in gold bars or foreign currency would instead be used to hoard commodities. Prices for food and other items would thus soar.[13]

The entire process, however, related to reports of corruption and insider trading. Because of this, Bei Zuyi, head of the Central Bank, was forced out of office and replaced by Chang Kia-ngau. Chang had headed the Bank of China from 1928 until 1935, when he was removed at the time that the fabi reform was adopted. But Chang had continued to serve in a variety of positions including minister of railways, and in wartime minister of communications, although he spent much of the later war years in the United States. Chiang Kai-shek had sent him to the northeast after the war, where he had to deal with the Soviet presence. Chiang turned to him during the scandal at the Central Bank. Press reports suggested that over fifty employees of the bank had been found to have engaged in illegal gold transactions.[14] Arthur Young lamented the political attacks on Bei, who appeared to have been forced to take the blame for the gold sales crisis. "How can China expect patriotic men to take responsibility if they will be treated like this," he lamented. Young also felt that T. V. Soong was receiving unfair criticism, because without the presence of Soong and Bei the situation would have been much worse. Still more fundamentally, Young did not agree with the exchange and gold policy.[15]

Could the new regulations stop the "gold rush"? Many Chinese observers were skeptical. The *Dagong bao* noted on February 8, 1947, that "the amount of smuggling done will be increased, and due to increased smuggling, there will be a greater demand for black-market foreign exchange," a pattern that had happened in the past. "When the black-market exchange-rate rises, the CN\$3,350 to US\$1.00 will become obsolete," which it quickly did.[16] Market frenzy peaked on Monday, February 10, when speculators unleashed a day of wild trading. As the *North-China Daily News* reported, "Local gold bar and U.S. dollar notes markets skyrocketted to new highs yesterday, with exchange shops and brokers' offices being filled to capacity and beleaguered by steadily growing bevies of excited speculators and traders." Finally, in the afternoon trading was suspended "by voluntary consensus of local financial circles who could not operate any longer considering the rapidly rising quotations which changed from minute to minute." US dollar rates for buying started the day with a surge to 11,000 yuan per dollar but reached 17,500 by the time trading stopped.[17]

The paper also had a different take on the prohibition on buying and selling gold. In a February 18 editorial, it noted that "during one day last month, the Central Bank of China sold as much as 5 tons of gold bars in an effort to press down gold prices [which] indicates that the financial authorities had quite a strong faith in their gold policy." But now the government had suddenly abandoned that policy and closed the gold market, at least the open market. For the *Dagong bao,* this was "tantamount to saying that the Central Bank has no more gold and that the Government has lost another instrument for absorbing currency." This move was clearly a result of another failure by financial authorities, the paper concluded.[18]

Reuters reported in late February that the government of China wanted to sell US$200 million of relief supplies provided by the United Nations Relief and Rehabilitation Administration (UNRRA) on the black market in order to raise revenue. T. V. Soong immediately denied that such a request had been made, but the report seemed credible enough that it was denounced by several American congressmen on the grounds that the supplies were to relieve those suffering because of World War II, not to fund the Chinese government. Not all in Congress were so opposed, however.[19] Additional bad publicity about the UNRRA effort surfaced in the summer of 1947 concerning the attempt to rehabilitate China's fishing industry. A convoy of thirty-four fishing boats provided by the agency had left Puget Sound for China the previous year. Yet a report in the *Seattle Times* in early 1947 stated that only eight of the thirty-four had actually been put into use. Queried by a senator, the director-general of the agency admitted that the fleet was only operating at 25 percent capacity.[20]

Whereas the hyperinflation was devastating for certain groups of people such as government employees, many others had been protected. Most industrial workers were granted cost of living increases which meant that their wages rose in tandem (if somewhat delayed) with commodity prices. This policy had been designed to curb labor unrest and prevent communist agents from exploiting labor grievances. In the early 1947 reforms, however, the government in effect froze the wage increases, announcing that they should not go beyond the level of January 1947. Since prices were rising almost daily, this meant a sharp decrease in real wages. Shanghai and other cities with industry had been plagued by labor unrest since the end of the war, and most industrialists feared these new controls would increase labor strife and lead to strikes.[21]

The *Wenhui bao* echoed these sentiments in an editorial of February 18, 1947. "What we are most worried about is that with the salaries and wages fixed at a certain level, if the Government cannot stabilize commodity prices at the January 1947 level, then labor strikes will become unavoidable. For this reason, one is worried about the future of peace and order in the country."[22] Indeed, as commodity prices rose despite the government's efforts to freeze them, workers upped their demands. On April 25, 1947, the *Dagong bao* wrote:

> with wild fluctuations of commodity prices here [Shanghai], the livelihood of the workers has been jeopardized. As wages are now under control while commodity prices are soaring all the time, the workers of all of the cotton mills in the fourth District unanimously urged the General Labor Union ... to petition the government for the unfreezing of the cost of living index.[23]

The government issued bans on strikes including one in July 1947, but they rarely were effective. The workers were living in dire conditions when the price freeze did not hold and were willing to take on the government in many cases.[24]

And economic conditions worsened during the year. A. Doak Barnett, who was in China at this time, commented that "A [Chinese] dollar is worth more today than it will be tomorrow; consequently all money is 'hot money.' As a general rule, people spend money as soon as they can get it."[25] When the government tried to mandate price controls, farmers and merchants refused to sell, hoarding the commodities themselves. Faced with shortages, the government had to all but abandon price controls by late spring. Rice riots became widespread, which alarmed Guomindang authorities, fearful that the communists could gain advantage. Even the official Guomindang organ *Zhongyang ribao* admitted on May 2, 1947, that "during the past week commodity prices in Shanghai have registered another mad hike. Rice, edible oils, vegetables, meats, cotton yarn and all other daily necessities have doubled in price." The system of freezing wages would likely have to give way or be adjusted.

"The problem of the pay of Government employees and schoolteachers has arisen."[26] In June, the government had to rescind the freeze on wage increases, which led to a spike in wages.[27] By October 1947, the free-market exchange rate for US dollars was over 80,000 yuan to 1 US dollar.[28]

ATTACKS ON T. V. SOONG

The economic crisis of January and early February 1947, with the sudden rise in the price of gold and the exchange rate for the US dollar, led to increased attacks on T. V. Soong. The communists, of course, remained hostile, but much of the severe criticism came from rival groups in the Guomindang, including Sun Ke (son of Sun Yat-sen), as well as Zhang Qun and Chen Lifu. The "CC" Clique headed by Chen Lifu and his brother Chen Guofu had been particularly aggressive in attacking Soong and earlier H. H. Kung.[29] Many of his enemies were based in the Legislative Yuan. When that body met in January 1947 in a meeting closed to the press, word of the sharp attacks on Soong leaked out. It was reported that, since he had taken over the leadership of the Executive Yuan in early 1945, China had issued 3 trillion-yuan worth of banknotes, fueling inflation. Soong was also lambasted for the issuing of larger-denomination banknotes that, the attacks alleged, stimulated inflation. One member of the body, Wei Dingsheng, went on record with the allegations, demanding that Soong appear before the body to answer questions. Soong had consistently refused to do so.[30] Others felt that Soong and his group had profited from the gold sales. In August 1946, the Central Bank had sold US$380 million worth of gold. Critics contended that Soong's group bought $151 million of the total and Kung's group $180 million. Whatever the truth of these reports, they were widely circulated within the Guomindang itself.[31]

One group behind many of the attacks was the Gexin movement, which was composed of younger Guomindang members who were mostly associated with the CC Clique or Whampoa group. Formed in 1944, they had initially attacked H. H. Kung during the period leading up to his resignation. They had opposed a coalition government with the communists that George Marshall had tried to arrange in 1946 and the Sino-Soviet Treaty negotiated in the final days of the war against Japan. By 1947, they had become very critical of T. V. Soong, blaming him for corruption. The group began using the phrase "bureaucratic capitalism" in their attacks, even though the communists were the likely source of this term. Their activities lay behind many of the newspaper attacks on Soong and criticism that emerged in the Legislative Yuan.[32]

A committee in the Legislative Yuan charged Soong with failing to control commodity prices, issuing bigger banknotes that contributed to inflation, and allowing government enterprises under his direction to spend lavishly. But it was the rapidly deteriorating value of the yuan after the suspension of the sale of gold that brought the criticism to a head.[33]

The noted scholar Fu Sinian suggested a probe into the property holdings of Soong and H. H. Kung.[34] When writing in the *Dagong bao* on February 21, 1947, Fu specifically called on Soong to resign. He cited his failed gold policy as a prime factor warranting his dismissal. Fu blamed the crisis on the rivalry between Soong and Kung, and he attacked the Central Bank of China for not allowing the Legislative Yuan to investigate the matter. The decision to issue large-denomination banknotes, taken on the eve of Chinese New Year, had been a disaster, he asserted. The short-lived program to subsidize exports violated the laws of Britain and the United States and had to be quickly abandoned. Soong refused to meet with officials except within his entourage, not attending meetings of the Executive Yuan and People's Political Conference. Fu even attacked Soong for his complete lack of understanding of Chinese culture and mocked his fluency in English. In truth, many who worked with Soong felt that he was more comfortable in an English-speaking environment than Chinese – that he preferred to read documents and write in English.

Fu noted that it was widely reported in the press that the current "gold panic" had been organized by Kung to create trouble for Soong. But if Kung returned, then Soong would do likewise to embarrass his rival. The Kungs and Soongs had to go, he suggested, or China was doomed. "The country can no longer tolerate him and the people can no longer forbear him. It is time he must go, otherwise all will collapse." He concluded that "The Chinese Communists welcome most heartily H. H. Kung and T. V. Soong's holding the reins of Government for it will hasten 'the end of everything' and the former will proceed to Nanking [Nanjing]."

Despite their rivalry, Fu saw Kung and Soong as sharing many character-istics. "The primary reason for the failure of Kung and Soong is their 'integrity.' H. H. will grab at anything, big or small, direct or indirect. T. V. cares only for his ego and muddles his public duties with his private interest. The former is more covetous than ambitious while the latter is just vice versa."[35]

Soong had been aware for some time that he would likely be forced out of office. On December 31, 1946, he wrote a confidential letter to William S. Youngman in Washington on the matter. Youngman had headed the China Defense Supplies during the war and would remain a close associate of Soong after he moved to America. Youngman later served as executor of Soong's estate and delivered a eulogy at his funeral. Soong stated that "There has been a great deal of open talk about changes in the government, including my own post as premier. ... Such being the circumstances the chances are that sometime during 1947 I would retire, for I would not move a finger to keep myself in office, and there are too many people who aspire to my post." Soong told Youngman that "when I retire I shall take at least a year out to recuperate and enjoy myself a bit."[36]

T. V. Soong would resign as president of the Executive Yuan on March 1, replaced by Zhang Qun in April 1947. Chiang Kai-shek himself served as acting president in the interim. In an address to the Legislative Yuan on March 1, Soong stated that "three times during the last year I submitted my resignation as President of the Executive Yuan. The Generalissimo has finally granted my request." Soong stated that the reason for his resignation was the financial crisis. "When the war ended, the course of inflation could have been stopped – that is if there had been international peace. Military expenditures could have been cut down and revenue increased." Soong placed the blame for the renewed fighting on the communists who plunged the nation into war.[37]

Soong took the opportunity to defend his record. He acknowledged criticism that Chinese Textile Industries had kept control of the Japanese mills seized at the end of the war rather than selling them to private interests. But he argued that he would have gotten very little for the mills at that point, and now they were much more valuable. "The truth can be told in one sentence. The present economic crisis is the cumulative result of heavily unbalanced budgets carried out through eight years of war and one year of illusory peace, accentuated to some degree by speculative activities."[38]

Soong had a lengthy meeting with Chiang on March 3, but Chiang would have little time to deal with the economic crisis. He was focused on military matters and the situation in Taiwan following the bloody uprising on February 28, 1947, by Taiwanese protesting against the military control established by the Chinese Nationalists and the ongoing riots there. Chang Kia-ngau, who had been serving in northeast China, returned to take over as governor of the Central Bank of China.[39] Chang brought more of the old private-bankers' group back into the operation of the Central Bank and its related functions. He made Li Ming the chair of the committee that regulated imports and Chen Guangfu director of the export development board. Chen was also thought to be the best candidate to negotiate a loan with the Americans because he continued to be well regarded in the United States.[40]

The fall of Soong also gave the CC Clique a chance to enhance its economic profile. It came to dominate the Agricultural Bank of China, one of the four big government banks. In the spring of 1945, Chen Guofu had replaced H. H. Kung as head of the board of directors of this bank. Another CC Clique member, Luo Jinghua, aggressively developed commercial enterprises affiliated with the clique. When the war ended, few of the Japanese firms taken over by the Guomindang government had come under CC control; Soong had been the dominant player. But with his eclipse, the CC gained momentum and by 1947 had made its presence felt.[41]

The Chinese press generally cited the gold panic as the immediate factor leading to Soong's resignation, as well as his ongoing dispute with the Legislative Yuan. But most of the Shanghai press was very critical of his performance in office. The *Shen bao* on March 2, 1947, noted that "because of the gold bar and green back crisis, Dr. Soong has aroused the dissatisfaction of all quarters, which has made it necessary for him to resign." The paper considered that T. V. was excessively self-confident and "will not easily take other people's advice . . . and he is sometimes too stubborn."[42]

The liberal *Wenhui bao* argued that "nobody will regret that he has had to 'quit with humiliation.'" However, the paper suggested that Soong was not solely to blame for the crisis. Fundamentally, Soong had stressed the raising of funds to cover military expenses as the top priority and the revival of the national economy to be secondary. "In order to attain the first objective, he has often sacrificed the second one." As long as the civil war continued, the paper concluded, the situation was unlikely to improve.[43] Still in a later article, the paper noted that when Kung turned the Ministry of Finance over to Soong, China had US$800 million and 5 million ounces of silver as reserves as well as 20 trillion Chinese dollars' worth of enemy property. When Soong resigned, the treasury was empty, forcing the government to turn to Chang Kia-ngau.[44] The *Dagong bao* noted that "formerly Dr. Soong enjoyed a very good reputation in financial circles, and at the time he assumed the post, people both at home and abroad had great expectations of him. But now, only a short time since then, he has had to quit his job in an embarrassing manner." While the paper recognized that the civil war was the basic problem, it concluded that "his way of doing things is dictatorial, and he seldom takes the advice of other people. . . . This is also one of the main reasons he has had to quit."[45]

One of Chang Kia-ngau's first tasks was to reevaluate the reforms of February, which had already been overtaken by events. Wages had been frozen at the time, but the rise in commodity prices made adjustments necessary. Labor became restive and demanded that the actual cost of living index be used to determine wages. Rice prices started to escalate as suppliers were unwilling to ship rice to Shanghai and other cities at the set prices and supplies dwindled. Widespread rice riots erupted, forcing the government's hand. In early May, Shanghai had to abandon the ceiling price on rice. The city agreed to sell rice to the local population on a rationed basis.[46] This was one of the problems with controlling commodity prices: producers began to hoard commodities rather than sell at a price they considered inadequate. Fu Sinian charged that the UNRRA sold cotton at the set price of 700,000 yuan per bale, but it was then being resold on the black market for 1.5 million per bale. The fixed-price system led to corruption and speculation.[47] The government finally permitted utility firms to raise rates on May 31, 1947, in part to cover higher wage costs now that the freeze on wages had been modified. The government provided some subsidies to the companies to keep them operating.[48]

BUREAUCRATIC CAPITALISM

The attacks on T. V. Soong that forced him out of office on March 1, 1947, as well as earlier attacks on H. H. Kung, included the charge of "bureaucratic capitalism" (*guanliao ziben*). Both men and their associates were accused of using government assets for personal, private gain. These charges are usually attributed to the communists, but they were endorsed by Soong's critics within the Guomindang, including many based in the Legislative Yuan. Yet these charges spread among foreign businessmen active in China as well as officials of Western countries. The ideas had a long life: Many years later, Soong and Kung were still referred to in the international press as two of the richest men in the world.

How could these charges have obtained so much traction? Were they true? It is evident that the Guomindang government was very active in the economy during the civil war period, running several enterprises such as cotton-textile firms confiscated from the Japanese. It is much less clear that Soong or Kung garnered much profit from these. The government also imposed controls on foreign exchange, import licenses, and the use of foreign capital. Because business conditions were so unfavorable at this time, many businessmen – both Chinese and foreign – found it easy to blame their failures on the government-connected enterprises that seemingly enjoyed special advantages. Yet the fact that Chiang Kai-shek dismissed both Kung and Soong suggests that these charges had considerable credibility with the public.

In October 2009, Sherman Cochran convened a conference at Cornell University on the theme "The Capitalist Dilemma in China's Communist Revolution: Stay, Leave, or Return?" Later published as a conference volume, the scholars involved examined the decisions by various capitalists and bankers on whether to leave China after the Communist Revolution or to stay.[49] In some cases, individuals who had left China for Hong Kong or elsewhere decided to return. The pattern which emerges from these essays is that many capitalists had become completely alienated from the Guomindang government and thought conditions under Chairman Mao would be an improvement. Few probably held that opinion by the mid-1950s and certainly not by the Cultural Revolution. Yet it does point to one of the puzzles of the civil war period in China: Why did so many of the capitalists desert the Nationalists? The abysmal record of the government's policies during the postwar period was certainly a factor.

China's capitalists did not have the benefit of hindsight in 1949 and could not know what Mao's China had in store for them. Yet they did know their experiences under the Guomindang, and a sizable number came to feel that they were being shut out of economic opportunity by government-connected individuals and enterprises. In many ways, the situation resembles that of contemporary China, where a wide variety of enterprises exist, but government ties are usually helpful in operating a successful business. Another comparison with contemporary China is that children of key officials ("princelings") and other family members came under attack for their business and political activity (Figure 5.2).

5.2. Madame Chiang Kai-shek was close to her sister Ai-ling's children. From left to right: Louis Lin-jie Kung, niece Jeanette Ling-jie Kung, Madame Chiang, and David Ling-kan Kung. Hulton Deutsch/Corbis Historical/Getty Images

Among the firms drawing criticism was the Fuzhong Industrial Company, which had been formed at the end of the war against the Japanese as a partnership between the Bank of Communications, the Jincheng Bank, and the China National Products Bank. The key figure in the enterprise was T. L. Soong, the general manager, although H. H. Kung was on the board of directors as well as Xu Xinliu, who represented the Bank of Communications. The firm was also registered in the United States as the business partner of Willis-Overland Motors of Toledo, Ohio, which specialized in exports of cars, trucks, and jeeps, as well as auto parts. The American firm was capitalized at US$600,000 while the headquarters established in Chongqing was capitalized in Chinese yuan.[50]

The Yangzi Development Company was formed in a similar fashion, but the key figure was David Kung, son of H. H. Kung. Established in the winter of 1945, the firm was registered in Shanghai in January 1946. Stockholders included David Kung and Shanghai "notables" such as Du Yuesheng. This company was established to be involved in international trade, and the young Kung served as an agent in China for numerous American firms. According to the scholar Zheng Huixin, these ties gave him a monopoly on the marketing of products of sixty American companies in the China market. Eventually, the company had offices in Shanghai, Hankou, Fuzhou, Nanjing, Hong Kong, and Tianjin and had an affiliate in New York registered as the Yangzi Trading Company. Imports included cotton, electrical equipment, medicine, and luxury items while exports included hog bristles, tea, and agricultural products.[51]

One of the major criticisms of the politically connected enterprises was that they had favorable treatment in receiving foreign exchange. The Control Yuan investigated this question and completed a report in early October 1947. It found that several firms associated with Soong and Kung received special privileges. These firms included Fuzhong, the Yangzi Development Company, and the China Development Finance Corporation. These firms "have obtained more than their allowed quotas of foreign exchange and have imported certain luxury items forbidden to be imported by others," the report found. The Control Yuan identified the family members involved. For Fuzhong, it named T. L. Soong, for the China Development Finance Corporation, T. A. Soong (Song Zi'an), and for the Yangzi Development Company, David Kung. Finally, the report stated that several banks including the Bank of Communications and the Jincheng Banking Corporation had invested in the China Development Finance Corporation, which violated banking regulations.[52] This report thus corroborated many of the charges made in the press about "bureaucratic capitalists."

In one of his many attacks on T. V Soong, the scholar Fu Sinian wrote that "T. V. is frightfully strict in granting foreign exchange for legitimate use, but in cases in which he is interested he makes no fuss about the expenditure of foreign exchange at all." Fu cited the examples of the Jiuda Salt Company and Yongli Chemical Company, which Soong had failed to assist even though they were major private firms that contributed to China's economy. But he argued, if they were "to join the China Development Finance Corporation (the nerve center of the Soong trust), then all questions will be resolved. T. V.'s ignorance and egoism will inevitably lead China's economy to total collapse."[53]

Yet there is some evidence that Soong's connections were not always helpful. His China Development Finance Corporation (CDFC) survived the war and began to make plans for postwar projects. Yet many of these stalled because of the foreign-exchange regulations. In a memorandum prepared by the company on August 31, 1947, it noted that during the war in 1943, the corporation and the United States Rubber Company had made plans for a postwar joint project to manufacture high-quality rubber products in China, perhaps a foretaste of the joint-venture projects of Deng Xiaoping's China. The company was finally incorporated under the Ministry of Economic Affairs in April of 1947. But as of August, the memorandum noted, although plans were made, the plant had not been established. That would happen "as soon as the raw rubber import restrictions will ease up." The Chinese portion of the investment was to come from the Bank of China and the corporation. In the meantime, the CDFC served as an agent of the American firm, marketing their products in China.[54]

A second venture that was stalled was an agreement between the CDFC and the Studebaker Corporation of the United States to begin a joint venture to produce automobiles in China. The plant had been shipped to China in autumn of 1946. But the report noted that "while preparing to start the semi-manufacturing operation and assembly of trucks, import and exchange control regulations became tightened, making it impossible to import truck parts and manufacturing materials in sufficient quantities. The large number of War Surplus trucks bought by the Government also affected the business adversely." The project had to be postponed: another failure by the CDFC.[55] In general, 1947 was the turning point as the accumulating problems with hyperinflation became to impact deeply the economy. But T. V. Soong's fall from power was critical. The CDFC was closely identified to him and his position.[56]

David Kung was a particular target of criticism. Was this unfair? Arthur Young, who was sympathetic to H. H. Kung, tended to lend credence to some of the charges in his private diary. On May 11, 1946, for instance he wrote "Hear DK brought 4,000 bales of cotton on speculation."[57] In 1946, to save foreign exchange, the government barred merchants from importing trucks unless they were already on the way. In the fall of 1947, David Kung acquired 700 jeeps, which he had reclassified from trucks to cars, allowing him to import these to China, evading the ban.[58] When a March 4, 1946, regulation prohibited the importation of vehicles priced over US$1,200, the Fuzhong Company got them reclassified to evade the rule. Fuzhong also exceeded the limit on importing radio equipment including receivers. It had become an agent for Westinghouse Corporation in America and shipped their products directly from New York, regardless of the quota.[59] Whatever the significance of the charges, they were believed by a wide group of people within the business community and damaged the Guomindang government.

Soong family members and their associates were charged with using their diplomatic passports when conducting private business in America. An investigation by officials of the Control Yuan in June 1947 revealed that during the war when they had official appointments, they had in fact received diplomatic passports. As scholar Zheng Huixin noted, T. L. Soong had received diplomatic passport D-2067 on July 3, 1940, when he represented the Executive Yuan in America. He had returned to the US in September 1946, where he remained on this passport. The assistant manager of the Fuzhong Company, Shen Hongnian, had received diplomatic passport D-2435 in April 1942 when he served as secretary to T. V. Soong, then minister of foreign affairs. But he returned to America on July 5, 1946, when he was working for the company.

T. A. Soong had received diplomatic passport D-2325 in November 1941 when he traveled to America representing the Military Affairs Commission. But he had remained there and like his brother was engaged in private business after Japanese surrender. In the view of Chinese critics, use of diplomatic passports when conducting private business was improper.[60]

Chiang Kai-shek himself received reports on many of these matters. According to Zheng Huixin, Chiang was aware of the charges that Fuzhong had exceeded the quota for importing vehicles, and both it and the Yangzi Development Company had violated the rules for importing radio and refrigerator equipment, as well as the regulation on jeeps. According to Chiang's diary, he was concerned about the issue, and when Zhang Qun took over the Executive Yuan, Chiang instructed him to correct the situation. Chiang noted that there was limited foreign exchange and many companies sought it. Because of criticism that government-connected firms enjoyed advantages in receiving foreign exchange, the entire process had to be open and public with a list of companies involved, the names of the head of the board of directors, and the list of the types of goods being imported. The process must be fair and open, Chiang insisted.[61]

But Zheng Huixin concludes that there was a contradiction in Chiang's attitude toward the matter of family corruption. He was not above removing both Kung and Soong from office, but he was reluctant to allow criticism aimed at his wife's family to go too far. He limited the publicity surrounding Kung's removal in 1945 and would do the same in 1948 when his own son, Jiang Jingguo, would target David Kung. He feared that the communists would take advantage of this information to attack him and the Guomindang.[62]

Following T. V. Soong's resignation, the government announced once again plans to sell many of the government enterprises, including 70 percent of Chinese Textile Industries. Several other enterprises had already been sold, the government announced, including a tobacco company operated by the Ministry of Economic Affairs, paper mills in the north and northeast operated by the National Resources Commission, and flour mills operated by the Ministry of Food, among others. Other enterprises operated by the government were to offer half of their stock to the public.[63] Yet despite this talk of turning these enterprises over to the private sector, little of this seemed to have been completed. By the time the government began to offer these enterprises for sale in 1947, many private businessmen were already focusing on getting capital out of China rather than risking more. The original plan to sell enterprises confiscated from the Japanese located in the former Manchukuo was suspended in the summer of 1947 because they were either in the war zone or had already been confiscated by the communists.[64]

State-owned enterprises were no better at obeying government decrees than private ones. In the fall of 1947, for instance, Arthur Young noted that the government-owned Chinese Textile Industries was deeply involved with the black market. It refused to sell cotton yarn at the mandated prices, selling only at the black-market rate. The inability to get this type of enterprise to accept government regulations clearly showed the lack of administrative control in China.[65]

CRITICISM BY FOREIGN BUSINESSMEN AND GOVERNMENT OFFICIALS

Western businessmen in China picked up the criticisms of "bureaucratic capitalists," often finding this a scapegoat for the failure of commerce and trade to revive in the postwar period. They were particularly critical of the China Merchants Steam Navigation Company, a government enterprise. This was a product of the exclusion of foreign merchants from the interior waters of China, a sensitive issue in the aftermath of Japanese surrender and the end of extraterritoriality. But American representatives in China still thought the Chinese were shooting themselves in the foot by blocking the revival of trade. The American assistant commercial attaché Carl H. Boehringer noted in a report from Nanjing on July 23, 1947:

> Because the Chinese are jealous of their newly-regained sovereign rights they prevent foreign companies to assist in economic revival. At Hankow [Hankou], for instance, where ocean steamers once lined the Bund to carry away products of the flourishing industries . . . there may now be seen

a few small river boats of the China Merchants Steam Navigation Company, a monopolistic, official concern which charges freight rates on cargo from Hankow to Shanghai which are in excess of those charged by foreign ships for the same cargo moved from Shanghai to New York.

The result, he noted, "industry is largely at a standstill."[66]

When foreign business failed to revive in 1947, many in the British and American commercial community stepped up their criticism, echoing the remarks coming from the Legislative Yuan. Businesses associated with the Soong family (including the Kungs) were referred to as "holy family" enterprises, a phrase that appeared in print. Although these officials denied getting special privileges, the Far East American Council of Commerce and Industry and the National Foreign Trade Council submitted a joint report to the State Department complaining of preferential treatment accorded to the "holy family" businesses. They repeated the domestic criticism of those such as T. L. Soong who traveled in the United States under diplomatic passports. By contrast, they charged, many private Chinese businessmen could not easily get passports at all. American firms, they contended, could not get the credits and licenses to trade with China. Meanwhile, the Universal Trading Corporation, a Chinese-government institution, maintained spacious offices in the Rockefeller Center in New York City and did not have to comply with licensing and foreign-exchange regulations. Other firms mentioned were the Fuzhong Company headed by T. L. Soong and H. H. Kung, the Nanyang Brothers Tobacco Company tied to T. V. Soong; the China Development Finance Corporation (T. A. Soong), China–US Rubber Company (T. V. and T. A. Soong), and the Yangzi Development Company (David Kung). The complaints by the American businessmen alleged that these companies could obtain foreign exchange and import licenses while others could not.[67]

Among the examples cited by the American businessmen was the almost complete failure of automobile dealerships in Shanghai owned by Americans, a group that had been very prominent before the war. The Cadillac dealership in Shanghai, for example, had been unable to get a license to import any cars because they were deemed luxurious. Yet a ship had just arrived with twenty-three Cadillacs, imported by the government-run Central Trust of China. The complaint also stated that many American firms had received orders for goods from China but had not been given the licenses to import them. Items such as textile spindles, structured steel equipment, and mining equipment were sitting in American warehouses.[68]

A delegation of American businessmen in Shanghai met with Albert Wedemeyer in July 1947 to air these grievances. He had been sent as a special envoy to China by President Truman. The group complained about anti-American sentiment and discrimination by the Chinese government while at the same time attacking the US State Department for failing to defend the interest of American businessmen in China. They contrasted the State Department's seemed indifference to the fate of American businessmen to the British Foreign Office, which worked closely with British business interests.[69] The new head of the Executive Yuan, Zhang Qun, issued a statement on August 13 inviting foreign investment in China, which was welcomed in manufacturing and other areas except for those sectors reserved for state control. Zhang pledged that foreign investors would be permitted to remit an appropriate portion of profits, and he pledged nondiscrimination between Chinese and foreign investors. A United Press reporter spoke with unidentified foreign businessmen who expressed to him interest in Zhang Qun's statement but considerable skepticism. They had heard much of this before and would reserve judgment until such time as change had actually occurred.[70]

T. V. Soong strongly denied these charges made by foreign businessmen, working with Dr. Wellington Koo in Washington to refute them. Soong stressed that he was not connected with any import firms.[71] H. H. Kung continued to defend his record as well. In a press statement on July 12, 1947, following a trip to north China, Kung vigorously denied reports in the American press that China had squandered the US$500 million loan. Such criticism occurred as China sought new American financial assistance.[72] Whatever the validity of the reports or what lay behind the delays in getting permission to do business, by the fall of 1947 many American businessmen concluded they were not wanted in China. And these groups had been among those most active in advocating a strong interest in China. As Washington became more focused on the situation in Western Europe and the Marshall Plan, China began to lose the attention of American political leaders.

Bruce Smith, head of the Shanghai American Chamber of Commerce, wrote to Shanghai mayor Wu Guozhen on July 24, 1947, complaining about the difficulties that faced foreign firms attempting to operate in China. Regulations governing import and export business were drawn up, he noted, without any consultation with the business community and implemented with no advance notice. This created chaotic conditions that made trade difficult. It was also almost impossible to import parts and supplies to keep manufacturing plants operating; power plants and transportation companies faced similar restrictions. Equipment needed to rehabilitate these facilities was often denied import licenses. Smith suggested that American businessmen were losing faith and interest in China.[73]

A few months later, in January 1948, Smith demanded that any future economic aid to China should carry the condition that the Chinese government curb the present tendency "to foster its own enterprises or companies in which officials have interest and to encourage rather than stifle private enterprise." Chinese-government-sponsored monopolies in trade, such as the Shanghai fish market, should be eliminated. Restrictions on foreign ships in inland waters should be reduced, and Chinese labor laws should reduce the advantage given to labor in the current climate. Finally, Smith argued, foreign capital should be encouraged to invest in China rather than the current policy of discouragement.[74]

Liddell Brothers and Company, which manufactured tools and equipment used by textile mills, took their case directly to Arthur Young. On November 27, 1947, they complained that "all import licenses are rigorously curtailed and the quota allotments to dealers and manufactures are quite below their requirements." In their own case, they stated, "although we are operating at only 30% of the capacity of our plant, we have barely enough materials available to fulfill our outstanding commitments to a number of Chinese cotton mills." They had on hand enough material to last through March 1948 but not after that. Their immediate request for Arthur Young was to enlist his aid in getting a large shipment of iron, steel bars, and steel sheet that had arrived at Shanghai but had not been released by customs. The memo emphasized that the customers who needed their output of machinery were Chinese textile mills who relied on their equipment.[75]

Businessman Edwin Chester Allan tried to revive his business enterprises in Shanghai after World War II but encountered severe difficulties. Before leaving the United States, he tried to buy an automobile to send to China but found it virtually impossible. He had to obtain a permit from the Chinese consulate to start the process. "They are asking $2,000 for a Ford Sedan here and by the time you pay 'squeeze' in every direction it would cost nearly $5,000 landed in Shanghai." Once he arrived in China, he wrote a letter to his wife Dolly on April 8, 1947. "Nothing but chaos everywhere you turn," referring to Shanghai. "Really a d– shame to see such a good place go to rack and ruin. Makes me sick when I think of it." He reported that he was wrapping up his business the best he could. "I have no idea what is going to happen to the exchange in the next few months."[76]

Among the critics was an individual considered to be a staunch supporter of Chiang Kai-shek and his government – Claire Chennault. Leader of the "Flying Tigers," Chennault was a popular wartime hero in China and America. He enjoyed a close relationship with both Chiang Kai-shek and Madame Chiang. Yet after the war when he tried to organize a commercial air transport line, he ran into numerous roadblocks. He felt that, with his knowledge of flying conditions in China and experience in leading aviators, he could create a company that would be beneficial to China and the Guomindang government. But he encountered little but obstacles. He unleashed his criticism in a private letter to General Albert Wedemeyer on July 27, 1947, in which he outlined the many problems facing private business in China. He started with an attack on the control over business exercised by the government banks. "Government banks today are actually running most of China's business, and I think this is unhealthy," he told Wedemeyer. The unrealistic rate of exchange drove most to the black market, "while the accompanying limits on importing foreign exchange drove most people overseas going to the black market when making remittances to China."[77]

The failed attempt by the Chinese government to regulate the exchange market had basically driven economic activity underground. "There are no important private exports from China today," Chennault declared. Most exports were smuggled from Guangzhou to Hong Kong. Nanjing simply lacked the ability to run a program of economic control, and the pay of civil service was too low, which meant that bribery was common. Chennault strongly complained about the daily burden of hyperinflation. "You may be interested to know," he told Wedemeyer, "that our airline payroll for the last two weeks weighed slightly over a ton in currency and that it took five men four days to count it out into bundles." Chennault tried to be hopeful. In the conclusion of his letter, he said that he thought China "was still a great country and I think that it would take a surprisingly small, well directed effort at this time to channel its future along sound lines."[78] That conclusion seemed very much like wishful thinking. But when an old friend of the Chiangs, one who was closely identified with the Nationalist government, had become so discouraged, the depth of the economic problems was clear.

Wedemeyer seemed to agree with many of Chennault's assessments. He was in China as a special envoy of President Truman and sent a memorandum to Chiang Kai-shek on August 20, 1947, that particularly discussed allocation of exports and imports, foreign exchange, and the general treatment of foreign firms and businessmen. "In most cases," he told Chiang, "the laws on the statute books were manifestly fair. However, in their implementation continued injustices and dishonest interpretations as well as bribery were all involved." Legitimate business, "be it foreign or Chinese ... cannot thrive under existing conditions. This of course encourages illegitimate business."[79]

By 1947, many American businessmen were opposed to another American loan to China. They were annoyed by what they perceived as favoritism for the Universal Trading Corporation, which allegedly exported a large volume of capital goods to China while Western merchants and Chinese private merchants were being shut out.[80] Merchants became less willing to cooperate with the government. By the autumn of 1947, when goods arrived in ports such as Shanghai but did not have the necessary foreign-exchange permission, government agencies began to confiscate the commodities. Importers then began shipping the goods to Hong Kong where they could be smuggled into China.[81]

American businessmen with an interest in China increasingly blamed the agents of their own government for not taking a harder stand in forcing the Chinese to accommodate American business. They again demanded that Yangzi ports be opened to foreign shipping, and they called for the abolition of the Universal Trading Corporation, which most viewed as a tool of government monopoly. Prominent government officials should be removed from the business sector. A May 1948 memorandum supported by American business groups expanded their complaints to include the difficulty of registering foreign businesses, the problem of remitting profits, and the general incompetence of Chinese officials. Although they acknowledged that black markets were illegal, they argued that such markets were an open and free normal part of business activity in China. US officials must use American aid as a tool to press China on behalf of American firms.[82]

Some news reports also suggested that China was misusing American aid. The *China Press* on September 21, 1947, noted a story that China was reselling for profit much of the US Army surplus property that had been provided at a fraction of its cost, and often selling to American firms. One of the hottest-selling items was tractors, which were in short supply in the United States and subject to a waiting period of up to two years. China sold 122 surplus tractors to an American firm for US$700,000. Presumably these had been provided to help agriculture in China.[83]

Corruption is a complex issue. Envy of government-connected individuals who personally profit from political ties unavailable to others is at its core. It becomes a political and perhaps even a moral issue for some. Its economic impact is less clear. There are many examples of societies that experience rapid economic growth despite rampant corruption, or what is commonly perceived as corruption. The Hu Jintao era in China is certainly a notable example. China's economy grew rapidly while government-connected individuals and their families garnered large wealth. But that was not the case of China in the civil war. A dysfunctional currency, a severely strained transportation system, and an ongoing civil war created a climate where economic growth was not going to happen.

Was corruption a key component in inhibiting economic growth? It certainly made the issue more politically sensitive. One reason Chinese businessmen were so irate over the "holy family" enterprises was that they perceived that those were flourishing while their own were languishing. But was that really true? If government-connected enterprises got first access to foreign exchange, was that the major reason private firms stagnated? In fact, many businessmen simply circumvented the rules and traded (smuggled) through Hong Kong. It is impossible to quantify the exact economic costs of bureaucratic capitalism.

The political costs are much clearer. The communists perceived the charges of corruption as a winning political issue, violating the sense of fair play in the economy and playing to the economic grievances of most Chinese. Opponents of the Soong/Kung group within the Guomindang saw an opportunity to advance their political position within the movement. Some might have seen the attacks as a subtle way of undermining Chiang Kai-shek himself since they involved his wife's family. And attacks from foreign businessmen vented to their own diplomatic and political leaders damaged the Chiang government's chances for foreign support. How badly corruption hurt the economy is unclear, but the damage to the standing of the Chiang government was much more obvious.

Finally, there was another key factor fueling the criticism of foreign businessmen in China. While they were correct that China did not make it easy for them to do business, at bottom their grievances were tied to the disappearance of the old treaty-port China. Gone were the days when a foreign businessmen could sell Cadillacs in Shanghai with little regard for the Chinese government. When many returned to China after the war, it was their old way of life – now vanished – that they were loath to accept. Hence their anger at Chinese authorities. But when Mao and the communists finally triumphed, the situation became much worse.

GETTING CHIANG KAI-SHEK'S ATTENTION

Ultimate power in the Guomindang government rested with Chiang Kai-shek. As Lloyd E. Eastman noted about the decade prior to the war with Japan, "regardless of the formal positions that Chiang Kai-shek held in the party, government or army, he wielded ultimate authority over the regime as a whole. He exercised that authority with minimal concern for the formal chain of command."[84] Thus, any major policy change in military, diplomatic, or economic areas required Chiang's stamp of approval. Odd Arne Westad added, "no other leader within the GMD had the authority to force through even the simplest decisions. A vital matter such as repairs to the railroads connecting the cities to the interior was held up by factional infighting within the government."[85]

Virtually everyone with a significant position in the Guomindang government realized that, ultimately, they needed Chiang's blessing for any substantial policy to be enacted. He Lian (Franklin L. Ho), the noted economist based at Nankai University, began work with the Central Planning Board in early 1944 under the direction of its chief secretary Xiong Shihui. Professor He had been tasked by Chiang Kai-shek with undertaking postwar planning. In his memoirs, he recounts that he needed broad instructions on several issues – how much public ownership of enterprises should occur versus private owners; what should be the regional distribution of capital investment; and what were the major goals of planning for economic development. After several weeks of wrestling with the questions, He Lian concluded that "frankly, there was no one capable of providing me with any instruction aside from the Generalissimo. My direct superior, Hsiung Shih-hui [Xiong Shihui], wasn't capable of finalizing any suggested resolution of the problem." He Lian was able to have a one-hour conference with Chiang during which he endorsed several ideas presented by He. "The meeting with the Generalissimo was very fruitful. After the meeting I was in a position to proceed with the organization of my work and the distribution of responsibility."[86]

Much has been made in recent years about the release of the Chiang Kai-shek diaries, which provide insights into Chiang's thought process (or at least how he wished that process to be seen by posterity). But in trying to understand how Chiang dealt with issues facing China, there is a better source. Chiang had established the Office of Personal Attendants (Shicong shi), which compiled voluminous records about his daily activities. The *Jiang Zhongzheng zongtong dang'an: Shilue gaoben* (The Chiang Kai-shek archives: draft working records) has now been published in dozens of volumes, with each covering two to three months. The *Shilue gaoben* contains daily records of virtually all of Chiang's activities including meetings, speeches, important documents sent or received, quotations from the diary, and even leisure activities (such as strolling in the evening with Madame Chiang). Important dates such as the twentieth wedding anniversary of Chiang and Soong Mei-ling or Madame Chiang's fiftieth birthday are mentioned along with details of any celebrations. Reading through these pages gives one a sense of what Chiang was doing at any given time.[87]

For example, on May 25, 1947, Chiang received a report about the high rice prices in Shanghai, with one picul topping half a million yuan. The increase had unsettled society. Then on May 31, 1947, the *Shilue gaoben* quotes from Chiang's diary that he understands that the financial crisis has gotten much worse, and the price of rice has continued to increase. He also commented on the difficulties with foreign exchange. Then on October 31, he noted that the price of rice had risen to 800,000 yuan and higher per picul. The striking thing about these entries, however, is how uncommon they are. During these weeks, Chiang's attention was almost entirely on military matters, including inspection trips to various military headquarters. He also dealt with political matters, student unrest, and diplomatic concerns. Far down on his list of activities was concern with financial matters. He met occasionally with financial officials such as Yu Hongjun, but his only consistent attention to the topic was his strong interest in obtaining an American loan. The *Shilue gaoben* contains frequent telegrams from Wellington Koo in Washington related to the negotiations for a loan. On June 20, 1947, Chiang had an afternoon meeting with Chen Cheng, Chang Kia-ngau, and Wang Shijie at which military training and foreign relations with America and the Soviet Union were discussed, as well as currency reform. But despite the rapid depreciation of the value of fabi, the topic did not absorb much of his time.[88]

Chiang did become concerned when scandal threatened to engulf those in his entourage. On March 5, 1947, Chiang received a report on the gold sales crisis in Shanghai that suggested that T. V. Soong and Bei Zuyi were involved in some way. Later in the month on March 22, 1947, Chiang held an afternoon meeting with Chang Kia-ngau, now director of the Central Bank, and Yu Hongjun, then minister of finance. That same day, Wu Tiecheng delivered a report on the party congress, particularly on criticism of T. V. Soong, H. H. Kung, and foreign minister Wang Shijie. What Chiang feared most was that much criticism would play into the hands of the communists. His family legacy must be kept clean. The *Shilue gaoben* does not provide any significant analysis of why T. V. Soong was dismissed.[89]

Although Chiang was aware of the financial crisis and hyperinflation, he did not make dealing with it a priority. In the context of the Guomindang government, that meant that little could be done to resolve the issue. Officials dealing with the matter would press Chiang to focus on it, but military matters always came first. On June 28, 1947, Shanghai mayor Wu Guozhen came to discuss the economic problems that were worsening daily as inflation continued. And on July 2, 1947, Chang Kia-ngau, general manager of the Central Bank, came to discuss reforming the currency and possibly replacing fabi. Yet it would be over a year before the gold yuan reform was attempted, too late to salvage the currency. Chang cautioned that a new currency would not succeed unless the deficit was brought under control.[90]

Shortly after these meetings, Chiang became preoccupied with the visit of Albert Wedemeyer as Truman's special representative and the related prospects of obtaining an American loan. Chiang held another meeting with Chang Kia-ngau on July 29, 1947, during Wedemeyer's visit, discussing how to increase the trust that China's banking community had in fabi. Chiang also dealt with the fallout from the scandal involving the Fuzhong and Yangzi Development Companies obtaining foreign exchange illicitly. But that involved a matter of family reputation, which was always a prime concern for Chiang. He ordered foreign-exchange issues to become more transparent and met with Zhang Qun and Chang Kia-ngau on August 14 to discuss its regulation. But he also wanted to avoid public criticism of the Soong and Kung families.[91]

FOREIGN-EXCHANGE WOES WORSEN

The smuggling issue between Guangzhou and Hong Kong became more severe in 1947 as little legitimate trade occurred. Because foreign exchange was difficult to obtain, most trade was carried on illicitly. Large numbers of goods from Hong Kong were regularly sold in Guangzhou with prices only slightly higher than in Hong Kong itself, indicating the ease of smuggling. The primary item smuggled in return was wolfram mined in Guangxi and Guangdong, which fetched a high price in Hong Kong.[92]

Of course, not everyone saw smuggling as a bad thing. The *China Weekly Review* noted that businessmen in South China had long complained that most of the foreign-exchange permits and import licenses went to Shanghai businessmen who had the right connections with Nanjing authorities. Southerners were left out. But the journal noted:

> it now appears that Chinese businessmen in Canton and other South China cities have – largely through smuggling – solved their import–export problems in a reasonably satisfactory manner. Foreign exchange is obtained by smuggling Chinese products such as Wolfram, tea oil, duck feathers, Chinese medicines and various food stuffs to Hongkong where they are sold for Hongkong dollars which in turn are used to purchase imports in the British crown colony. ... This "illegal" trade has now developed into such a well-organized two-way affair that some observers believe that South China nearly enjoys a balance of trade.[93]

Philip Thai, in his study of smuggling in modern China, noted that "as its supply of foreign exchange reserves steadily eroded, the government correspondingly reduced import quotas," which further constricted legitimate trade. Measured in US dollars, import quotas shrank from $172 million for February to July 1947 to only $42 million for September 1948 to March 1949, a decrease of 75 percent. Thai notes that small firms found it almost impossible to get quotas and were "reluctant to register with the government or apply for import permits."[94] Thai cites an observation by the Chinese trade commissioner at Kowloon that there was a shift in the economics of smuggling from trying to avoid the payment of duty to evading trade controls. This was especially true in south China, since importers had to apply directly to the Central Bank in Shanghai.[95]

In June 1947, several economic experts led by Fang Xianting and Yang Yinpu publicly urged the government to simply lift controls on foreign exchange and allow foreign-exchange rates to fluctuate freely. They argued that doing so would increase China's exports, as they would be priced competitively. Remittances by overseas Chinese would no longer be going entirely into the black market, and capital that had fled overseas could be returned to China to help revive the economy. They argued that this would serve to ease the economic crisis.[96] Their arguments held little traction with authorities, however.

In August 1947, the government announced a new Foreign Exchange Equalization Fund Committee to govern the exchange rate for the Central Bank of China. The committee, which operated August 1947 until May 1948, consulted with and supervised the rate of exchange with the Bank of China, Bank of Communications, National City Bank of New York, and the Hongkong and Shanghai Banking Corporation.[97] The rate for August 18 was set at 39,000 yuan for US$1. The committee had more flexibility to keep the official rate in line with the black-market rate, although the maximum increase was set at 5 percent per month. One immediate result was a sudden growth in exports. For several months, export goods had accumulated in warehouses because the exchange rate was too unfavorable to sell overseas. But with the new rate, exporters leaped to take advantage, creating a short-term rush.[98] But the growth was only temporary. For about a month, the exchange system worked reasonably well, but starting on September 21, the black-market rate began suddenly to rise. The committee felt that if it raised rates to match, this would simply accelerate inflation; but if it held firm, then legitimate traders would turn to smuggling to evade the unrealistic exchange rates. Ultimately, the new policy did not stabilize the foreign-exchange value of the yuan, which in fact worsened.

The head of the stabilization committee, Chen Guangfu, a prominent banker, sent a confidential letter to Chang Kia-ngau, governor of the Central Bank, on October 25, 1947. He complained that the group had been subject to severe criticism in the press and by public officials. Chen felt that the committee was wrongly blamed for increasing prices which it could not control. If "the Committee does not command confidence," he stated, "the Committee would be glad to withdraw."[99]

A report of November 27, 1947, noted that the black-market foreign-exchange rates had increased 50 percent since November 15. On that date, the black-market rate was 95,000 yuan for one dollar and by November 27, it reached 140,000.[100] Arthur Young prepared a memo on the issue on December 1, 1947, and remarked that official remissions to China from overseas Chinese were drying up because the rate was simply too unfavorable. In all likelihood, people were using the black market.[101] Young also sent a memo to Chang Kia-ngau warning that the rapid rise in the black-market rate in the first two weeks of November was a sign of serious problems. "Money is being sent abroad in growing volume by persons including officials."[102]

On his return to China in 1947, Arthur Young stayed at the Cathay Hotel in Shanghai. In his papers, he saved a printed form from the hotel stating that "we regret to inform you that due to circumstances beyond our control, we are reluctantly compelled to raise rates in this hotel." The line for the rate was left blank so the new amount could be written in. On his arrival, the room was 900,000 yuan nightly.[103] Newspapers began to make the inevitable comparison with Weimar Germany in 1923, when it completely collapsed. When the value of 1 yuan in 1936 was equal to 50,000 yuan in October 1947, the *Shen bao* felt that moment had come.[104] By late October, rumors began to spread that China was on the verge of attempting to return to the silver standard by issuing silver coins. The United States was rumored to loan China a substantial amount of silver to permit the coinage.[105]

In an editorial of November 19, 1947, the *Dagong bao* called the government's foreign-exchange equalization effort begun in August a complete failure. When the gap between the open market and black-market exchange rate varied by 40 percent, the board seems to have given up trying to close the difference. One obvious problem was that remittances from overseas Chinese continued to flow into the black market. The paper concluded:

> We admit that under existing economic conditions in China, it is impossible for us to have a very sound foreign exchange policy. All we can hope for is . . . a policy that will more or less encourage exports. This is about time that the Government authorities considered lifting conditionally the foreign exchange controls.

The buying and selling of foreign exchange should be open and left to the market to determine the rate. This policy should encourage exports and reduce smuggling. It might even be possible, the *Dagong bao* suggested, that some remittances might flow into legitimate banks.[106]

Despite the serious deterioration of the currency, Chiang Kai-shek's attention still lay elsewhere. Throughout November 1947, the log of his daily activities reveals an almost-total focus on military matters, with occasional references to concerns over student demonstrations and their communist leanings. With the impending meeting of the national assembly, Chiang met regularly with Chen Bulei and Chen Lifu to discuss political mobilization. Conspicuously missing from his schedule were regular meetings with financial officials. Finally on November 25, 1947, Chiang noted the increase in prices of commodities in Shanghai, which he found troubling. He blamed speculators for the rise in cotton-textile prices. He also condemned the black market in American dollars, noting that the going rate was 130,000 yuan for 1 dollar. But Chiang was quickly diverted when he flew to Beiping the following day accompanied by his son Jiang Jingguo, where he met military officials.[107] On his return to the capital, he held meetings with Zhang Qun, head of the Executive Yuan, and Arthur Young to discuss the financial crisis. In mid-December, he met with the leaders of the four government banks to formulate a solution. But ultimately, Chiang seemed to have pinned his hopes on a loan from the United States.[108]

DETERIORATION OF THE BATTLEFIELD SITUATION OF THE GUOMINDANG

Over the course of 1947, the Guomindang government's military position began to weaken. Large portions of the countryside in the north and northeast fell under Chinese Communist Party control. Odd Arne Westad argues that "the most spectacular military operation of the civil war was Liu Baocheng's 1947 sweep across the Yellow River toward his former base in the Dabie Mountains. This was a new type of offensive for the Communists. . . . The operation was a startling success that awoke all Chinese to the possibility of the Communists ultimately topping the government of Jiang Jieshi."[109] The worst defeats were to come in the following two years, but there was a shift in public perception in 1947, recognizing that the communists might indeed win the civil war.

Communist success on the battlefield also had a profound economic impact. The urban bases of the Chiang government became further isolated from the countryside. Cotton and foodstuffs could not reach Shanghai and Tianjin. The cities became further dependent on foreign imports, adding to the strain of the foreign-exchange problem. Solutions to the problem that might have been viable in 1946, such as allowing foreign shipping access to the interior, were no longer options. The military and political divide was separating the rural and the urban economies, and the latter was failing.

Wedemeyer returned to the United States without arranging a new American loan, so US cash could not be used to cover the imports to keep Chinese cities alive. The Truman administration had simply lost faith in the economic competence of the Guomindang government. In December 1947, the government planned to set up finance and currency bureaus in Shanghai, Tianjin, Guangzhou, and Hankou, with the announced goal of preventing banks from engaging in speculation and illegal activities. Few expected significant results. A severe tightening of credit by government banks was to be initiated.

CHAPTER 6

1948

The Collapse of Fabi and the Gold Yuan Reform Disaster

B Y THE SPRING OF 1948, THE FOREIGN BUSINESS COMMUNITY had all but written off the Guomindang government and its ability to salvage the economy. A secret report of March 26, 1948, by D. F. Allen, the British shipping representative for the Far East noted, "the mood of the British Community in Shanghai today is without question more despondent than it was four months ago." The deteriorating military situation was critical, but Allen focused on the weaknesses of the Guomindang government. "The dominant feature of their mood is complete disgust with the Kuomintang [Guomindang] and all it stands for in corruption, feebleness and chauvinism." He concluded that fabi was on its last legs, and that the real currency in Shanghai was the American dollar and in Guangzhou, the Hong Kong dollar. Allen's report argued that the communists would not make much of a difference if they won, a perspective that many Chinese businessmen had come to adopt.[1]

For some months, many of the financial leaders in Nanjing had also become convinced that people had lost confidence in fabi and that the currency was doomed. Something completely new was needed. The price of commodities was rising substantially faster than the increase in the amount of fabi in circulation, an indication that people were not holding on to the rapidly depreciating currency. But the basic question was that, if a new currency was issued, what would prevent it from going the way of fabi? American help was deemed essential. On January 14, 1948, a delegation led by Bei Zuyi left for the United States with the hope of enlisting American aid in the creation of a new currency. The *Xinwen bao* stated that with a US$300 million loan, all fabi could be redeemed and replaced by a new currency. The *Dagong bao* was more skeptical, stating that "stabilization of commodity prices cannot be achieved by merely replacing the existing currency with a new one. Success or failure of the currency reform will depend mainly upon whether the State budget can be balanced." That prospect seemed remote, which meant that the new currency would fail as well. "It is possible that when and if public confidence in the new currency is shaken, commodity prices may rise even more rapidly than they have done in the past," a statement that was remarkably prescient.[2] At the end of February 1948, the market rate for the US dollar reached 300,000 yuan; it had started the year at 150,000. A picul of rice rose to 3.3 million yuan by February 27.[3]

Meanwhile, the government continued its cycle of raising the exchange rate to match the black-market rate only to find the new official rate completely inadequate. On April 6, 1948, the Foreign Exchange Equalization Fund Committee increased the official rate of exchange for US$1 to 324,000 yuan. Almost immediately, the black-market rate reached 565,000, and prices continued to surge.[4] By June 7, the black-market rate for dollars reached 1.4 million and on June 15 reached 1.95 million yuan per dollar.[5] By June 25, it hit 3.7 million and by July 13 rose to 6 million per dollar. The end was clearly near.[6] Bad news from the battlefield accelerated the decline of fabi. With the fall of Kaifeng to the communists in late June, prices on some commodities in Shanghai doubled in less than twenty-four hours.[7]

The cover price for the *China Weekly Review* in Shanghai was 300,000 yuan on July 10, 1948; 600,000 for July 17; 800,000 for August 7; and 1.5 million for August 21.[8] In late May, the government introduced an Exchange Certificate System that was supposed to let the exchange rate fluctuate with the market. But as in the past, the black-market rate continued to soar.[9] And in mid-July, the government issued the 5 million-yuan note to cope with the higher prices, a move that the *Dagong bao* stated would simply fuel price rises.[10]

The worst consequence for urban residents was the soaring price of rice, which the government could not control. In early March 1948 the price of rice in Shanghai was 3.3–3.5 million yuan per picul. The government could simply not get more rice on the market without paying a higher price to producers. As L. K. Little noted on March 11, 1948, the day had arrived when "the farmers won't bother to bring their produce to the city because, by the time they can spend money they receive at the market, prices of what they want to buy have gone up so fast that the money won't bring them anything worthwhile."[11] As the price index continued to soar, even government enterprises could not resist the trend. In early April, the government transportation enterprises raised passenger fares, as did other government-owned enterprises.[12] Because the government itself did not have enough foreign exchange to purchase petroleum from overseas, most vessels in the China Merchants Steam Navigation Company had to suspend operations at the end of April.[13]

The United States began a program of sending relief supplies to China to alleviate the shortage in urban areas. In January 1948, Congress provided US$125 million for the purchase of commodities including cotton, petroleum, foodstuffs, and other items. The goal was not only to alleviate shortages in China but also to absorb currency and reduce inflation. The first shipment of flour arrived in Shanghai in mid-January 1948. The relief items could be sold on the open market, but the proceeds were to go to relief efforts. The program delivered some benefits but could not stem the tide of hyperinflation.[14]

The Chiang government continued to press for more American financial aid, including funds that could be used to stabilize the currency. The Truman administration and George Marshall as secretary of state had been hesitant to provide aid to the Chiang Kai-shek government, which they saw as increasingly inept and corrupt. But the success of the Chinese Communists on the battlefield and the tense relationship between Washington and Moscow changed the equation in Washington. Republican leaders in Congress pressed Marshall to find funds for Chiang, and Truman himself began to see the Cold War as extending beyond Europe. Marshall asked Congress for an aid program for Chiang. The China Aid Act passed in early April 1948, providing $388 million for economic aid to China over a one-year period and an additional $125 million for military aid.[15]

Much of the assistance was to be in the form of commodities that would be sold, as had earlier relief supplies. The *Shen bao* urged the government to use the proceeds from these sales to close the budget deficit and discontinue printing excess banknotes.[16] The new loans were attacked by communists and leftists. Feng Yuxiang, the old "Christian General," denounced the loans, stating that Chiang had already lost the support of the people and American efforts to shore up the Chiang dictatorship would not be effective.[17]

The collapse of fabi also brought an end to Zhang Qun's tenure as head of the Executive Yuan. Weng Wenhao emerged as a surprise choice, in part because he was thought to have a better chance of obtaining American aid than some of the other candidates.[18] Yu Hongjun was out as minister of finance; Weng brought in Wang Yunwu for the position. The general manager of the Commercial Press for many years, Wang had served as minister of economic affairs from May 1946 to April 1947, a tenure fraught with conflict with T. V. Soong. Now Wang would have responsibility for salvaging China's sinking currency, and he advocated a major change.[19]

Yet changing personnel could not solve the underlying problem. On June 15, 1948, Weng admitted that the government could not balance the budget because of the expense of the war against the communists. After his remarks, the *Xinwen bao* editorialized that "it is tantamount to admitting in advance that inflation is going to become worse and that the inevitable result is that the financial problem will become a mess. At this time when commodity prices are soaring, this will at least accelerate the price hike."[20] On June 26, rice prices increased 30 percent to 23 million yuan per picul; the US dollar increased to 4.8 million yuan per 1 dollar.[21] Many felt that the government had simply given up halting the price rises. As the *Xinwen bao* noted on June 27, 1948, "what is most surprising in the current frantic price hike is that the Government has taken an attitude of aloofness toward it. ... This phenomenon has increased the people's apprehensions and given them the impression that the different kinds of Government control agencies have already stopped functioning."[22]

Capital continued to flow into Hong Kong despite all efforts to control exchange. One indication was a sharp growth in the number of bank accounts in the Crown colony. The Hongkong and Shanghai Banking Corporation, the dominant British-controlled bank, noted that before the war only one or two depositors had accounts of more than 10 million Hong Kong dollars, but in June 1948, over 1,000 had such accounts, and

10,000 had at least 5 million in deposits. The assumption was that most of these deposits had come from Chinese seeking to get capital out of China.[23]

Even the *Zhongyang ribao* (Central daily), generally considered the voice of the government, expressed despair. "The illegal activities of Chinese banks, both Government and private, have now become anarchic. How many of these banks dare to declare that they have never violated any of the decrees and regulations promulgated by the Ministry of Finance? How many of them dare to declare that they have only one set of books?" The government banks were singled out as particular targets. "The capital of Government banks and bureaus is the property of the state and the sweat and blood of the people. Do these banks and bureaus have the right to use these funds in any way they like and to buy a large amount of real estate in China or abroad?"[24]

On July 22, 1948, the exchange rate for the dollar reached 6.5 million yuan per 1 dollar. Livingston T. Merchant, economic adviser to the American Embassy in Nanjing, noted in a report to the secretary of state on July 30, 1948, that "there is no doubt in my mind that the Central Bank is absolutely out of dollar exchange. The inflation is now taking on an explosive form with the first signs beginning to appear of the actual physical slowdown of the conduct of business which characterizes its final stages." He noted that CNAC flights from Shanghai to Nanjing had been suspended because the official rate did not cover the rising cost of obtaining aviation fuel. Many stores in Shanghai were staying closed rather than risk holding fabi for even a few hours. "The rate went over eight million in Shanghai yesterday and until this morning the largest denomination bill in circulation was worth only slightly over one cent gold."[25]

On July 29, Chiang Kai-shek met with officials at his mountain retreat in Zhejiang to discuss the matter. Among those attending were Weng Wenhao (head of the Executive Yuan), Wang Yunwu (minister of finance), Yu Hongjun (the head of the Central Bank), and Wang Shijie (the foreign minister). They decided that a reform plan would be developed in secret. Chiang returned to Nanjing on August 18 and the following day he would approve the regulations for the new currency.[26]

SOONG HEADS SOUTH

Although T. V. Soong had been forced out as head of the head of the Executive Yuan in March 1947, he had one final role to play in Guomindang China. Chiang Kai-shek appointed him governor of Guangdong province in September of that year, with the added title of pacification commissioner. Soong's appointment gave rise to speculation that Chiang was preparing a base in the far south in the event the communists continued their military march. Communist sources suggested that the United States wanted Chiang to secure this area so that it could become a base for American aid to counter the communist triumphs.[27] But others in Washington realized that Chiang might be on the way out and that the United States should support regional regimes in south and southwest China. Soong was seen as a candidate for such a government in Guangdong province. This was not to be, for when Chiang resigned the presidency in January 1949 (if perhaps not giving up actual political power), Soong also stepped down and left for the United States, never returning to mainland China. But when Soong undertook his new position in the fall of 1947, he did so with typical energy, frantically trying to undertake multiple economic projects. And he took the daring step of using Japanese advisers and technicians as he saw fit.[28]

Soong's appointment was heavily criticized by the same groups that had attacked him a few months earlier. The National Socialist Party, headed by Zhang Junmai (Carsun Chang), one of the Third Force groups, saw the appointment as revealing Chiang's unwillingness to purge the government of corrupt individuals. An editorial of October 4, 1947 in their major journal stated, "today, all the people throughout the country are hungry and emaciated, but he and H. H. Kung and a small number of bad eggs are growing fatter and fatter, richer and richer, so much so that even high-class foreigners are envious of their material abundance." The article concluded that "we express the strongest protest against the assumption of governorship by T. V.! We believe that this protest of ours also represents the wish of all the wise, great and law-abiding people throughout the length and breadth of the country."[29]

Ling Wusu, a representative of the Democratic Socialist Party on the provincial council, attacked Soong for his failure to assist private industry and mining in Guangdong. Ling charged that Soong was signing secret agreements with the United States that would allow for military bases in south China and for the reduction of tariffs on US products.[30] In October 1948, the Control Yuan – a center of opposition to Soong – sent two representatives to Hong Kong to investigate charges that Soong had been engaging in unlawful transactions in Hong Kong currency as well as building unauthorized airfields in Guangdong.[31]

Soong was deeply upset at the criticism he received and continually protested that he had not accumulated large sums of money. In October 1947, T. V. had made a very public donation of his shares in the Yangzi Development Company to a charity that aided dependents of Guomindang members who had died in the defense of the country. His opponents in the party downplayed the donation, calling it a "drop in the bucket," and suggested it was all for show.[32]

When Soong heard a rumor that someone at a dinner party at the British Embassy in Nanjing had stated that an official with connections to the Guangdong provincial government was conducting unauthorized business between Guangzhou and Hong Kong, he became sufficiently outraged to write to the British ambassador himself on January 12, 1948. He asked the ambassador to please assist in providing information about the charges. "I feel sure that you will sufficiently sympathize with a public servant who has frequently been under fire without justification to accede to my request." The ambassador replied on January 24 that he had made enquiries but had not been able to find out any information about the alleged remarks.[33] Soong obviously felt compelled to try to dispel charges of corruption leveled at him.

When the gold yuan reform was introduced in August 1948, the new currency was not successful in the south. Because Hong Kong and Macao imported foreign goods with no or little duty, smuggling into China was virtually inevitable. It seems that 70–80 percent of the trade between Hong Kong and south China was done through smuggling.[34] When Jiang Jingguo (Chiang Ching-kuo) imposed his "reign of terror" in Shanghai after the gold yuan reform, the terms were rigorously enforced there. But Soong seemed unwilling to use those methods in Guangdong.

Some in the Legislative Yuan raised the issue of why this was not the case. The British consul-general at Guangzhou in a report to the colonial secretary in Hong Kong on September 27, 1948, noted that "Dr. Soong says he will not have a reign of terror in Canton, and there seem to be a reluctance here to copy Shanghai methods." Jiang Jingguo enforced the rules by methods that alienated many of the business community. The British consul noted that "commodities disappear if police try to prevent sales at black market rates." But in explaining this, the consul simply assumed that the rumors about Soong were true. "One possible reason for this is, of course, the fact that it is common knowledge that Dr. Soong has a sizable fortune salted away abroad and that he should be responsible for the local enforcement of the economic programme strikes the Cantonese merchant community as somewhat anomalous."[35] Clearly, Soong had not succeeded is dispelling rumors about his wealth.

Soong's tenure in Guangdong shows that he had great ambitions for the province and assumed the Guomindang government would control the area in the future. He worked closely with the National Resources Commission (NRC) to develop large-scale projects. In April 1948, an American engineer, Martin T. Bennett, completed a study for the NRC for the development of ammonium sulfate fertilizer plants for Guangzhou and for Taiwan. The Guangzhou plant was to be located outside of the city between it and the Pearl River along the Guangzhou–Kowloon Railway. Budgeted at over US$20 million, the plant would have produced over 121,000 pounds of ammonium sulfate and additional ammonium nitrate. The plant assumed that an American loan would be forthcoming to be repaid over fifteen years.[36] The project was not, of course, completed before the communists seized the area, but it reveals that the Soong regime was still making long-term plans for the province in 1948.

A second major project promoted by Soong was the development of Hainan Island. A sweeping proposal would have funded development of agriculture, fishing, mining, industry, and transportation. Because Japan had invested substantial resources in the island during the war, Soong decided to invite Japanese experts and assistants to come to Hainan to assist in the project. The proposal included reasonable pay for the Japanese, security for their living arrangements, and provision for a Japanese-style education for their children. With the war only three years in the past, Soong seemed unconcerned by possible public reaction to the employment of these Japanese experts. But like the fertilizer project, Soong's ambitions were not realized.[37] A major difficulty in getting the Japanese experts to China was General Douglas MacArthur's office, Supreme Commander Allied Powers, in Tokyo. When Soong requested twenty Japanese engineering experts be sent to Guangdong for the repairs to the Kokusaku Paper Mill, he was advised by John Leighton Stuart, then American ambassador to China, that the Far Eastern Commission had not cleared the process. China would have to appeal directly to the commission, which had not heretofore allowed Japanese engineers to participate in work overseas.[38]

The ambitious plans for Guangdong reflected a sense of optimism that was not warranted under the circumstances. Both the military and economic situations were rapidly deteriorating. An official who had served under Soong in the Ministry of Finance and continued working there sent a private message to Soong on June 28, 1948. Tax revenues were not improving, he noted. An increase in import tariffs produced negligible revenue because so few items were legitimately imported. The government had pledged to improve collection of the income tax, but "we do not have the organization or trained staff to administer properly an income tax. Prices continue to rise. The rapidity and extent of the rise are terrifying. People have been wondering what will happen. Unless the deterioration of the military situation could be checked, even U.S. aid will not be of any avail. Some momentous crisis may develop." Soong's informant suggested that the business community had no confidence in the in the new finance minister. "I am sorry I have nothing encouraging or hopeful to report to you except that I still manage to get along."[39]

INTRODUCTION OF THE GOLD YUAN

On August 20, 1948, Chiang Kai-shek suddenly announced a new currency – the gold yuan. The use of the term "gold" was a bit of salesmanship, as the government had less than US$100 million in gold reserves at this point and it was not used to back the new issue.[40] The plan had been prepared in secret during the previous weeks. Weng Wenhao, head of the Executive Yuan, and Wang Yunwu, minister of finance, both promoted the policy, finally convincing Chiang. Wang, who had only a limited background in finance, was the most enthusiastic architect of the reform. However, T. V. Soong and Chang Kia-ngau cautioned Chiang against the change.[41] By government decree, all gold and silver held by individuals and banks had to be surrendered to the Central Bank of China in exchange for the new currency. All banks were to close for two days to facilitate the exchange. Old fabi notes were to be converted at banks at the rate of one gold yuan per three million fabi yuan (Figure 6.1). The government announced that the amount of the new currency would be strictly limited and that rigid price controls would be enforced in major cities.[42] Overnight, there was a stunning change in market prices. The cost of a tram ticket, previously 300,000 yuan fabi, became 10 cents in the gold yuan currency. The street price of the *North-China Herald* dropped from 800,000 yuan to 25 cents.[43]

6.1. People crowd banks to exchange the old fabi notes for the new gold yuan notes, August 1948. Bettmann/Getty Images

The total of the new currency to be issued was 2 billion yuan, while 700 trillion yuan of the old currency circulated. The exchange rate for the American dollar was set at four gold yuan for one dollar. Chiang considered the key to success of the reforms to be Shanghai, more than ever the financial center of Guomindang China. Chiang sent his son, Jiang Jingguo [Chiang Ching-kuo], to Shanghai on August 20 to oversee the process in the metropolis. Jingguo had made a trip to Shanghai a few weeks earlier to study the economic situation in the city. He wrote to his father on June 26 to report that conditions were quite serious. On June 28, he began a series of personal meetings with his father that continued until August 3 to discuss the situation.[44] The reform was prepared with such secrecy that even key government officials were caught off guard. Wu Guozhen, then mayor of Shanghai, which would be central to the success or failure of the gold yuan, was one such official. He only learned of the change on August 19 when Yu Hongjun, then head of the Central Bank, phoned him with the news.[45]

Some in the press indicated hope that the reform would be successful. On August 21, 1948, the *Dagong bao* noted "the publication of the size of the note issue and the independence of the note issue constituted one of the important reasons why the fapi [fabi] was able to enjoy the confidence of the public in the early days, and now those have been restored."[46] The *Shen bao* likewise stressed the importance of independent power to control the issue of banknotes. "The Government must not issue a single Gold Yuan note without first obtaining the written approval of the responsible officers of the supervisory committee." It this rule was violated, the paper continued, inflation would resume.[47] Jiang Jingguo himself was optimistic when the project started. On August 22, 1948, he wrote in his diary that most people seemed supportive of the new currency and felt that it would succeed. Government personnel, he noted, were not as optimistic.[48]

And skepticism abounded. Even before the currency was introduced, much of the Chinese press pronounced it a failure. The *Shidai gonglun* (Modern critique) on February 15, 1948, wrote that today's China did not have the basis for a successful new currency. It lacked the ability to back currency in either silver or gold. The "new fabi will quickly become the old fabi." The article was triggered by reports that Chiang had sent Bei

Zuyi to America to attempt to get US backing for the new currency.[49] When asked about the reform, economist He Lian (Franklin Ho) recalled, "I thought that it was plainly impossible! You cannot achieve monetary reform merely by adopting a new currency to replace the old one. You cannot achieve monetary reform without fiscal reform."[50] Upon learning of the new policy, Shanghai mayor Wu Guozhen headed to Nanjing on August 20 to attempt to convince Chiang Kai-shek that the gold yuan reform would not work. His stance simply angered Chiang. Wu returned to Shanghai without even meeting with the minister of finance, sensing that it was a lost cause.[51]

The British consul in Shanghai sent a confidential report to the embassy in Nanjing that stated, "in view of the slight prospects of the new currency succeeding in the present circumstances, the question may well be asked why did the Government introduce it at the present juncture?" The general view was that, if the government was going to succeed, it should have tried the change before things had deteriorated so seriously. "With wholesale prices tripling in the month of June and retail prices similarly tripling in the month of July, there was a general feeling that the situation had become untenable. It is believed that the leaders of the Shanghai banking community informed the Generalissimo to that effect about a month ago."[52] The issuing of the new currency was done in tandem with a series of policies including the freezing of most commodity prices at the level of August 19, 1948. Similar policies in the past had proven unsuccessful.

To bring in funds to back the new currency, the government tried once again to interest the public in purchasing shares in government enterprises. Among the firms touted were the Chinese Textile Industries, China Merchants Steam Navigation Company, Taiwan Sugar Corporation, Taiwan Paper Company, and Tianjin Paper Company. Yet according to a report from the American Embassy in Nanjing sent to Washington in mid-September 1948, sales were sluggish. After a month, apparently sales of stock had only brought in 4 million gold yuan, as opposed to the projected sales of 564 million. As in 1947 when the government announced such sales, the credibility of the investment was low, so the public was wary of purchasing the stock.[53]

Equally troubling was the difficulty of setting the exchange rate at a realistic level. On August 18, 1948, the official exchange rate was 7.5 million yuan fabi to 1 US dollar. At the time of the currency reform decree, this was suddenly raised to 12 million yuan to 1 dollar. When the gold yuan reform was introduced, the exchange rate had been set at four gold yuan for one American dollar, a rate set by Chiang Kai-shek himself.[54] In May 1948, the Central Bank had introduced a flexible exchange rate designed to reflect market values. They had tried to keep the rate above 70 percent of the black-market value. But after the gold yuan reform, the government tried to maintain a fixed exchange rate. But this effort, too, quickly failed. In November 1948, Nanjing could no longer maintain the four-to-one rate. As the communists won a series of major victories in late 1948 and early 1949, the Central Bank was also in retreat.[55]

For the gold yuan reform to succeed, Nanjing authorities believed, banks, enterprises, and individuals had to surrender their gold, silver, and foreign currency assets to the Central Bank. Li Ming, then chair of the Shanghai Bankers Association, stated that all modern and native banks in Shanghai would comply with the new order.[56] Thanks to the harsh methods used by Jiang Jingguo in Shanghai, a substantial amount was surrendered. But the situation in the rest of China was much less successful. Shanghai residents supplied 64 percent of the total value of surrendered gold, silver, and foreign currency, but estimates were that only 20–30 percent of the national total of these items had been turned in by the September 30 deadline.[57] The situation in south China was particularly bad. The Hong Kong dollar continued to be hoarded by the local population, and T. V. Soong refused to use the harsh methods of Jiang Jingguo. So the gold yuan never caught on in Guangdong and surrounding areas. As Chou Shun-hsin noted, "even at best, the Chinese currency only supplemented and never superseded the role of Hong Kong dollars as the *de facto* standard money in south China."[58] In an editorial on September 15, the *Dagong bao* echoed this theme. "The nation's economy is an organic whole, so if economic conditions in other parts of the country cannot be made entirely satisfactory, Shanghai will eventually be adversely affected." The government's focus on Shanghai would not work in the long run, the paper concluded. "We urge that the

Government give special attention to measures which are nation-wide in scope, instead of thinking that by improving conditions in one city alone, it will be able to improve conditions in the whole country."[59]

Ultimately, the gold yuan reform could not succeed unless the government abandoned the policy of covering deficits by printing currency. But the continuation, indeed the acceleration, of the civil war in the latter half of 1948, made this nearly impossible. As the *Shang bao* predicted on August 20, 1948, when the reform was issued "we are convinced that no currency reform measures can have any success as long as order is not restored and as the budget is not able to be balanced. . . . [But] bandit suppression will certainly continue even after the currency reform. . . . Bandit quelling and a stable currency cannot exist side by side." The only hope was that "this most wasteful war must be stopped if we are to have effective currency reform."[60] That, of course, was not going to happen until the communist victory.

JIANG JINGGUO'S REIGN OF TERROR

The gold yuan reform worked remarkably well for several weeks in the Shanghai and Nanjing areas. Commodity prices remained stable at the August 19 ceiling levels, and approximately US$170 million in gold, silver, and foreign exchange was surrendered to the Central Bank in exchange for the new currency.[61] But there was a cost for this success. Chiang had placed his son Jiang Jingguo in charge of enforcing the reform in Shanghai. As Chang Kia-ngau noted, "for six weeks Shanghai was more or less terrorized into a state of monetary equilibrium. Commodity prices remained at ceiling levels except for perishable goods, and the black market in foreign currencies and gold passed out of existence."[62] Jiang used his own agents to make these arrests, subordinating the Shanghai city police. His nominal boss, general manager of the Central Bank Yu Hongjun, had little control over Jiang Jingguo. He wrote to his father on a regular basis to report on the situation, and the backing of the elder Chiang was the source of Jingguo's authority.[63]

Jiang Jingguo relied on two outside organizations that were relatively new and answered directly to him. The Sixth Battalion of the Bandit-Suppression National-Reconstruction Corps (Kanluan jianguo dadui) was brought in to search warehouses for hoarded goods. They also put up "secret-report boxes" that allowed citizens to report violations anonymously, and they carried 45 caliber pistols while on patrol. The second organization that assisted Jingguo was the Shanghai Youth Service Corps (Da Shanghai qingnian fuwu zongdui), which enrolled approximately 12,000 youth. The younger Jiang considered it to be essential for the success of his endeavors in Shanghai. Although they were loyal to him, most of the young people had limited or no training in the tasks that they had been given.[64]

Doak Barnett, then in China, noted that the "methods used by Chiang [Jiang] have been described as 'reform at pistol point.' His energy, fearlessness, and honesty were admired by many, but it soon became apparent that his methods were antagonizing key groups whose cooperation was absolutely necessary for the success of such a program."[65] But Jingguo felt that he was launching a social revolutionary movement that would overcome economic inequality in society. His target was to be the big, wealthy "traitorous merchants." "Those who disturb the financial markets ... are not the small merchants, but the big capitalists and big merchants. Therefore, if we are to employ severe punishments, we should begin with the chief culprits."[66]

Jiang Jingguo became convinced that many business and banking leaders were only giving superficial support to his program. On September 11, he met with several bankers with whom he was dissatisfied, including Li Ming, who was head of the Shanghai Bankers Association, and Qian Xinzhi, head of the Board of Directors of the Bank of Communications. Reportedly, Jiang was particularly rude to Zhou Zuomin, manager of the Jincheng Bank, who had voluntarily spent the war in occupied areas, demanding more foreign exchange. Zhou fled to the Hongqiao Hospital to escape the pressure.[67] The capitalists, Jingguo reported, were friendly to him in person, but "behind one's back there is no evil they do not commit."[68] Chiang Kai-shek issued a statement affirming that he believed several private banks had not submitted all of their foreign exchange. On September 12, Jingguo held a rally for officials implementing the policy and spoke for over an hour to applause and cheers. But the following day, he summoned business leaders to a meeting at the Central Bank of China building and informed them that if they slowed down production or suspended operations because they felt that the fixed price was too low, the government was prepared to confiscate their enterprises.[69]

Jiang's special agents arrested Li Ming, one of the most prominent bankers of the Republican era, on the grounds that he was secretly holding US$3 million. Shanghai mayor Wu Guozhen went to Nanjing to plead his case with Chiang Kai-shek, arguing that Li's bank did not have nearly that much capital. Chiang replied that his son had the evidence. Still, Li was released after filling out a police report and promptly fled to New York. Jingguo was alienating the Shanghai business community. Many of the Shanghai capitalists gave up on the Guomindang government at this point. Altogether, nearly sixty prominent business leaders were swept up in the campaign.[70]

But Jiang's reign of terror could not work outside of the urban areas and Shanghai in particular. Mayor Wu Guozhen noted that the new currency was not accepted in the villages where commodities were produced. Farmers simply refused to sell at the prices fixed by the reform and were dubious about holding gold yuan notes. Textile leaders in Shanghai who were arrested by Jiang's agents protested that they could not obtain cotton from the interior, so that the only way to continue to operate was to import foreign cotton. Jiang Jingguo had Rong Hongyuan, China's leading textile magnate, arrested for hiding foreign exchange. Rong claimed that he had no real alternative to obtain cotton other than overseas purchases. He was sentenced to seven years in prison but later released when the gold yuan reform failed.[71] Both textile production in Shanghai and the use of electric power declined from August to September 1948 because of the lack of raw materials. Estimates put the decline in output at 30 percent. Fearful that merchants would simply transport commodities outside of Shanghai to the interior where price controls were not enforced, Jingguo began to impose stringent rules on exporting goods from Shanghai. Since the big city had long relied on sales of commodities in its hinterland, this further depressed the economy.[72]

Cotton textiles were hit doubly hard because prices of cotton products had been fixed on August 19, 1948. As Juanjuan Peng noted in her study of the Yudahua business group, "unfortunately, August happened to be the low season for the textile manufacturers; the cotton price hit the peak just before the new cotton was picked and the yarn price was still low because the farmers, the ultimately consumer of cotton products, usually waited until after the harvest to make purchases."[73] The legal price for textile goods was set at an unfavorable level and could not be adjusted.

Jiang Jingguo targeted Zhou Zuomin of the Jincheng Bank, placing him under house arrest. Zhou apparently then admitted that his bank held significant deposits in foreign currency and other assets in the United States. According to He Lian, who had earlier been a professor at Nankai University but began working for the Jincheng Bank in 1946, Jiang targeted Zhou because he had stayed in Shanghai and Hong Kong during the war and was suspected of working with the Japanese. He Lian recalled that Weng Wenhao and Chang Kia-ngau both spoke up on Zhou's behalf. With their support, and assistance from Claire Chennault, Zhou escaped to Hong Kong.[74]

Du Yuesheng had been one of the most powerful underworld figures in Shanghai for several decades. He had worked with Chiang Kai-shek on earlier occasions, and he invited Jingguo to dine with him on his arrival in Shanghai. Jingguo not only declined but shortly thereafter had Du's son Du Weiping arrested and sentenced to eight months in prison for hoarding and violating the stock exchange rules.[75] Another victim was the son of Aw Boon Haw, the famed Tiger-Balm king, who was arrested for gold and foreign currency smuggling. Although several hundred were arrested in the crackdown, Jiang was most concerned with the "Big Tigers," labeling himself as the "Big Tiger hunter." But some were beyond Jingguo's reach. T. V. Soong was rumored to have purchased a large amount of Hong Kong currency on August 18 on the eve of the announcement of the gold yuan reform. No charges were filed in the latter case.[76]

Still, Jiang Jingguo was fearless in his sweep of those suspected of corruption. Among those targeted was H. H. Kung's son, David Kung [Kong Lingkan], who had stayed in Shanghai to manage the Yangzi Development Company. Jingguo's forces, the Youth Service Corps personnel, military police, and officials from the Central Bank raided the warehouses of the company and seized control. David Kung was accused of holding foreign exchange, and several employees of the company were arrested. According to the British Embassy in Nanjing, Kung was also accused of hoarding 100 motor cars, 500 cases of woolen piece goods, and 200 cases of medicine.[77] Jingguo's move was risky because David was a favorite of his aunt, Madame Chiang Kai-shek, whom David Kung contacted shortly after the raid on the Yangzi Development Company. Madame Chiang protested directly to her husband, and she called Jingguo directly. He was forced to back off in tackling the "Big Tigers." Madame Chiang had the upper hand.[78]

On October 8, the Generalissimo flew from Beiping, where he had been assessing the military situation in the north, to Shanghai to meet with his son. Ten days later, the problem was dumped on Wu Guozhen, mayor of Shanghai.[79] He received a telegram from Chiang Kai-shek telling him to deal with the matter. Wu tried to dodge the issue, replying that he had not been responsible for David's arrest and that others should be held responsible. Wu had been unhappy from the start with Jingguo's role in Shanghai, feeling that the young Jiang was moving into his turf. Three days later, Wu received a phone call from Madame Chiang herself stating that Chiang wanted Wu to handle the matter. Faced with the pressure from the top, Wu began an independent investigation of the matter. By the time he finished his work, the gold yuan had collapsed, and the matter was largely overshadowed. He concluded that David Kung's actions were legal and followed the rules of the gold yuan reform. His company had simply ceased importing anything after the new currency was issued. But Wu felt that even though his actions were not illegal they were unethical. He had relied on influence and position to obtain foreign exchange before the reform, much as his father H. H. Kung had done.[80]

Chiang Kai-shek persisted in the approach he had used in the past when faced with reports of corruption among the Soongs and Kungs. Although he acknowledged the possibility of some wrongdoing, he felt the communists were attempting to take advantage of this, so the issue should not be aired too publicly. He particularly disliked attempts by those within the Control Yuan to target his in-laws. In his telegram to Wu Guozhen, Chiang noted that the Yangzi Development Company was a private firm, not a government institution. Therefore, it was not a proper target for investigation by the Control Yuan. Wu agreed and had the Shanghai police notify the personnel from the Control Yuan that they must withdraw the team they sent to investigate the firm. The Control Yuan's mandate was to investigate government agencies only.[81] Jiang Jingguo was frustrated that he could not punish David Kung. He wrote in his diary on October 16, 1948, "in the case of the Yangzi Development Company, I was not able to carry it through to the end because of limitations on my mandate." The general feeling was that if Jingguo could not punish David Kung, he could not really be effective.[82]

Jiang Jingguo's "reign of terror" did have one major impact – many of the prominent capitalist leaders in Shanghai left for Hong Kong and beyond. David Kung headed first to Hong Kong and then New York. His departure infuriated several members of the Control Yuan, who believed that he should not have been allowed to leave while the Yangzi Development Company case remained unsettled. At a meeting of the Legislative Yuan on November 2, 1948, some members unleashed an attack on the Kung family and specifically blamed the corporation for hoarding commodities.[83] Du Yuesheng made a substantial payment to the government and was allowed to leave for Hong Kong with his son. Later, he declined to go to Taiwan but chose to remain in Hong Kong, as did industrialist Liu Hongsheng. And the Guos (Kwoks) of the Yong'an Company also departed for the British Crown colony. Others would choose the People's Republic over Taiwan, including Zhou Zuomin. Jingguo's brief reign was felt long after the gold yuan collapsed.[84]

As the capitalists left, they attempted to take as much of their money with them as they could. The official *Zhongyang ribao* (Central daily news) noted on September 9 that the government had shut down illegal direct remittances from Shanghai to Hong Kong. But gold yuan notes were increasingly being sent from Shanghai to Guangzhou, where they could be converted to Hong Kong dollars and eventually US dollars in many cases.[85]

The *Shidai piping* (Modern critique) published in Hong Kong by the China Democratic League was blunt. The attacks on the Zhejiang–Jiangsu financial clique, it noted, had disrupted Shanghai's economy; there was no market for manufactured goods, and many banks closed as capitalists left for Hong Kong. Jingguo had threatened confiscation for any enterprise that closed, the journal concluded, so many shops remained open but with no goods to sell. Still, the journal concluded that the crackdown excluded the "four great families" associated with Chiang Kai-shek.[86] *Shang bao* (Commercial press), a Shanghai paper associated with the C. C. Clique, was more circumspect but noted that "while it is necessary to stabilize commodity prices and prohibit speculation, yet in trying to achieve these objectives, the Government must not act in such a way as to hinder the normal operation of the system of production. We sincerely support the economic supervisory work, but we also love the industrial and business enterprises."[87]

A few days later, the *Shang bao* noted that the cost of production for most items now exceeded the price which merchants could charge, which was set at August 19 levels. "The replacement of raw material supplies has become difficult. Foreign supplies cannot be imported. Wages and other expenses cannot be reduced, while taxes are being increased. Thus, the present ceiling prices are sometimes far below production or importation costs."[88] The *Shishi xin bao* (Current affairs news) noted in the evening edition on September 21, 1948, that "during the past month everybody has been living under great nervous strain, fearing that what he or she did might be contrary to the law. The merchants have not dared to do business, so that a state of depression have prevailed in the markets and economic activities have partly come to a standstill."[89] Jiang Jingguo had come down hard, and the economy suffered.

The August 19 price level held for approximately seventy days before it suddenly fell apart. The government itself triggered the collapse when in an ill-timed effort to raise revenue it increased the tax on a wide range of consumer items including tobacco and alcohol on October 2. Merchants would be permitted to raise prices to cover the new taxes. Tobacco shops closed for two days and reopened with the higher prices. When people saw the new prices, they assumed this was only the beginning and started a wild buying spree. Since merchants could not easily get new stock, many were left with empty shelves. As Lloyd E. Eastman wrote, "within three weeks the buying spree abated, for virtually nothing remained to be purchased. Then Shanghai became like a besieged city, shortages being far more critical than at any time within memory, including the last stage of the war with Japan. The poor went for weeks without rice, meat, or cooking oil."[90] Stores began to run out of commodities but were not legally permitted to close. Shoppers on Shanghai's famed Nanjing Road found empty shelves in the Sincere (Xianshi), Wing On (Yong'an), and Xinxin Department Stores. Factories were idle because they had no raw materials but could not declare bankruptcy.[91] Many stores, worried when they could not restock, simply started closing earlier, which increased the frenzy of the shoppers.[92]

By mid-October, even Jiang Jingguo recognized that most textile mills in Shanghai were in a paralyzed state because they could not get raw materials. With domestic sources unavailable, imports of cotton became essential. The *Dagong bao* reported on October 15 that Jingguo had agreed that the ban on privately held foreign exchange be eased so that raw cotton could be imported by the textile mills. He personally telephoned Weng Wenhao to ask the Executive Yuan to deal with the matter. Jingguo noted in his diary on October 17 that Weng was very concerned about the situation in Shanghai and was likely to support abandoning the price controls.[93] On October 20, the *Zhongyang ribao* reiterated that the August 19 price levels for daily necessities had to be held so that people could maintain their livelihood. But the government should study the production costs for raw materials and fuel and adjust prices so that production of commodities such as textiles would be possible. How this was to be done without gutting the price controls was unclear.[94]

COLLAPSE OF THE GOLD YUAN

The key to the gold yuan reform was a promise by the Ministry of Finance that the government would not continue to print money to cover deficit spending. When the new currency was introduced, the government pledged to reduce the portion of the budget covered by deficit from 70 percent to only 30 percent. In October, they reduced that portion to 50 percent, but the following month the deficit soared to 75 percent of the budget. The plan to absorb capital by selling shares in government enterprises and issuing bonds had largely failed to bring in substantial revenue. Once the dam broke and people lost confidence in the gold yuan, they quickly converted cash into commodities which led to a reboot of hyperinflation.[95] As the *Shang bao* noted on October 6, 1948, "from the point of view of the emergency measures, it is evident that the present state of confusion – the buying spree and the closing of shops earlier than usual – indicates that the measure taken by the Government have already reached the limit of effectiveness."[96] On October 21, Jiang Jingguo went to Nanjing to meet with Weng Wenhao and sensed that the government was ready to abandon the price controls.[97]

By late October, rumors spread that the price ceilings would be broken. On October 28, the *Dagong bao* noted that "since the buying spree began ... the economic situation in this city has been especially grave." The end was clearly near. "The fact today is that in places outside of Shanghai, the ceiling price dyke has long been breached, and even in Shanghai, it is also difficult to obtain goods at ceiling prices. Viewing the situation as a whole, we see that the sources of supply have been cut off and frozen."[98] Stores were virtually empty. "There are no medicines for the sick, no coffins for the dead, no milk powder for babies, and not even toilet paper and cotton for women in labor. Even more serious is the shortage of rice, cooking oil, and fuel. All essential daily necessities have disappeared. What can one do?"[99]

Financial leaders in the government gathered in Nanjing on October 27 and 28 and heavily criticized Jiang Jingguo for his handling of the crisis. Chiang Kai-shek was still in Beiping at that point, attending to the military situation in the north. In his monthly reflections for October in his diary, Jingguo noted the tobacco-tax increase, and the large issuance of the gold yuan notes. That situation set up a tidal wave of buying in early October that had destabilized the marketplace. The fundamental problem, he concluded, was that the amount of notes issued had been too large. Summoned to Nanjing for the meeting with government leaders, Jingguo was one of the few to advocate continuing with the plan. He had to deliver the bitter news to his supporters in Shanghai that the campaign was over.[100]

On November 1, 1948, the government abandoned the August 19 ceiling level on prices. Weng Wenhao and Wang Yunwu both announced their resignations, taking responsibility for this debacle. Jiang Jingguo publicly apologized. On November 11, Chinese citizens were now permitted again to hold gold, silver, and foreign exchange, and the exchange rate for the American dollar was increased from the old four gold yuan for one dollar to twenty to one. The freeze on wage increases was dropped, and they were to be adjusted to meet the needs of livelihood of the workers. Wages and prices surged.[101]

The gold yuan regulations were abandoned after only seventy days; the new currency had been a complete failure. Law-abiding citizens who had surrendered their gold and silver when asked suffered great losses, while those who had hoarded these metals were rewarded. As Lloyd E. Eastman argued, "the termination of price controls on October 31 marked the beginning of the final collapse of the National Government on the mainland. ... Largely by coincidence, the full extent of the debacle on the battlefield also became apparent at this time." Hyperinflation resumed with a vengeance. Farmers would not supply rice to Shanghai, which resulted in a series of rice riots in early November. By November and December industrial production in Shanghai was only 50–60 percent of the level of early 1948.[102] Increasingly, the Chinese resorted to a barter economy, avoiding currency altogether. In early November, for instance, it was reported in Shanghai that two cans of kerosene (ten gallons) could be exchanged for one picul of rice.[103]

Why had the reforms failed? Continued military setbacks by Nationalist forces in the civil war undermined popular confidence in the currency. But the basic cause was that the government had totally abandoned its pledge to limit the quantity of notes issued. On November 20, 1948, the total issuance of gold yuan notes was 2.47 billion; on December 29, 7.85 billion; on February 4, 1949, 25.5 billion; March 16, 98.487 billion; and April 20, 1.1 trillion. The result was a rapidly weakening yuan.[104]

From the beginning, the gold yuan had a fatal flaw. The premise of the new currency was that the amount issued would be limited to avoid the rapid increase in money supply and attendant inflation. When citizens surrendered their gold, silver, and foreign currency, they were issued gold yuan notes. They had other options, including depositing these items in an account in the Central Bank. But few Chinese trusted the government institutions and took a chance on the new currency instead. The government did a reasonable job of restraining deficit spending during the seventy days of price controls. As of September 30, only 23 percent of the new notes had been created to finance the government; 63 percent were printed to exchange for surrendered gold, silver, and foreign exchange. The latter was much greater than anticipated. As Lloyd Eastman wrote, "the result was that U.S. $190 million worth of gold, silver, and foreign currencies that had hitherto been held off the market were now suddenly converted into money and became an active inflationary ingredient." Ironically, this represented a complete reversal of the government policy during 1946 and early 1947, when the Central Bank sold gold to pull currency out of circulation. The gold yuan had taken gold and silver out of circulation and replaced it with paper currency – a recipe for disaster.[105]

With the ceiling prices abandoned, the rate of inflation soared to levels that surpassed what had occurred with fabi. As the *Shen bao* noted on November 9:

> commodity prices have virtually become unbridled horses, free to gallop at a speed beyond the reach of human attempts to stop them. . . . Although only seven or eight days have elapsed since the ceiling prices were unfrozen, values of rice, edible oil, flour, coal, and other daily necessities have appreciated more than tenfold, while prices differ at different times during the same day. The soaring tendency has been startling.[106]

On November 9, 1948, the British Consulate in Shanghai reported that rice prices in Shanghai had tripled over the weekend and continued to rise.[107] Farmers in the lower Yangzi were still reluctant to ship rice to Shanghai because they did not wish to hold the gold yuan notes even for the briefest period. But as the *Dagong bao* noted, "Shanghai's rice problem is entirely man-made. . . . There are bumper crops in China this year, and the autumn harvest is now being gathered." But farmers would not ship rice to Shanghai if they must take the gold yuan notes which were rapidly becoming worthless.[108]

When the new currency had been introduced, the official exchange rate had been set at 4 gold yuan to 1 US dollar. But away from Shanghai, the black-market rate began to increase within days. Starting in Tianjin, rate increases followed in Guangzhou, Chongqing, and Hankou. By November 11, the black-market rate had reached five times the official rate. In early November, the American authorities negotiated a special exchange rate for US organizations in China of 15 gold yuan to 1 dollar. The day after on November 5, the rate was raised to 20 to 1. The government revised the official public rate upward to 28 to 1 on November 30, 1948. This was increased to 2,660 to 1 on February 28, 1949, and 205,000 to 1 on April 25, 1949. The black-market rate for that day was 813,880. The gold yuan had collapsed.[109] When the communists arrived in Shanghai, the rate had reached 7 million to 1.[110]

As the black-market rate soared once again, even the foreign embassies began to give up on the new currency. The American consul general in Shanghai had alerted the secretary of state as early as mid-September that "the currency reform is going very badly." He warned that "production and commerce [are] coming to a standstill. Imports also greatly curtailed primarily as a result of freezing of retail prices." Exports had surged briefly at the start of the reform but now stalled because at the official rate of exchange domestic prices were above world rates for most export commodities. The feeling was that the gold yuan had at most a month before hyperinflation resumed.[111] On November 10, 1948, the American ambassador to China John Leighton Stuart notified the secretary of state that – in light of the thoroughly disorganized economy in China with the gold yuan cascading hourly – the embassy "has reluctantly authorized all Consulate China to make local arrangement through recourse to black market for gold yuan requirements."[112]

A similar attitude prevailed among the British. In a telegram from the British embassy in Shanghai to the Foreign Office in London on October 19, 1948, the embassy noted that the black-market rate for prices had soared, and that the embassy was going to the black market. "I am aware that the Central Bank [of China] will notice immediately when we cease to purchase funds through official channels and that we may consequently incur some slight political odium if we do so." But the view from Shanghai was that it would not matter. "I cannot help feeling that the days of the Government in its present form once currency collapse are numbered and that any odium we may incur will soon be forgotten in subsequent changes." The reply from London was more cautious. It suggested that the British consult with the Americans and attempt to act in concert. Also, before resorting to the black market the ambassador should try to get a renewed subsidy rate. If that failed they might turn to the black market but should warn the Chinese in advance.[113]

Paul Frillman, working for the US Information service in Shanghai, in
a letter of December 1, 1948, noted that after the introduction of the gold
yuan, "for a while prices held ... but then in their own mysterious way, black
markets began to appear, to grow, and finally mushroom until the malig-
nancy was once more beyond control. In a few weeks all gold yuan became
worthless."[114] On November 15, Jiang Jingguo wrote to his father that his
mission in Shanghai was a failure.[115] The gold yuan reform really destroyed
China's small middle class, with many businesses in Shanghai closing. Chiang
Kai-shek never admitted the gold yuan was a mistake, blaming communist
victories in Shandong as the culprit.[116] The government began selling gold
and silver at select offices with the stated goal of drawing down the gold yuan
notes. But when long queues formed, this became a sign of people's eager-
ness to dump the failing currency. Violence erupted on occasion, with forty-
five people injured and seven killed in the frenzy (Figure 6.2).[117]

After Weng Wenhao resigned as head of the Executive Yuan and
Wang Yunwu as minister of finance, Sun Ke replaced Weng and Xu
Kan took over for Wang. Sun immediately checked into a hospital in
Shanghai and received few visitors as he tried to put together a cabinet.[118]

6.2. Frenzied crowds surge into banks attempting to dump the gold yuan notes as their
value plummets. ullstein bild Dtl./ullstein bild/Getty Images

Meanwhile, the treasury halted sales of gold on January 17, 1949, and hyperinflation continued.[119]

Wu Guozhen, who had opposed the gold yuan reform from the beginning, was still angry about it in an interview of 1953. "The whole trouble about the gold yuan was that it embittered every part, every segment, of the Chinese people against the government," lamented the former mayor of Shanghai. "The bankers and businessmen like Li Ming got embittered and hated the government. And the middle class got entirely bankrupt because they surrendered what little savings they had." Even the poor were impacted. "Chinese poor people always had some ornament, gold you know, and so on, but they had to surrender those things too and finally the currency they got became worthless. So you can say the gold yuan was a fatal blow."[120]

ECONOMIC CONSEQUENCES OF MILITARY COLLAPSE

The collapse of the gold yuan had in fact paralleled the military collapse of the Guomindang and the triumph of the communist forces. Two events were clearly related. A classified report done by the American Department of State's intelligence division December 1948 stated that "the outstanding economic development in China during 1948 was the progressive contraction of the area under the control of the National Government." It cited two cases, coal and food production, to illustrate that point. Coal production in China in 1948, it noted, was similar to that of 1947. However, supplies reaching consuming areas were sharply reduced, particularly during the latter half of the year, as mining areas fell into communist hands and transportation lines were destroyed or lost.[121] The Shanghai Power Company normally used 19,000 tons of coal a month, but in September 1948 the company only received 7,300 tons. It began to draw down its emergency stocks.[122]

A similar situation prevailed in food production. The intelligence report indicated that food production in 1948 reached a postwar peak and was probably comparable to prewar levels. Yet it noted:

in the face of this recovery in the agricultural regions, China's urban centers were able to meet their food requirements only with the assistance of receipts from abroad. Factors contributing to this situation were Communist captures of producing areas as in Manchuria; the disruption of distribution patterns, a general phenomenon in the area north of the Yangtze affected by military operations.

The report also cited the sharp depreciation of currency and in the face of government attempts to fix prices, "an increasing unwillingness on the part of farmers to market their crops."[123] The American commodity relief program, which shipped foodstuffs directly to urban areas such as Shanghai, was designed to alleviate the shortages created by the isolation of cities from the rural areas.

In cotton textile production, the output held up for the first half of 1947 and then began to drop sharply. In the months since then, major cities in north and central China had become isolated economically from the surrounding countryside. "At the present time [December 1948] it is evident that the government's economic position is extremely precarious," the report concluded.[124] Much of the cotton grown in China was in communist-held areas by late 1948.

WHY DID THE NANJING GOVERNMENT WAIT SO LONG FOR COMPREHENSIVE CURRENCY REFORM?

The collapse of the gold yuan was hardly a surprise; many observers – Chinese and foreign – assumed the effort was doomed from the start. The currency situation had simply deteriorated too far to permit the gold yuan to succeed. What was unexpected was that Jiang Jingguo's methods delayed the collapse. But what if the effort had been undertaken a few months earlier before fabi had fallen so precipitously and the military situation turned so strongly against the Guomindang? Obviously, we can never know the answer to this question, but what of the related question: why did not Nanjing act sooner? For the Guomindang government to have launched a new currency in the summer of 1947 rather than 1948 would have required a strong push from Chiang Kai-shek himself. Nothing of that significance could be done without his personal attention. But during the months in question, Chiang paid only limited attention to the financial/inflation situation.

The opening of the *Shilue gaoben*, the draft of Chiang's daily activities by the Chiang Kai-shek archives, allows us unprecedented access to his activities, including a list of his visitors, important documents, and tele-grams he sent and received, and even sections of his diary. Mention is usually made of his morning study lesson and sometimes the evening one of the Bible or Chinese classics, dining arrangements, strolls, and sight-seeing with Madame Chiang, and even "gazing at fish," an occasional occurrence. The record reveals that virtually all his attention was cen-tered on the military situation, reading reports from the field, communi-cating with military commanders including personal conferences, and frequently traveling to cities around China where he met almost exclu-sively with military leaders. Other topics of interest included Guomindang and communist politics and foreign relations, particularly with the United States.[125]

Among the few occasions on which Chiang did turn to financial matters were when the Soongs and Kongs were involved or when connections to the United States and potential American aid were at stake. Otherwise, he showed little interest. After departing from his Lushan summer getaway in early September 1947, Chiang stopped briefly in Shanghai. He held a short meeting with Shanghai mayor Wu Guozhen, who was deeply disturbed by the rise in commodity prices. But the visit appears more of a courtesy call by Wu, and no details of the meeting are listed. A similar meeting occurred on October 22, 1947, when Chiang passed through Shanghai again. The early morning meeting merits only one line with no topic of discussion listed.[126] In early October, Chiang and Madame Chiang flew to Beiping, where he dealt with the battlefield situation in north and northeast China. He later flew to Shenyang and then Qingdao for a firsthand look. Only on October 12 did he meet with Zhang Qun, then head of the Executive Yuan, to discuss the grain market in Shanghai. Chiang wanted to reduce con-sumption and promote austerity.[127]

Even as the value of fabi sank in 1948, Chiang paid little attention to the issue, although he still held out hopes for an American bailout. He worried about secretary of state George Marshall's views on the Guomindang government, feeling that he was not supportive and that the hopes for substantial American aid were fading. Bei Zuyi had led a delegation to the United States seeking financial aid and reported back to Chiang on a regular basis. As preparations continued for the national assembly, Chiang broadened the range of his meetings to include

political preparation for the gathering. He met with Guomindang delegates and Chen Bulei, a key political operative. Finally on April 8, 1948,
he met with Chang Kia-ngau, then manager of the Central Bank, to
discuss the crisis of foreign exchange. But they would not meet again
until May 6 to discuss the price of gold, and the introduction of the new
currency would not occur for over three more months. Although he
noted the surging price of rice and the market turmoil on June 10, the
crisis in currency and commodity markets in China simply did not draw
much of Chiang's time.[128]

Finally, in the summer of 1948 Chiang had to deal with the issue of the
collapsing of fabi. Chiang met frequently with his son Jiang Jingguo, to
whom he would entrust the handling of the situation in Shanghai. But the
younger Jiang did not really have any expertise in financial matters.
Chiang's meetings with financial leaders were still relatively rare in the run-
up to the gold yuan reform. On June 28, 1948, he consulted Yu Hongjun,
director of the Central Bank, to set in motion the reform, and on July 5, he
discussed financial matters with the mayor of Shanghai, Wu Guozhen.
During July 13–15, he held a series of meetings to develop a concrete
proposal for currency reform, and during the final days of July he held
additional talks with Yu Hongjun. But Chiang focused as usual on military
matters until August 13–14, when he made the final decisions with Weng
Wenhao, now head of the Executive Yuan, and Wang Yunwu, the new
minister of finance. After he returned from his excursion in north China
on August 18, he issued the rules for the gold yuan the following day.[129] So
the fateful decisions that led to the disastrous gold yuan reform were made
with only the limited attention of Chiang Kai-shek.

As the gold yuan reform unfolded and his son riled the capitalists in
Shanghai, Chiang Kai-shek had good reason to turn his attention elsewhere, because it was during these weeks that the Guomindang's military
position began to unravel in the northeast and in the central plains of
north China. Chiang frequently absented himself from Nanjing as he
visited northern commanders attempting to shore up the resistance to
the communists. On September 5, he did meet with Yu Hongjun, Weng
Wenhao, and Wang Yunwu to receive a report on market conditions in
Shanghai, foreign-exchange issues, and the wave of arrests of individuals
such as Du Weiping undertaken by his son. Jiang Jingguo himself

reported to his father on September 7, and a week later Jingguo went to Nanjing to report personally to Chiang. The elder Chiang did turn his attention to the matter after the flare-up over David Kung and the Yangzi Development Company that so alarmed his wife. Chiang turned the matter over to Wu Guozhen, the mayor of Shanghai, who would deliver his report to Chiang on November 4, even as David Kung left for the United States. Wu Guozhen met personally with Chiang on November 12 to discuss the handling of the David Kung matter. Chiang was concerned about the reputation of the Kung family and possible damage to the position of the Guomindang. Meanwhile on October 29, Jiang Jingguo returned to Nanjing from Shanghai with the gold yuan plan now completely defeated.[130]

Chiang's attention was thus only tangentially focused on the gold yuan reform. In mid-October, the fighting at Jinzhou in northeast China had turned against the Guomindang, and the communists took the city. Meanwhile the 60th corps at Changchun defected to the communists, and the city surrendered with a decisive battle. Further south in Shandong, the city of Jinan fell in September, eventually placing much of the province in communist hands. By early November, the fateful Huaihai campaign was underway. The military situation was crumbling for the Nationalists. Almost simultaneously came the news from the United States that Truman had been reelected against predictions by most pundits. Chiang was deeply unhappy with the result, as he was certain a Republican administration under Dewey would have been more receptive to aiding his government. Then on November 13 came the shocking suicide of Chen Bulei, one of Chiang's most trusted lieutenants. All seem to be crumbling around him.[131]

GUOMINDANG SHANGHAI'S FINAL WEEKS

On December 30, 1948, the *Xinwen bao* noted that only the very wealthy were surviving in this final economic crisis:

> The earlier reform measures and the purchase of gold and foreign currency by the Government had virtually robbed the middle class of the very last cent of their purchasing power. Today those with purchasing

power are mostly members of the super-powerful class. They had not only refrained from parting with their gold and foreign currency, but on the other had bought in more gold and foreign currency from the black market at the time of reform.

The paper concluded that despite soaring prices, the actual sale of commodities for consumption was small. Only the speculators were in the market.[132] The cost-of-living index for Shanghai municipal workers had registered as 294 percent for the last half of January. Cyril Rogers, the British adviser to the Central Bank of China, told a British official on February 9, 1949, that the rate of inflation of the gold yuan had now surpassed that of fabi. He was preparing to leave China.[133]

On January 22, 1949, Chiang Kai-shek resigned and left Nanjing for his native Fenghua. This development caused a slight but brief improvement in the value of the gold yuan, which went from 300 gold yuan to one dollar to 250 to one. On January 27, 1949, the Ministry of Finance staff, about 1,500, arrived in Shanghai having abandoned Nanjing. The government itself moved to Guangzhou in early February.[134]

In what would be the final weeks of Guomindang China on the mainland, much of the gold, silver, and foreign exchange accumulated as reserves for the gold yuan notes would be transferred to Taiwan or overseas. According to records held by the Central Bank of China, between November 1948 and April 1949, a total of over US$49 million was moved from China to banks in the United States. During the same period, almost 77 million in Hong Kong currency was moved from China to banks in the British colony. By May of 1949, almost 2.3 million ounces of gold had been moved to Taiwan, nearly 245.3 million ounces moved to banks in New York, and 9.27 million ounces to London. Substantial quantities of silver had been shipped to New York and London as well. As historian Wu Jingping concluded, the gold yuan reform had led to a concentration of gold, silver, and foreign exchange in the Central Bank for the purpose of providing backing for the new currency. But after November 1948, little was used for that purpose. Instead, the concentration allowed people to prepare to move capital to Taiwan or overseas.[135]

By early March 1949, the gold yuan remained in circulation but often bypassed even by the government itself. Military pay and food allowances were calculated on the silver dollar. Customs duty was payable in the Customs Yuan, which was pegged to the American dollar. And land, salt, and commodity taxes were increasingly collected in kind. The commodity taxes on cotton yarn, matches, cement, cigarettes, and sugar were likewise collected in kind, indicating a barter economy taking hold. For all intents and purposes, Guomindang China ceased to have a functioning currency.[136]

Shortly after the communists took control of Shanghai on May 28, 1949, authorities issued a decree that henceforth the renminbi (people's currency) issued by the People's Bank of China would be the sole legal tender. The populace had until June 5 to convert their old gold yuan notes at the People's Bank. The exchange rate was set at 100,000 gold yuan to 1 yuan in the new currency. New China had arrived.[137]

AFTERWORD: A BITTER EXILE FOR THE SOONGS

The ad hominem attacks on the Soongs and Kungs continued even as they left China for America. In May of 1949, the Legislative Yuan adopted an emergency measure to request of Soong, Kung, and Chang Kia-ngau that they contribute US$1 billion to finance the war against the communists. The assumption was, of course, that these "bureaucratic capitalists" had that level of private income. Although it was recognized that Soong had lost much of his China-based wealth during the war years, press reports suggested that he had property valued at over US$1 billion stashed in America, Canada, and Chile.[138]

Soong bitterly resented the lingering attacks on his reputation even as he pursued a comfortable life in America. After *The Saturday Evening Post* published a column by Stewart Alsop, entitled with "Why We Lost China," in which he highlighted a feud between Madame Chiang and her brother, T. V. fired off a letter to the magazine bitterly complaining about the flimsy basis for the article. Alsop's source was identified as "a witness on the scene during the tragic feud" over the Stilwell issue.[139] And even though the two had clashed over that matter and other issues, the Soong archives at the Hoover Institution at Stanford contain several warm letters from "May" in Taiwan to "my Dear Brother" in America. She would sometimes send gifts to his daughters with an intermediary such as Wellington Koo and acknowledge gifts that he had sent her. In the summer of 1956, she noted that T. A.'s sons were visiting, and she was helping them learn Mandarin Chinese. She sometimes included details of her projects in Taiwan such as finding housing for veterans. Ultimately, T. V. Soong helped his sister obtain medical specialists from the United States to treat Chiang Kai-shek's medical problems as well as her own. They continued to have a strong if not always harmonious relationship, as is often the case with siblings.[140]

Even after Soong left for the United States, having lost his holdings of real estate and business interests in China, he was still routinely referred to as one of the richest men in the world. His assets did include a portfolio of American stocks such as Alcoa, General Electric, Polaroid, Monsanto, General Dynamic, Lockheed, Hilton, and Reynolds Metal, among others, as well as an apartment on Fifth Avenue.[141] When Soong died in 1971, his executor was William S. Youngman, Jr. who worked with Soong as the head of China Defense Supplies from 1941 until the end of the war. The final probate of the estate filed in New York listed the value of his assets as somewhat over $10 million. Aside from legal and funeral expenses, the estate was dispersed among several family members, including Soong's widow, Laura Chang Soong, and his daughters and their families.[142] Critics claimed that Soong's assets were hidden in accounts all over the world as well as in the Bank of Canton in San Francisco. Still, the evidence suggests that Soong was a wealthy man but certainly not one of the wealthiest men in the world.

Madame Chiang had earlier requested T. V. Soong to come to Taiwan. In a February 14, 1951, letter she wrote, "I wish you were here. I think it was a great mistake that you did not come back when I repeatedly asked you to come. When another opportunity comes for you to return you ought to do so."[143] But Soong had decided to remain in America. The bitterness of earlier disputes with Chiang and many Guomindang stalwarts who had attacked him and were then in Taiwan made him wary of the trip. Despite pleas from Mei-ling, Soong only made one brief visit to Taiwan in 1963, when he was received rather coolly by Chiang.[144] From his base in America, however, he continued to support the Nationalist cause. He still had strong contacts in Washington with individuals such as

Averill Harriman. He often visited his youngest brother T. A. Soong and occasionally Ai-ling. Mei-ling encouraged T. V. and his sister to stay in touch, reminding her brother to call her on her birthday, for example. That warmth did not extend to H. H. Kung, with whom T. V. never seemed to have reconciled.[145] Soong died suddenly on a trip to San Francisco in April 1971 at the age of seventy-nine.

William Youngman became something of a guardian of Soong's legacy, sometimes writing to the Soong family members about new publications relating to their patriarch. On January 22, 1984, in a letter to Laurette and Ivan Feng, he noted "I have read lately one interesting book about T. V.'s work before I knew him. It is called 'The Shanghai Capitalists and the Nationalist Government 1927–1937,' by Parks M. Coble, Jr., published by Council on East Asian Studies, Harvard University." In a handwritten note added at the bottom of the page, he did add, "Doesn't mean that I agree with the book, but the facts are interesting." Youngman concluded the letter with the statement, "while the cause that we were for did not succeed, T. V.'s efforts to make a great China were, in my opinion, unparalleled in modern history."[146]

Youngman and the Soongs were particularly upset by the publication of Sterling Seagrave's bestselling book, *The Soong Dynasty*. Seagrave essentially portrayed Soong and the entire family including the Kungs as thieves who had looted vast fortunes from China. Seagrave stated that the entire clan devoted the years from 1944 on to building what was "probably the largest fortune, collectively, on the planet a fortune probably in excess of $2 billion U.S., perhaps more than $3 billion."[147] Elsewhere he stated that T. V. "energetically pursued his reputation he was earning 'as one of the richest men in the world.'"[148] Youngman wrote directly to Seagrave on March 18, 1985, challenging his assumptions. He informed Seagrave that as the sole executor of Soong's estate he knew that the charges against T. V. were false. "T. V. Soong was not 'the richest man in the world' or anything like it. He brought little out of China after the war. He died possessed of a very modest fortune which he honestly acquired mostly in the U.S.A. by sound investment and hard work. ... With the able assistance of Sullivan and Cromwell I examined all his financial records and those of his banks and can say as certainly as anyone can that there were no undisclosed assets as you suggest." He also challenged Seagrave's use of sources. "Much of your account about T. V. Soong's activities in China before World War II is a distortion of the very able book by Parks Coble, Jr., a Harvard University Press publication." Youngman noted that Seagrave (and in fact most critics of Soong) conflated his control of government enterprises with his private assets, which Youngman felt was false. "It was easy for you to distort many of these activities using hearsay and rumors, particularly because of some of the ventures that Soong ran, such as some of the Bank of China operations and the China Development Finance Corporation had both government and private participation. It does not follow from this fact alone that Soong did anything improper."[149] Youngman sent copies of the letter to Soong's widow, his daughters, the book-review editor of the *New York Times*, and Professors Edwin Reischauer and John Fairbank at Harvard and Jonathan Spence at Yale. The latter had written a review of the Seagrave volume in the *New York Times* Sunday book-review section.[150]

Youngman was not the only one stirred up by the book. Madame Chiang Kai-shek wrote to Michael Feng, Soong's grandson, urging him to refute the book. She noted that Donald Gillin, an academic generally favorable to the Chiangs, had written a rebuttal. She urged Feng to obtain papers from his grandmother about Soong's career. She also noted that Youngman had been head of the China Defense Supply and that all the major staff had been Americans. She made other suggestions and concluded that "I think what I have given you will give you quite a lead toward refuting Seagrave's groundless accusations. I am glad that you have taken it upon yourself to rebut so much deceitful calumny against your grandfather's good name."[151]

H. H. Kung and his wife had moved to the New York area, where he lived, except for visits to Taiwan, until his death on August 16, 1967. The Kungs generally kept a low profile during their American years. David (Lingkan) Kung dropped the English name "David," and reverted to using only his Chinese name in America, distancing himself from his earlier identity. When Albert Wedemeyer, who corresponded with David Kung on occasion, accidentally used the old name, Lingkan reminded him that he was establishing an all-Chinese identity.[152] He spent much of his time in America helping Madame Chiang Kai-shek and assisting in promoting the interests of the Chiang government in Taiwan.

The one exception to this low profile was Louis (Lingjie) Kung, who moved to Houston and founded the Westland Oil Company. Kung achieved some notoriety when he married a twenty-eight-year-old movie actress, Debra Paget, in April 1964. Kung was her third husband and produced her only son, Gregory Kung. The two divorced in 1980. Paget had starred in Cecil B. DeMille's *The Ten Commandments* and opposite Elvis Presley in *Love Me Tender*. Madame Chiang Kai-shek is said to have visited the couple in Houston on occasion.[153] Louis Kung gained considerable attention in the early 1980s when he became convinced that a nuclear war was eminent. He had a massive compound built that was designed to have space for 1,500 people to seek shelter for ninety days after a nuclear attack. Rumors about the compound – security cameras, private police, body bags, soundproof conjugal chambers, as well as its extraordinary cost – circulated in the Houston press. Kung perhaps overspent, for Westland Oil had to seek chapter 11 bankruptcy protection in 1987. He lost the compound, which remained vacant after 1993.[154]

Louis Kung was the one Kung held in high regard by his uncle T. V. Soong. In January 1947 he had toyed with the idea of creating an elite guard service of 2,000–3,000 soldiers to be headed by Louis Kung. At the time, he told L. K. Little that Louis "is the best of the whole family."[155]

When T. V. sent a private letter to Madame Chiang to be hand delivered, he discussed the situation with Louis. Apparently, Mei-ling had expressed some concerns that Louis was "not very stable." But T. V. felt that although "like every human being Louis has his faults, but he has a capacity of dreaming." Soong alluded to the fact that Louis had been very close to Richard Nixon and had expressed his faith in him when he not only lost in 1960 but then was defeated when running for governor of California. "The close ties between him and Nixon is one of our most precious assets. It should not be wasted." Soong was concerned that the following autumn would see another attempt to seat the Beijing government in the United Nations in China's seat (then held by the Taiwan-based Republic of China). He urged Mei-ling to have Chiang invite Louis to Taiwan to work out a campaign to block this. "His part in the so-called 'China lobby' of a few years back was very effective as you recall." A postscript added "If you want to, you may show this letter to Sister E., [Ai-ling] but to no one else."[156]

The Chiang government was fighting a rearguard action. Ultimately, the tide of history had turned against him. Ironically, it would be his supposed ally, Richard Nixon, who was most responsible with his sudden and shocking visit to Beijing. The Soongs' and Kungs' role in mainland China was essentially over, even though they continue to attract attention not simply in the academic world but in popular publications, an indication of the enduring fascination with the family dynamics.[157] Ironically, the attacks by the communists against "bureaucratic capitalism" and corruption resurfaced in a wealthy People's Republic of China. But now wealthy Chinese billionaires are indeed among the richest men and women in the world.

Conclusion

I N THE CONCLUSION OF HIS BOOK SEEDS OF DESTRUCTION: *Nationalist China in War and Revolution, 1937–1949*, Lloyd E. Eastman posited the question "if a building collapses in a windstorm, what is the cause of the collapse?" Is it the weak building or the strong wind? The weak building referred to the Guomindang government, the strong wind to the communists. In Eastman's telling, the Guomindang government was a weak structure indeed by the late 1940s. "Never did the Nationalists succeed in creating a sound, sturdy political structure."[1]

This study has said very little about the strong wind – the formidable communist movement that forced Chiang into his exile in Taiwan. But a substantial scholarly literature on this topic is readily accessible. During the years covered by this study, the social, political, and military power of the Chinese Communist Party increased steadily. The shocking victories of the communist armies in winter of 1948 to 1949 were the culmination of this growth, often obscured from international gaze. Instead of replowing this ground, I have instead looked at the weak structure – the Guomindang–and focused on one key issue – hyperinflation. I would argue that the evidence reaffirms Eastman's view that the Guomindang government was a fragile structure in this period. Throughout the war against Japan, but particularly after the Japanese Ichigo offensive, the Chongqing government simply could not pay its bills. The acceleration of inflation in the war opened the door to rampant corruption among government bureaucrats and the military. As Eastman argued, "inflation was a major reason why corruption reached unprecedented levels . . . and why the army became dispirited and ineffective."[2]

As the salaries of those in government service, whether military or civilian, lost buying power at dizzying rates, the only option for most was pilfering from government supplies. Ammunition, medicine, kerosene, foodstuffs, anything movable began to disappear into the barter economy. Those at the bottom with little access to such commodities suffered the most. While officers got by, ordinary soldiers suffered malnutrition or deserted. American intelligence reports thought that the spending for the military by the Nationalist government was substantially more than was needed for the size of its army. Their analysis was that officers and regional militarists pilfered much of the money and supplies.

Until the autumn of 1948, Guomindang forces still seemed to have the upper hand in China, at least viewed from afar. Then, in a sudden series of military reverses in northeast China followed by the disastrous defeat in the Huaihai campaign, Chiang's position seemed to crumble like a house of cards. One crucial feature of these communist victories was the large number of Nationalist forces that changed sides in the middle of the conflict. Entire segments of the Nationalist Army defected and were suddenly gone. Although there is no simple answer to why this happened, one obvious cause was that so many of the officers and common soldiers had lost faith in the Chiang government. The long years of inflation and corresponding corruption had eroded trust in the Nationalists and left many to view the communists as a better alternative. Just as with the capitalists who moved their bodies and their capital out of China, soldiers deserted and officers surrendered.

China's vast rural population of peasant farmers, although mired in poverty, were in a better position to evade the damage of hyperinflation by avoiding the monetary economy. When not forced to give up their harvest at gunpoint, most farmers chose to hold onto grain rather than exchange it for what they perceived to be paper currency of dubious value. But those in the civilian and military service of the Nationalist government – the building that collapsed in the wind – were the most impacted.

The military were not the only group to desert the Nationalists. In the fight between communists and the Nationalists, one natural ally for the latter would seem to be private business and banking, China's capitalists. Yet as this study has revealed, by the end of the civil war period – certainly by the time of the gold yuan reform – many of China's private capitalists had become deeply disillusioned with the Chiang Kai-shek government. Some left China for Hong Kong, Taiwan, the Americas, or elsewhere. Some stayed or even returned to China, believing that Mao's New Democracy offered them a place in the "new China." Chiang Kai-shek's government had managed to alienate the one group that should have been natural allies against communism. When many came to realize that they had little place in Mao's China, it was too late. Their enterprises, their wealth, and their ability to emigrate were lost. But during the civil war, many felt that Chiang's China offered little opportunity for private business; they hoped that Mao's China would be better.

What led to this disastrous situation for the Guomindang government? A study of the single issue of hyperinflation can identify crucial flaws within the structure of the Chiang government that reveal why it ultimately crumbled before the strong wind. When the war against Japan ended in the summer of 1945, many inside observers, including financial adviser Arthur Young, felt that China might be able to turn the corner on inflation. They believed that, however bad things had gotten during the war, the fault lay with wartime conditions. The isolation of Free China and the severe strains of funding eight years of warfare provided few alternatives to simply printing money. But all of that could have theoretically changed after the war ended. The return to the east coast – the economic heart of Nationalist China before July 1937 – provided an opportunity to restore a tax base. The restoration of international trade opened the possibility of tariff revenue being revived. American and UNRRA aid would be forthcoming. And many hoped that peace would lead to a lowering of military expenses. A stable currency might be possible. But this was not to be. Chiang's financial policy was a disaster of staggering proportions. The currency collapsed not once, but twice – first fabi and then the gold yuan. The result was a stunning failure of the urban economy.

The origins of this failure go back to the beginnings of Chiang's leadership of the Nanjing government in 1927 to 1928. Chiang rose to power out of the warlord era in China – a time when regional militarists ruled. One's political clout was tied to the size and perceived strength of one's military. Chiang deftly maneuvered his way to supreme power within the party following the premature death of Sun Yat-sen from cancer in 1925. He bested such political opponents as Hu Hanmin, Sun Ke (son of Sun Yat-sen), Wang Jingwei, Comintern representatives, and even his future sister-in-law Soong Ching-ling, the widow of Sun Yat-sen. But once he established a government in Nanjing, he still faced formidable military challenges.

Chiang completed the Northern Expedition, capturing Beijing in the summer of 1928, by allying with militarists who had ties to the Guomindang such as Yan Xishan and Feng Yuxiang. They had vanquished warlords such as Sun Chuanfang, Wu Peifu, and Zhang Zuolin, warlord of Manchuria. But after a failed effort at disarmament, Chiang found himself merely the first among equals in the Nationalist military. Over the next decade, he managed to increase his hold over China by sometimes confronting his former allies and sometimes buying them off. When he challenged Feng and Yan on the battlefield in 1930, he made a shrewd overture to Zhang Xueliang, the "young marshal" of Manchuria who allied with Chiang and become the vice-commander of the armed forces of China. When Chiang finally took control over Guangdong province in 1936, he appeared on the verge of gaining nearly full control over China at least south of the Great Wall. Had the war with Japan not intervened, he would likely have succeeded. But it was precisely his success in unifying China that led Japan's right-wing militarists to push for war before Chiang became too strong.

The outbreak of war changed the equation for Chiang. On the eve of the war, the Nationalist military was still a coalition of many provincial armies but anchored by Chiang's own well-armed and trained "central" units. Those were devastated in the battle of Shanghai-Wusong in the last half of 1937, shattering the strength of the forces on which Chiang's status depended. Particularly damaging was the loss of so many of his officers, who could not be easily replaced. When the Nationalists' military units regrouped at Wuhan for a vigorous defense, Chiang found himself once again merely first among equals. As Stephen MacKinnon has argued, the result was a genuine coalition-style government that worked together to resist Japan.[3] After Wuhan fell in October 1938, Chiang's military moved to Chongqing, where he was determined to rebuild his own military units.

Over the course of his career Chiang Kai-shek had a variety of foreign military advisers – German, Soviet, and especially American. Nearly all believed that Chiang's military was simply too large. He had more soldiers than he could train, equip, keep healthy, and feed. They frequently urged him to reduce troop size so that the remaining units could be more effective. After the defeat of Japan and the increasing inflation of the civil war period, American advisers doubled down on this point. All was to no avail. Chiang still clung to the old warlord belief that the bigger your army, the stronger your political position. All suggestions that he balance the budget by reducing military expenses fell on deaf ears. In Chiang's mind, more soldiers meant political strength.

In his rise to power, one crucial advantage Chiang enjoyed was greater revenue. At the start of the Northern Expedition, he relied on Soviet military and economic aid. When his armies captured Shanghai and the lower Yangzi, this gave him access to the wealthiest region of China, so he broke with Moscow and drew on income from taxes, tariffs, and the selling of government bonds. He had greater financial assets than any of the military rivals within his coalition so could offer his opponents "silver bullets" to defect and join his group. This became an essential part of his strategy to unite China.

For most of the Nanjing decade, Chiang had to use "real money" to attract the support of regional militarists. When China was on the silver standard, government expenses had to be balanced by tax and other receipts and sale of government bonds. All of this had changed in November 1935 when fabi was introduced and China went to a fiat currency. Chiang simply decided how much money he needed for his military and ordered H. H. Kung to supply the currency. When the war with Japan began, government receipts declined while expenses skyrocketed. As Arthur Young had noted in his diary, when Chiang wanted more defense money, he simply sent a note raising the defense budget. When regional militarists needed to be given funds to ensure their loyalty, he had Kung order the appropriate branch of the Central Bank to provide the banknotes. Chiang did not seem troubled that issuing unsecured notes led to a steady erosion of their value.

Chiang was notoriously stubborn and once he made his mind up on an issue if was difficult to persuade him to a different point of view. When

Chiang decided on an exchange rate for the yuan into dollars and British pounds, he was loath to adjust it. It became almost a matter of pride or face to keep the façade of the nation intact. Chiang never seemed to have understood the harm that the huge gap between the exchange rate and the black-market rate could do to China. Nor could his officials, including his own brothers-in-law, persuade him on this or other points.

When Chiang constructed his civilian government in Nanjing, he created an authoritarian regime under his personal power. His authority was not absolute even within this structure and elusive elsewhere because he did not control the treaty ports that included the financial center of the International Settlement in Shanghai. Areas away from the lower Yangzi River were often under the control of regional militarists who were not inclined to accept his commands unless cash was forthcoming. Chiang centered many agencies of the new government under his personal command by always holding multiple positions. As Lloyd E. Eastman commented about the Nanjing years, "responsibility was concentrated in a few leading figures in the regime. Chiang Kai-shek, for example, at one time held twenty-one offices."[4]

Another part of Chiang's strategy was to set up rival institutions or cliques to compete with one another. Observers often commented on factions in the Nationalist government. These were fostered by Chiang because it gave him the ultimate authority; no one faction could become too powerful. An example of this strategy, noted earlier in this study, was in intelligence agencies. Chiang set up two, rival groups. The Juntong was under the Military Affairs Commission and headed by Dai Li. The Zhongtong was under the Party Central Office and controlled by the C. C. Clique. Both agencies engaged in investigation and covert operations. Chiang played them off against one another until it appeared that Dai Li had become too powerful.[5] But the energy used in competing with each other inhibited their effectiveness. Both the Japanese and the communists infiltrated the Guomindang structure and had excellent intelligence information. This strategy of divide and rule was pervasive during the entire time he ruled on the mainland; it was clearly a deliberate approach.

In setting financial policy, Chiang had the ultimate, inside rivalry. T. V. Soong and his brother-in-law, H. H. Kung vied for power and control during the entire period from the establishment of the Nanjing government. Chiang fostered the rivalry turning to Kung when Soong resigned in October 1933, a pattern repeated until the civil war period. Kung was more compliant and loyal; but Soong was more capable and more popular with Americans. He could not dispense with either but could play them against each other. The impact of this rivalry has been noted throughout this study. Both men maintained their own supporters and thwarted those in the other camp. Bei Zuyi was perceived as a Soong man; Yu Hongjun as closer to Kung. Their jealousy and suspicion, fostered by Chiang, haunted policy making. Soong used private correspondence carried by foreign friends or through his wife to avoid the diplomatic pouch, fearful that Kung would become aware of the contents.

The rivalry between the two men meant that Chiang held the ultimate authority. As Arthur Young discerned, Chiang understood little about finance and banking but knew what he wanted – money for his military. When Soong tried to trim military spending in 1933, Chiang dismissed him for the more pliant Kung.[6] Kung remained minister of finance until his political unpopularity threatened the government and Soong seemed to offer a greater hope for American aid. But with Kung in eclipse, Chiang then allowed others such as the C. C. Clique and Weng Wenhao to play a larger role. Even criticism from the Legislative Yuan by such luminaries as Fu Sinian could be useful as a constraint on Soong.

Because of this rivalry, both men felt vulnerable. After the fight between Chiang and Soong during the war over the Stilwell issue, Soong realized how precarious his position was, how dependent on Chiang for his power and position. Nonetheless, it is doubtful that even if Soong and Kung had cooperated and put up a united front to get Chiang to reduce military spending that such a ploy would have worked. Likely neither man would have retained his position had they attempted this. So even though the disastrous nature of printing paper currency became obvious to all, neither of the two key financial officials of the Nationalist government were willing to risk all to persuade Chiang to act. So like a slow-moving train wreck, no one could halt the disaster in time.

Even in the final months of fabi, Soong could not get Chiang Kai-shek to focus on the issue of inflation. As the diary of Chiang's daily activities reveals, he was interested in the military and only occasionally turned his attention to financial matters. When the government finally attempted to issue the new gold yuan currency, it was simply too late. Jiang Jingguo's coercion worked for only a short time before the new currency went the way of the old.

The entire aftermath of Japanese surrender was a failure of fiscal and economic policy. From the decision to undervalue the currency of the Wang Jingwei regime to the inability to revive tax revenue, the government was truly inept. International trade was stifled; customs revenue was minuscule. Reliance on America was ultimately not enough and not always helpful. The decision to purchase large stocks of US surplus military material saddled China with debts for unneeded items.

With the end of extraterritoriality, the Chinese government could restrict foreign access to the China market, and it did. Pent-up resentment of decades of foreign privilege in China took front and center stage with many officials. Foreign firms became wary of investing in China, and domestic capital was insufficient to revive the economy. Warehouses and docks, railway lines and stations, power plants – all had been badly damaged in the war but could not be repaired because of the shortage of capital. Although some sectors such as cotton textiles showed life after the end of the war with Japan, they too went flat. Energy shortages, inability to import foreign equipment, and lack of access to domestic cotton were among the culprits. Finally, the failure to manage foreign exchange properly badly damaged relations with the United States and often hurt China's exports. This study has been a long litany of failed policies.

When the final collapse of Nationalist armies occurred in late 1948 and early 1949, it appeared shockingly rapid to the outside world. But it mirrored the collapse of Nationalist forces in Henan during Operation Ichigo in the war against the Japanese. Corruption meant that ordinary soldiers were ill trained, fed, and housed. Medical care was minimal. Desertions were high and morale low. The failure to pay for the bloated military during both the war against Japan and the civil war had spawned corruption among the officer corps. The regular soldiers, mostly the least powerful group in society – peasants – suffered accordingly.

Ultimately, the failure of the Nationalist government to deal with the issue of hyperinflation is a cautionary tale about centering too much authority on one individual. No leader has unlimited energy, time, and knowledge to control everything. Chiang Kai-shek lacked an understanding of banking and finance and could not seem to look beyond military matters. When confronting a daunting crisis like the Japanese invasion, his lack of knowledge and unwillingness to follow the advice of others proved disastrous. Had World War II in Asia ended in a different way with a more gradual surrender of Japan, perhaps American help would have created a smoother transition. But in the sudden aftermath, Chiang was not able to lead China to recovery.

Glossary

Bai Chongxi 白崇禧
Bei Zuyi 贝祖诒
Chen Boda 陈伯达
Chen Bulei 陈布雷
Chen Cheng 陈诚
Chen Gongbo 陈公博
Chen Guangfu 陈光甫
Chen Guofu 陈果夫
Chen Lifu 陈立夫
China Development Finance Corporation (Zhongguo jianshe yin gongsi) 中国建设银公司
Chuli hanjian anjian tiaoli 处理汉奸案件条例
Da Shanghai qingnian fuwu zongdui 大上海青年服务纵队
Diweiye chuli ju 敌伪业处理局
Du Weiping 杜维屏
Du Yuesheng 杜月笙
Feng Yuxiang 冯玉祥
Fu Sinian 傅斯年
Fuzhong gongsi 孚中实业公司
Gexin 革新
Gu Weijun (V. K. Wellington Koo) 顾维钧
guanliao ziben 官僚资本
gudao 孤岛 Guo Jinkun 郭锦坤
hanjian 汉奸
He Lian 何廉
Jiang Jingguo 蒋经国
Juntong 军统

Kanluan jianguo dadui 戡乱建国大队
Kong Lingkan (David Kung) 孔令侃
Kong Xiangxi (H. H. Kung) 孔祥熙
Li Ming 李铭
Li Shizeng 李石曾
Liang Hongzhi 梁鸿志
Liu Bocheng 刘伯承
Lu Zuofu 卢作孚
Ma Yinchu 马寅初
Qi Chunfeng 齐春风
Qian Xinzhi 钱新之
Shanghai hangye gonghui 上海行业公会
Shen Hongnian 沈鸿年
Shi Zhaoji (Alfred Sze) 施肇基
Song Ailing (Madame H. H. Kung) 宋蔼龄
Song Meiling (Madame Chiang Kai-shek) 宋美龄
Song Qingling (Madame Sun Yat-sen) 宋庆龄
Song Yaoru (Charles Soong) 宋耀如
Song Zi'an (T. A. Soong) 宋子安
Song Ziliang (T. L. Soong) 宋子良
Song Ziwen (T. V. Soong) 宋子文
Sun Ke 孙科
Wang Chaoguang 汪朝光
Wang Jingwei 汪精卫
Wang Kemin 王克敏
Wang Shijie 王世杰
Wang Yunwu 王云五
Weng Wenhao 翁文灏
Wu Guozhen (K. C. Wu) 吴国桢
Wu Jingping 吴景平
Wu Tiecheng 吴铁城
Xi Demou 席德懋
Xiong Shihui 熊式辉
Xu Kan 徐堪
Xu Xinliu 徐新六
Xuan Tiewu 宣铁吾
Yang Tianshi 杨天石
Yangzi jianye gongsi 扬子建业公司
Yu Feipeng 俞飞鹏
Yu Hongjun (O. K. Yui) 俞鸿钧

Zhang Fakuei 张发奎
Zhang Jia'ao (Chang Kia-ngau) 张嘉敖
Zhang Junmai 张君劢
Zhang Qun 张群
Zheng Huixin 郑会欣
Zhongguo fangzhi jianshe gongsi 中国纺织建设公司
Zhongguo jianshe yin gongsi 中国建设银公司
Zhongtong 中统
Zhou Fohai 周佛海
Zhou Zuomin 周作民

Notes

INTRODUCTION

1. On this argument see Rana Mitter, *China's Good War: How World War II Is Shaping a New Nationalism* (Cambridge, MA: Harvard University Press, 2020), and Parks M. Coble, *China's War Reporters: The Legacy of Resistance against Japan* (Cambridge, MA: Harvard University Press, 2015), *passim.*

2. Some examples of the new scholarship include Hans Van de Ven, *China at War: Triumph and Tragedy in the Emergence of New China* (Cambridge, MA: Harvard University Press, 2018); Harold M. Tanner, *The Battle for Manchuria and the Fate of China: Siping, 1946* (Bloomington: Indiana University Press, 2013); Daniel Kurtz-Phelan, *The China Mission: George Marshall's Unfinished War, 1945–1947* (New York: W. W. Norton, 2018); Odd Arne Westad, *Decisive Encounters: The Chinese Civil War, 1946–1950* (Stanford, CA: Stanford University Press, 2003); Diana Lary, *China's Civil War: A Social History, 1945–1949* (Cambridge: Cambridge University Press, 2015). Other examples include *China 1945: Mao's Revolution and America's Fateful Choice* (New York: Alfred A. Knopf, 2014) by journalist Richard Bernstein.

3. Chang Kia-ngau, *The Inflationary Spiral: The Experience in China, 1939–1950* (Cambridge, MA: MIT Press, 1958); Arthur N. Young, *China's Wartime Finance and Inflation* (Cambridge, MA: Harvard University Press, 1965). See also Chou Shun-Hsin, *The Chinese Inflation, 1937–1949* (New York: Columbia University Press, 1963).

4. Chang Kia-ngau, *The Inflationary Spiral*, p. 49.

5. Young, *China's Wartime Finance and Inflation*, p. 152; Yang Peixin, *Jiu Zhongguo de tonghuo pengzhang* (Currency inflation in old China; Beijing: Renmin chuban she, 1985), pp. 30–31.

6. Wu Jingping, "Jinyuan quan zhengce de zai yanjiu" (On the study of the gold yuan policy), *Minguo dang'an* (Republican Archives), 1 (2004), pp. 99–110 (p. 99).

7. Adapted from Chang Kia-ngau, *The Inflationary Spiral*, p. 372.

8. T. V. Soong Papers, Hoover Institution Archives, box 25, folder 1, "Report on Money and Banking," unpublished draft, by Frank M. Tamagna, October 10, 1946, p. 28.

9. Yang Peixin, *Jiu Zhongguo de tonghuo pengzhang*, pp. 75–76.

10. Adapted from Chang Kia-ngau, *The Inflationary Spiral*, p. 372; Yang Peixin, *Jiu Zhongguo de tonghuo pengzhang*, pp. 30–31.

11. Lin Meili, *Kangzhan shiqi di huobi zhanzheng* (The currency war during the war of resistance period; Taibei: Guoli shifan daxue lishi yanjiu so, 1996).

12. Matthew T. Combs, "Chongqing 1943: People's Livelihood, Price Control, and State Legitimacy," in Joseph W. Esherick and Matthew T. Combs, eds., *1943: China at the Crossroads* (Ithaca, NY: Cornell East Asian Series, 2015), pp. 282–322.

13. Arthur N. Young, *Cycle of Cathay: An Historical Perspective* (Vista, CA: Ibis Publishing Company, 1997).

14. Chang Kia-ngau, *The Inflationary Spiral*, p. 8.

15. Chang Kia-ngau, *The Inflationary Spiral*, p. 8. See also Yang Peixi, *Jiu Zhongguo de tonghuo pengzhang*, pp. 23–24.

16. Cited in Lincoln Li, "An Alternative View on Occupation Policy: China's Resistance Potential," in David Pong, ed., *Resisting Japan: Mobilizing for War in Modern China, 1935–1945* (Norwalk, CT: EastBridge, 2008), pp. 79–104 (p. 90).

17. Young, *China's Wartime Inflation*, p. 153.

18. Qi Chunfeng, "Kangzhan shiqi da houfang yu lunxian qujian de huobi liudong" (The flow of Guomindang currency between Chinese-controlled and enemy-occupied areas during the Resistance War against Japan), *Jindai shi yanjiu* (Modern Chinese History Studies) 5 (2003), pp. 137–169.

19. *Yinhang zhoubao* (Bankers' weekly) 22, no. 31 (August 9, 1938), p. 3.

20. Robert W. Barnett, *Economic Shanghai: Hostage to Politics, 1937–1941* (New York: Institute of Pacific Relations, 1941), pp. 112–113; Yin Xiqi, "Waihui tongzhi xin zhengce zhi jiantao" (An examination of the new policy to control foreign exchange), *Dongfang zazhi* (The Eastern Miscellany) 36, no. 2 (February 1, 1938), p. 19.

21. Lin Meili, *Kangzhan shiqi de huobi zhanzheng*, pp. 65–69.

22. Lincoln Li, *The Japanese Army in North China, 1937–1941: Problems of Political and Economic Control* (Tokyo: Oxford University Press, 1975), pp. 141–142; Ma Yinchu, quoted in *Zhanshi jingji lunwen ji* (A collection of essays on the wartime economy; Chongqing: Zuojia shushi, 1945), p. 197; United Kingdom, Foreign Office Files for China, PRO.FO 371/23445 F/806/75/10, Letter of November 3, 1938 from E. L. Hall-Patch in Tianjin to the British Ambassador at Shanghai, Sir Archibald Clark Kerr, Re currency situation in north China; Arthur N. Young Papers, Hoover Institution, box 68, memo of March 31, 1941; Zhu Chuxin, "Sannian lai di women de huobe zhan" (The war of the enemy against our currency in the last three years), *Dushu yuebao* (Readers monthly) 1, no. 11 (January 1, 1940), pp. 485–488.

23. Lin Meili, *Kangzhan shiqi*, p. 55.

24. Wu Jingping and Guo Daijun [Kuo Tai-chun], eds., *Song Ziwen zhu Mei shiqi dianbao xuan, 1940–1943* (Select telegrams between Chiang Kai-shek and T. V. Soong, 1940–1943; Shanghai: Fudan daxue chuban she, 2008), p. 303.

25. Lauchlin Currie Papers, Hoover Institution Archives, Stanford University, box 3, folder "Report by Lauchlin Currie, February 24, 1941; box 4, folder "Currie: First Visit to China," Hollington Tong translated for Currie.

26. Lauchlin Currie Papers, Hoover Institution Archives, Stanford University, box 1, folder "Correspondence," H. H. Kung to Lauchlin Currie, February 26, 1941.

27. Young, *China's Wartime Finance and Inflation*, p. 169.
28. Young, *China's Wartime Finance and Inflation*, p. 235.
29. Young, *China's Wartime Finance and Inflation*, p. 236.
30. Young, *China's Wartime Finance and Inflation*, p. 238.
31. Young, *China and the Helping Hand*, p. 158; Takafusa Nakamura, "The Yen Bloc, 1931–1941," in Peter Duus, Ramon H. Myers, and Mark Peattie, eds., *The Japanese Wartime Empire, 1931–1945* (Princeton, NJ: Princeton University Press, 1996), pp 171–186 (p. 181); Barnett, *Economic Shanghai*, pp. 121–125, 133–135.
32. Shou Jinhua, *Zhanshi Zhongguo de yinhang ye* (China's wartime banking industry (n.p., 1944), pp. 78–79; Young, *China's Wartime Finance and Inflation*, p. 180.
33. Ke-wen Wang, "Collaborators and Capitalists: The Politics of 'Material Control' in Wartime Shanghai," *Chinese Studies in History* 26, no. 1 (Fall 1992), pp. 42–62 (p. 47); Eleanor Hinder, *Life and Labour in Shanghai* (New York: International Secretariat, Institute of Pacific Relations, 1944), p. 46.
34. United States, Office of Strategic Service, *Programs of Japan in China with Biographies*, vol. 1, pp. 124–126.
35. Wellington Koo, "Wellington Koo Memoir," vol. 4, part 2, "Sojourn in China," p. 326.
36. Combs, "Chongqing 1943," pp. 292–293.

CHAPTER 1 ICHIGO AND ITS AFTERMATH

1. Cao Juren, *Caifang waiji, Caifang erji* (A record of covering the news, a second record of covering the news; Beijing: Sanlian shudian, 2007), pp. 122, 212.
2. Hara Takeshi, "The Ichigo Offensive," in Mark Peattie, Edward Drea, and Hans van de Ven, eds., *The Battle for China: Essays on the Military History of the Sino-Japanese War of 1937–1945* (Stanford: Stanford University Press, 2011), pp. 392–402 (p. 392). This discussion of the Ichigo campaign is also based on Hans van de Ven, *China at War: Triumph and Tragedy in the Emergence of the New China* (Cambridge, MA: Harvard University Press, 2018), pp. 179–190; Wang Qisheng, "The Battle of Hunan and the Chinese Military's Response to Operation Ichigo," in Peattie, Drea, and van de Ven, *The Battle for China*, pp. 403–418; Hsi-sheng Ch'i, *Nationalist China at War: Military Defeats and Political Collapse, 1937–1945* (Ann Arbor: University of Michigan Press, 1982), pp. 74–79; and Parks M. Coble, *China's War Reporters: The Legacy of Resistance against Japan* (Cambridge, MA: Harvard University Press, 2015), pp. 116–126.
3. Van de Ven, *China at War*, p. 179.
4. Van de Ven, *China at War*, p. 181.
5. Van de Ven, *China at War*, pp. 182–185; Hsi-sheng Ch'i, *Nationalist China at War*, pp. 74–79; Lloyd E. Eastman, *Seeds of Destruction: Nationalist China in War and Revolution, 1937–1949* (Stanford: Stanford University Press, 1984), p. 141.
6. Paul Preston and Michael Partridge, eds., *British Documents on Foreign Affairs: Reports and Papers from the Foreign Office Confidential Print* (Bethesda, MD: University Press of America, 1997), part II from 1940 through 1945; Series E Asia, vol. 7, ed. Anthony Best, "Monthly Summary from Chungking Embassy of Great Britain, June 1944," p. 365.

7. Hsiao-ting Lin, "Wartime Sino-U.S. Relations Revisited: American Aid, Persona and Power Politics, 1938–1949," in Wu Jingping, ed., *Song Ziwen shengping yu ziliao yanjiu* (T. V. Soong: personal wartime archives; Shanghai: Fudan daxue chuban she, 2013), pp. 260–285 (p. 282).

8. Preston and Partridge, *British Documents on Foreign Affairs*, Series E, Asia, vol. 7, pp. 468, 471, 489, 504–505; Zhongguo renmin kangri zhanzheng jinian guan, ed., *Kangzhan jishi* (Memoranda on the war of resistance; Beijing: Zhongguo youyi chuban she, 1989), pp. 218–221.

9. Lary, *The Chinese People at War*, pp. 154–155; van de Ven, *China at War*, pp. 188–189.

10. In Song Shiqi and Yan Jingzheng, eds., *Jizhe bixia de kangri zhanzheng* (The writing of reporters in the war of resistance; Beijing: Renmin ribao chuban she, 1995), pp. 318–321.

11. Preston and Partridge, *British Documents on Foreign Affairs*, Series E, Asia, vol. 7, pp. 468, 471, 489, 504–505; Zhongguo renmin kangri zhanzheng jinian guan, ed., *Kangzhan jishi*, pp. 218–221.

12. *China at War*, vol. 13, no. 6 (December 1944), p. 2.

13. T. V. Soong Papers, Hoover Institution Archives, box 8, folder 24, telegram from Alfred Sze to T. V. Soong in Chongqing, October 17, 1944.

14. Roger B. Jeans, ed., *The Marshall Mission to China, 1945–1947: The Letters and Diary of Colonel John Hart Caughey* (Lanham: Rowman & Littlefield, 2011), p. 51.

15. Van de Ven, *China at War*, pp. 179–180.

16. Wang Qisheng, "The Battle of Hunan," p. 403.

17. Eastman, *Seeds of Destruction*, pp. 50–56.

18. The government banks extended advances to the government of 1,261,921 million yuan during the war era. Arthur N. Young, *China's Wartime Finance and Inflation* (Cambridge, MA: Harvard University Press, 1965), pp. 12, 15. In her study, Lin Meili gives slightly different figures: for 1943, the deficit was 41,943,703,152; for 1944, 138,726,128,798; and for 1945, 1,202,205,543,309. See Lin Meili, *Kangzhan shiqi de huobi zhanzheng* (The currency war during the war of resistance; Taibei: Guoshi guan, 1996), p. 38.

19. Chang Kia-ngau, *The Inflationary Spiral: The Experience in China, 1939–1950* (Cambridge: MIT Press, 1958), p. 58.

20. Joseph W. Esherick, ed., *Lost Chance in China: The World War II Dispatches of John S. Service* (New York: Random House, 1974), p. 134.

21. Young, *China's Wartime Finance and Inflation*, p. 141.

22. Young, *China's Wartime Finance and Inflation*, p. 141.

23. Young, *China's Wartime Finance and Inflation*, p. 152.

24. Chen Yung-fa, "Chiang Kai-shek and the Japanese Ichigo Offensive, 1944," in Laura De Giorgi and Guido Samarani, eds., *Chiang Kai-shek and His Time: New Historical and Historiographical Perspectives* (Venice: Sinica venetiana, 2017), pp. 37–74 (p. 67); Li Huang, "The Reminiscences of Li Huang," Chinese Oral History Project, East Asian Institute of Columbia University, 1975, p. 698.

25. Chen Yung-fa, "Chiang Kai-shek and the Japanese Ichigo Offensive," p. 68.

26. Chihyun Chang, *The Chinese Journals of L. K. Little*, vol. 1, p. 88.

27. Eastman, *Seeds of Destruction*, pp. 149–152.

28. Eastman, *Seeds of Destruction*, pp. 149–156.

29. H. H. Kung Papers, Hoover Institution Archives, box 17, folder 6, "Central Bank, 1944," letter from Pingwen Kuo (Guo Bingwen) to H. H. Kung, August 10, 1944; cable of August 8, 1944, Pingwen Kuo to Bernard Westall, London; letter from H. G. McHeary to Hsi Te-mou (Xi Demou), Bank of China, August 29, 1944; letter from H. W. Scruton to Hsi Te-mou, September 8, 1944.

30. Young, *China's Wartime Finance and Inflation*, pp. 160–161.

31. H. H. Kung Papers, Hoover Institution Archives, box 17, folder 6, "Central Bank, 1944," letter from Lt. General Joseph T. McNarney, Lt. General, US Army, to General Shang Chen (Shang Zhen), Chief, Chinese Military Mission to the United States, September 19, 1944; McNarney to Shang Chen; Lauchlin Currie Papers, Hoover Institution Archives, box 3, folder "China – Economic Conditions," memorandum to the President, April 2, 1943.

32. Chihyun Chang, *The Chinese Journals of L. K. Little*, vol. 1, p. 118.

33. Arthur Young Papers, Hoover Institution Archives, box 94, folder "US aid, post war."

34. Chang Kia-ngau, *The Inflationary Spiral*, p. 12.

35. T. G. Li, *A China Past: Military and Diplomatic Memoires* (Lanham: University Press of America, 1989), pp. 222–223.

36. Chou Shun-Hsin, *The Chinese Inflation, 1937–1949* (New York: Columbia University Press, 1963), p. 195.

37. Chou Shun-hsin, *The Chinese Inflation*, p. 199.

38. Linsun Cheng, *Banking in Modern China: Entrepreneurs, Professional Managers, and the Development of Chinese Banks, 1897–1937* (New York: Cambridge University Press, 2003), pp. 118, 125.

39. Chang Kia-ngau, *The Inflationary Spiral*, p. 75.

40. Obayashi jimusho, ed., *Dai Toa senso daiichi nendo ni okeru Shanhai Keizai no hensen* (Economic changes in Shanghai during the first year of the Great East Asia War; Shanghai: Obayashi jimusho, 1943), pp. 81–83; Masuda Yoneji. *Shina senso keizai no kenkyu* (Research on China's wartime economy; Tokyo: Daiyamonda sha, 1944), pp. 29–30.

41. Chang Kia-ngau, *The Inflationary Spiral*, p. 75.

42. Arthur Young, *Cycle of Cathay: An Historical Perspective* (Vista, CA: Ibis Publishing, 1997), p. 241; Wang Chaoguang, *Zhongguo mingyun de juezhan, 1945–1949* (The decisive war for China's fate, 1945–1949; Nanjing: Jiangsu renmin chuban she, 2006), p. 235.

43. United States, Department of State. Office of the Historian, *Foreign Relations of the United States: Diplomatic Papers: 1944*, vol. 6, *China*, p. 843.

44. Chihyun Chang, *The Chinese Journals of L. K. Little*, vol. 1, p. 31.

45. Theodore White and Annalee Jacoby, *Thunder Out of China* (New York: William Sloane, 1946), pp. 115–116.

46. Arthur Young, *Cycle of Cathay*, p. 241.

47. *Foreign Relations of the United States: Diplomatic Papers: 1944*, vol. 6, *China*, p. 853.

48. Gregory Scott Lewis, "Shades of Red and White: The Life and Political Career of Ji Chaoding, 1903–1963," unpublished PhD dissertation, Arizona State University, 1999, p. 172.
49. Lewis, "Shades of Red and White," p. 172.
50. Chihyun Chang, *The Chinese Journals of L. K. Little*, vol. 1, p. 31.
51. Preston and Partridge, *British Documents on Foreign Affairs*, Series E, Asia, vol. 7, pp. 284, 306.
52. *Foreign Relations of the United States: Diplomatic Papers: 1944*, vol. 6, *China*, pp. 928–929.
53. Hsiao-ting Lin, "Wartime Sino-U.S. Relations Revisited" p. 264.
54. Wu Jingping and Guo Daijun, Song Ziwen zhu Mei shiqi dianbao xuan, 1940–1943 (Select telegrams between Chiang Kai-shek and T. V. Soong, 1940–1943; Shanghai: Fudan daxue chuban she, 2008), p. 320.
55. *Foreign Relations of the United States: Diplomatic Papers: 1944*, vol. 6, *China*, p. 948.
56. Arthur Young, *Cycle of Cathay*, p. 252.
57. *Foreign Relations of the United States: Diplomatic Papers: 1944*, vol. 7, *The Far East*, p. 1063.
58. Lewis, "Shades of Red and White," p. 172.
59. T. V. Soong Papers, Hoover Institution Archives, box 25, folder 4; Yang Peixin, *Jiu Zhongguo de tonghuo pengzhang* (Currency inflation in old China; Beijing: Renmin chuban she, 1985), pp. 66–67.
60. Chihyun Chang, *The Chinese Journals of L. K. Little*, vol. 1, pp. 117–118. The Control Yuan report was leaked to the Chinese press in early May and mentioned Yu Hongjun as one of the officials responsible. Chihyun Chang, *The Chinese Journals of L. K. Little*, vol. 1, p. 120. Arthur Young, who knew Yu quite well, believed him innocent. He was "a true patriot, honest and sincere," Young wrote. He also admired Bei Zuyi, whom he labeled "the best of 400 million." Cited in Chihyun Chang, *The Chinese Journals of L. K. Little*, vol. 2, p. 8. See also H. H. Kung Papers, Hoover Institution Archives, box 9, folder 3, "Foreign Ministry," cable from Wellington Koo in London to H. H. Kung and Foreign Office, Chongqing, March 5, 1944; reply from H. H. Kung to Wellington Koo on March 15, 1944.
61. T. V. Soong Papers, Hoover Institution Archives, box 6, folder 36, memorandum from Henry Morgenthau to T. V. Soong, March 8, 1935.
62. T. V. Soong Papers, Hoover Institution Archives, box 6, folder 36.
63. Arthur Young Papers, Hoover Institution Archives, box 111, folder "Graphs from 1937–1945."
64. *Foreign Relations of the United States: Diplomatic Papers: 1944*, vol. 7, *The Far East*, pp. 1084–1086.
65. T. V. Soong Papers, Hoover Institution Archives, box 4, folder 27, Hsi Te-mou (Xi Demou) to T. V. Soong, May 21, 1945, Hsi Te-Mou to T. V. Soong, August 17, 1945.
66. T. V. Soong Papers, Hoover Institution Archives, box 25, folder 4, "Morgenthau," Notes on the Conference between Dr. T. V. Soong and the Secretary of the Treasury, May 9, 1945.
67. T. V. Soong Papers, Hoover Institution Archives, box 25, folder 4, "Morgenthau," Notes on the Conference between Dr. T. V. Soong and the Secretary of the Treasury, May 9, 1945.

68. T. V. Soong Papers, Hoover Institution Archives, box 25, folder 4, "Morgenthau," Notes on the Conference between Dr. T. V. Soong and the Secretary of the Treasury, May 16, 1945.

69. T. V. Soong Papers, Hoover Institution Archives, box 8, folder 18, T. V. Soong to Edward Stettinius, April 20, 1945.

70. T. V. Soong Papers, Hoover Institution, box 6, folder 36, letter from Henry Morgenthau to T. V. Soong, May 16, 1945.

71. T. V. Soong Papers, Hoover Institution, box 25, folder 4, "Morgenthau," Notes on the Conference between Dr. T. V. Soong and the Secretary of the Treasury, Washington, D. C., May 16, 1945.

72. Arthur Young Papers, Hoover Institution Archives, box 4, folder "Hsi Te-mou," cable from O. K. Yui (Yu Hongjun) to Hsi Te-mou, April 23, 1945.

73. T. V. Soong Papers, Hoover Institution Archives, box 26, folder 6, Hsi Te-mou to T. V. Soong, July 3, 1946. An additional $10 million was used to purchase cotton textiles on July 18, 1945, and $13.5 million in raw cotton on March 13, 1946. Of the total $220 million in gold purchased under the $500 million line of credit, all but $13.8 million had arrived in China by July 3, 1946.

74. Arthur Young Papers, Hoover Institution Archives, box 84, folder "Planning for Postwar, 1945," letter from Arthur Young to O. K. Yui, Minister of Finance, March 15, 1945.

75. T. V. Soong Papers, Hoover Institution Archives, box 25, folder 4, "Morgenthau," excerpt from Raymond Swing's Broadcast, May 14, 1945.

76. T. V. Soong Papers, Hoover Institution Archives, box 8, folder 23, "Raymond Swing."

77. Margaret Mih Tillman, *Raising China's Revolutionaries: Modernizing Childhood for Cosmopolitan Nationalists and Liberated Comrades, 1920s–1950s* (New York: Columbia University Press, 2018), pp. 131, 133, 157; C. X. George Wei, *Sino-American Economic Relations, 1944–1949* (Westport, CT: Greenwood Press, 1997), p. 56; Xiao Ruping, "Kangzhan shengli hou Zhejiang de shanhou jiuji" (Relief aid in Zhejiang after the victory in the War of Resistance), *Kangri zhanzhen yanjiu* (Research on the War of Resistance against Japan) 1 (2013), pp. 126–128.

CHAPTER 2 HYPERINFLATION AND THE RIVALRY BETWEEN
T. V. SOONG AND H. H. KUNG

1. *The China Weekly Review*, April 20, 1946, p. 169.

2. *Dagong bao*, August 30, 1946, cited in *Chinese Press Review*, US Consulate Shanghai, August 30, 1946.

3. Suzanne Pepper, *Civil War in China: The Political Struggle, 1945–1949* (Lanham, MD: Rowman and Littlefield, 1999), p. 128.

4. T. V. Soong was the moving force behind the China Development Finance Corporation, but when the company was organized in June of 1934, H. H. Kung was the chair of the board of directors. This was Chiang Kai-shek's decision. At the time, Chiang was pursuing his appeasement policy of Japan. Soong was then persona non grata by Japan, so Chiang insisted Kung be the head. See Zheng Huixin (Cheng Hwei-sheng), *Cong touzi*

gongsi dao "Guanban shangxing"; Zhongguo jiangshe yin gongsi de chuangli ji qi jingying huodong (From private investment company to state enterprise: The development and operation of the China Development Finance Corporation; Hong Kong: Zhongwen daxue chuban she, 2001), pp. 68–71.

5. Zheng Huixin, *Cong touzi go dao "Guanban shangxing,"* p. 272.

6. For details on Soong's career, see Wu Jingping, *Song Ziwen zhengzhi shengya biannian* (A chronology of the political career of T. V. Soong; Fuzhou: Fujian renmin chuban she, 1998). Material on the Nanyang Brothers Tobacco Company is found on p. 322.

7. See Shou Chongyi, *Kong Xiangxi qiren qishi* (H. H. Kung, the man and his affairs; Beijing: Zhongguo wenshi chuban she, 1987).

8. Yang Tianshi, *Kangzhan yu zhanhou Zhongguo* (Wartime and postwar China; Beijing: Zhongguo renmin daxue chuban she, 2007), pp. 490–492.

9. Wu Jingping and Guo Daijun [Kuo Tai-chun], eds., *Song Ziwen zhu Mei shiqi dianbao xuan, 1940–1943* (Select telegrams between Chiang Kai-shek and T. V. Soong, 1940–1943; Shanghai: Fudan daxue chuban she, 2008), pp. 428, 432.

10. Henry Morgenthau III, *Mostly Morgenthaus: A Family History* (New York: Ticknor and Fields, 1991), pp. 270–271.

11. John Morton Blum, *From the Morgenthau Diaries: Years of Crisis, 1928–1938* (Boston: Houghton Mifflin, 1959), pp. 220–227.

12. Blum, *From the Morgenthau Diaries*, pp. 479–480.

13. John Morton Blum, *Roosevelt and Morgenthau: A Revision and Condensation from the Morgenthau Diaries* (Boston: Houghton Mifflin, 1970), pp. 221–223.

14. On this point, see Kuo Tai-chun and Hsiao-ting Lin, "Introduction," in Lin Xiaoting and Wu Jingping, eds. *Song Ziwen yu waiguo renshi wanglai handian gao* (T. V. Soong important wartime correspondences, 1940–1942; Shanghai: Fudan daxue chuban she, 2009), pp. 247–250.

15. Hsiao-ting Lin, "Wartime Sino-US Relations Revisited, American Aid, Persona and Power Politics, 1938–1949," in Wu Jingping, ed. *Song Ziwen shengping yu ziliao wenxian yanjiu* (T. V. Soong: personal wartime archives; Shanghai: Fudan dauxue chuban she, 2010), pp. 262–267.

16. Lauchlin Currie Papers, Hoover Institution Archives, box 4, folder "Second trip to China."

17. Howard L. Boorman, editor, *Biographical Dictionary of Republican China* (New York: Columbia University Press, 1970), vol. 3, pp. 137–153.

18. Boorman, *Biographical Dictionary of Republican China*, vol. 1, pp. 192–196.

19. Boorman, *Biographical Dictionary of Republican China*, vol. 4, pp. 63–64.

20. Boorman, *Biographical Dictionary of Republican China*, vol. 3, pp. 438–440.

21. Boorman, *Biographical Dictionary of Republican China*, vol. 2, pp. 316–319.

22. Boorman, *Biographical Dictionary of Republican China*, vol. 2, p. 255.

23. Sao-Ke Alfred Sze, *Reminiscences of His Early Years*, as told to Anming Fu (Washington DC: n. p. 1962), pp. 4, 7, 12, 16; Boorman, *Biographical Dictionary of Republican China*, vol. 3, p. 126.

24. United States, Department of State. Office of the Historian, *Foreign Relations of the United States: Diplomatic Papers: 1944*, vol. 6, *China*, p. 241.

25. Wu Guozhen, *Cong Shanghai shichang zhi "Taiwan sheng zhuxi"* (From mayor of Shanghai to chairman of Taiwan province; Shanghai: Shanghai renmin chuban she, 1999), pp. 240, 247.

26. Ch'en Li-fu, *The Storm Clouds Clear Over China: The Memoir of Ch'en Li-fu, 1900–1993* (Stanford, CA: Hoover Institution Press, 1994), p. 181.

27. Arthur N. Young, *Cycle of Cathay: An Historical Perspective* (Vista, CA: Ibis Publishing, 1997), pp. 1–4.

28. T. V. Soong Papers, Hoover Institution Archives, box 7, folder 14, "Cyril Rogers," letter from Soong to Rogers, August 18, 1946.

29. T. V. Soong Papers, Hoover Institution Archives, *passim.* The archives contain numerous thank-you notes from individuals such as George Marshall for the gift. Other letters were for gifts made in the United States.

30. Hsiao-ting Lin, "Wartime Sino-US Relations Revisited," in Wu Jingping, *Song Ziwen shengping*, pp. 262–67.

31. Lauchlin Currie Papers, Hoover Institution Archives, box 4, folder "Second trip to China."

32. Robert E. Sherwood, *Roosevelt and Hopkins: An Intimate History* (New York: Harper and Row, 1950), pp. 16–17, 289.

33. Charlotte Brooks, *American Exodus: Second-Generation Chinese Americans in China, 1901–1949* (Oakland: University of California Press, 2019), p. 3.

34. Charlotte Brooks, *American Exodus*, p. 190.

35. Grace C. Huang, "Madame Chiang's Visit to America," in Joseph W. Esherick and Matthew T. Combs, eds., *1943: China at the Crossroads* (Ithaca, NY: East Asia Program Cornell, 2015), pp. 41–74 (p. 60).

36. Wu Jingping, "Kangzhan shiqi Song Ziwen yu Kong Xiangxi zhi guanxi zhi shuping" (A review of the relationship between T. V. Soong and H. H. Kung during the war period), in Wu Jingping, *Song Ziwen shengping yu ziliao yanjiu*, pp. 189–208 (pp. 202–206); Hsiao-ting Lin, "Chiang Kai-shek and the Cairo Summit," in Esherick and Combs, *1943: China at the Crossroads*, pp. 426–458 (p. 432); Joseph W. Esherick, "Prologue: China and the World in 1943," in Esherick and Combs, *1943: China at the Crossroads*, pp. 1–40 (pp. 34–36).

37. T. V. Soong Papers, Hoover Institution Archives, box 6, folder 38, letter from Mountbatten to Soong, October 25, 1943.

38. T. V. Soong Papers, Hoover Institution Archives, box 35, folder 17, telegram from Rajchman to T. V. Soong on December 6, 1943, and reply on December 10, 1943.

39. T. V. Soong papers, Hoover Institution Archives, box 35, folder 31, telegram of November 11, 1943.

40. Hsiao-ting Lin, "Chiang Kai-shek and the Cairo Summit," p. 433.

41. Joseph W. Esherick, ed., *Lost Chance in China: The World War II Despatches of John S. Service* (New York: Random House, 1974), pp. 78–82.

42. *Foreign Relations of the United States: Diplomatic Papers: 1944*, vol. 6, *China*, pp. 70–71.

43. Lauchlin Currie Papers, Hoover Institution Archives, box 4, folder "Second trip to China."

44. Lauchlin Currie Papers, Hoover Institution Archives, box 4, folder "Second trip to China." Currie noted that regarding the air service over the Hump, Soong agreed to General Arnold's suggestion of turning much of this over to the private aviation firm, CNAC. Currie felt that this was a mistake, because a commercial firm could not properly operate a military service. The original draft contains the sentence, "As General Arnold does not like China he will do anything to embarrass her." This is scratched through (although clearly legible), so would have been deleted from the report sent to the president. In his report to Roosevelt on his trip, dated August 24, 1942, Currie also gave the President blunt advice on Stilwell. "I am convinced that General Stilwell cannot function effectively as our chief military representative in China. I recommend therefore that he be recalled" (p. 37).

45. T. V. Soong Papers, Hoover Institution Archives, box 1, folder 38, From T. V. Soong in Chongqing to F. Chang, February 6, 1945; see also Wu Guozhen, *Cong Shanghai shichang*, pp. 237–238.

46. *Foreign Relations of the United States: Diplomatic Papers: 1944*, vol. 6, *China*, p. 51.

47. Wu Guozhen, *Cong Shanghai shichang*, p. 240.

48. Wellington Koo, "Wellington Koo Memoir," vol. 5, pp. 301–302.

49. *Foreign Relations of the United States: Diplomatic Papers: 1944*, vol. 6, *China*, p. 241.

50. *Foreign Relations of the United States: Diplomatic Papers: 1944*, vol. 6, *China*, p. 260.

51. Xu Bingsheng, "Guomin dang xingzheng yuan yuanhui jianwen" (Information on the meetings of the Guomindang Executive Yuan), *Shanghai wenshi ziliao xuanji* (Selections from literary and historical material, Shanghai), 43 (1983), pp. 122–132 (pp. 127–28).

52. Yang Tianshi, "Jiang Kong guanxi tanzheng" (An examination of the Chiang–Kung relationship), *Mingguo dang'an* (Republican archives) 4 (1992), pp. 115–120 (pp. 115–119).

53. T. V. Soong Papers, Hoover Institution Archives, box 30, folder 16, cable from T. V. Soong to H. H. Kung, March 15, 1943.

54. Albert C. Wedemeyer Papers, Hoover Institution Archives, box 83, folder 7, letter from Wedemeyer to T. V. Soong, November 26, 1945.

55. The family seems to have pronounced this Kong Lingkai. See for instance, T. V. Soong Papers, Hoover Institution Archives, box 64, folder 7, letter from T. V. Soong in New York to Madame Chiang Kai-shek, Taibei, March 22, 1965, and Albert Wedemeyer Papers, Hoover Institution Archives, box 46, folder 6, Kung Ling-kai (David).

56. H. H. Kung Papers, Hoover Institution Archives, box 9, folder 6, English correspondence files, letter from H. H. Kung to David Kung, October 28, 1939. The original letter was in English.

57. Norwood Alman Papers, Hoover Institution Archives, box 18, folder 23, David Kung file. T. V. Soong Papers, Hoover Institution Archives, box 64, folder 7, letter from T. V. Soong in New York to Madame Chiang Kai-shek, Taipei, March 22, 1965, and Albert Wedemeyer Papers, Hoover Institution Archives, box 46, folder 6, Kung Ling-kai (David).

58. Zheng Huixin, "Zhanhou zhongguo de 'guanban shanghang'" (Bureaucratic capitalism after the war), *Minguo dang'an* (2014), 1, pp. 134–143 (p. 136).

59. Arthur Young Papers, Hoover Institution Archives, Box 113, folder "China Diary," entry for May 11, 1946; United Kingdom, Foreign Office Files for China, 1918–1980, Adam Mathew, Archives Direct, FO 371/53747, Commercial Activities of David Kung.

60. Zheng Huixin, "Zhanhou zhongguo de 'guanban shanghang,'" pp. 136–137.

61. See, for example, Wang Chaoguang, "Jianbuduan libuluan – Kangzhan zhong houqi" (Unending chaos: The relationship between Chiang Kai-shek, H. H. Kung, and T. V. Soong during and after the war of resistance), pp. 209–232 (pp. 221–225) and Wu Jingping, "Kangzhan shiqi Song yu Kong Xiangxi guanxi zhi shuping" (A review of the relationship between T. V. Soong and H. H. Kung during the war period), pp. 189–208 (pp. 191–207), in Wu Jingping, *Song Ziwen shengping yu ziliao yanjiu.*

62. T. V. Soong Papers, Hoover Institution Archives, box 57, folder 19, letter from Brigadier General T. G. Hearn to T. V. Soong in Chongqing, November 27, 1942.

63. Wellington Koo, "Wellington Koo Memoir," vol. 5, "Sojourn in China," p. 189.

64. T. V. Soong Papers, Hoover Institution Archives, box 61, folder 31, letter from Madame Chiang Kai-shek to Laura Soong, June 22, 1941; letter from Madame Chiang Kai-shek to Laurette Soong, June 22, 1941; letter from Madame Chiang Kai-shek to T. V. Soong, January 5, 1944. In the last letter, she requested that Laura Soong send as many twelve-inch zippers as possible as well as different-colored velvet ribbons for hair bows. Soong cabled his wife on January 7, 1944, with the request. A more frequent request was for medicine, however. Among those requested by Madame Chiang from T. V. were drugs to treat amoebic dysentery, chloral hydrate, and vitamin B. T. V. Soong Papers, Hoover Institution Archives, box 62, folder 4, cables from Madame Chiang to T. V. Soong, September 13, 1943, and September 23, 1943.

65. T. V. Soong Papers, Hoover Institution Archives, box 35, folder 33.

66. T. V. Soong Papers, Hoover Institution Archives, box 61, folder 30, letter from Soong Ching-ling to T. V. Soong, January 12, 1942. Soong Ching-ling (Song Qingling) was incensed that the *Dagong bao* published a report that they had brought a vast amount of luggage, seven poodles, and many servants. She noted that the airplane had twenty-three passengers so that it would have been impossible for there to have been much luggage. "I could not even bring along my documents and other priceless articles, let along my dogs and clothings," she noted. See also *Zaisheng* 124 (August 3, 1946), p. 2.

67. T. V. Soong Papers, Hoover Institution Archives, box 61, folder 30, letter from Soong Ching-ling to T. V. Soong, October 24, 1941; cable from Soong Ching-ling to T. V. Soong, April 28, 1943; cable from T. V. Soong to Soong Ching-ling, April 26, 1943.

68. Lauchlin Currie Papers, Hoover Institution Archives, box 4, folder "Second trip to China, notes," September 3, 1942.

69. T. V. Soong Papers, Hoover Institution Archives, box 61, folder 31, Madame Chiang Kai-shek, personal letters. She often sent best wishes to Laura Soong, T. V.'s wife, as well.

70. T. V. Soong Papers, Hoover Institution Archives, box 30, folder 16, letter from H. H. Kung to T. V. Soong, February 3, 1945.

71. T. V. Soong Papers, Hoover Institution Archives, box 30, folder 16, cable from T. V. Soong to H. H. Kung, March 1, 1943.

72. T. V. Soong Papers, Hoover Institution Archives, box 30, folder 16, cable from Madame H. H. Kung to T. V. Soong, September 21, 1943.

73. Lauchlin Currie Papers, Hoover Institution Archives, box 3, folder "Madame Chiang Kai-shek," folder "China: Economic Conditions, Banknotes."

74. Lauchlin Currie Papers, Hoover Institution Archives, box 3, folder "China: Economic Conditions," memorandum of September 13, 1943.

75. Lauchlin Currie Papers, Hoovers Institution Archives, box 5, folder "Notes on T. V. Soong," Currie conversation with Li Ming, recorded April 24, 1943.

76. Lauchlin Currie Papers, Hoover Institution Archives, box 5, folder "U.S. Department of the Treasury, October 14, 1943."

77. T. V. Soong Papers, Hoover Institution Archives, box 1, folder 1, cables from T. V. Soong in Chongqing, December 25, 1944.

78. H. H. Kung Papers, Hoover Institution Archives, box 8, folder 6, letter from Robert T. Huang to H. H. Kung, February 13, 1941.

79. T. V. Soong Papers, Hoover Institution Archives, box 25, folder 15, letters from Bei Zuyi to T. V. Soong, July 19, 1942; July 21, 1942.

80. T. V. Soong Papers, Hoover Institution Archives, box 25, folder 15, letter from Bei Zuyi to T. V. Soong, June 9, 1943.

81. See for instance, T. V. Soong Papers, Hoover Institution Archives, box 25, folder 15, letter from Bei Zuyi to T. V. Soong, October 25, 1944.

82. Chihyun Chang, ed., *The Chinese Journals of L. K. Little, 1943–1954: An Eyewitness Account of War and Revolution,* vol. 1, *The Wartime Inspector General, 1943–1945,* pp. xxviii, 4. Little had generally good relations with T. V. Soong.

83. Chihyun Chang, *The Chinese Journals of L. K. Little,* vol. 2: *The Last Foreign Inspector General, 1946–1949,* p. 5.

84. T. V. Soong Papers, Hoover Institution Archives, box 16, folder 5, cable from T. V. Soong to Ambassador Patrick Hurley, March 12, 1945.

85. Chihyun Chang, *The Chinese Journals of L. K. Little,* August 26, 1943 entry, vol. 1, p. 13.

86. Arthur Young Papers, Hoover Institution Archives, box 113, folder "China Diary," entry for August 22, 1947.

87. T. V. Soong Papers, Hoover Institution Archives, box 1, folder 39, "F. Chang," letter of August 17, 1944, from F. Chang in Washington, DC to T. V. Soong.

88. Gregory Scott Lewis, "Shades of Red and White: The Life and Political Career of Ji Chaoding, 1903–1963," PhD dissertation, Arizona State University, 1999. Quotation from page 168, see also pp. 22, 101, 140, 169–170.

89. Ji Chaoding had extensive personal ties with H. H. Kung. During the war period in Chongqing, Ji lived on the top floor of Kung's compound, referred to Kung as "uncle," and often played bridge with Soong Ai-ling, Kung's wife. See Gregory Lewis, "Shades of Red and White," pp. 159, 178, 180–181.

90. Wang Chaoguang, "Sheng yu moshi yunbian xiao: Song Ziwen churen xingzheng yuan qianhou jingwei zhi yanjiu" (Fading away in the final years: Research on T. V. Soong before and after heading the Executive Yuan), in Wu Jingping, ed., *Song Ziwen yu zhanshi Zhongguo* (T. V. Soong and wartime China; Shanghai: Fudan daxue chuban she, 2008), pp. 284–300 (pp. 290–296).

91. Chen Boda, *Zhongguo sida jiazu* (China's four great families; Hong Kong: Changjiang, 1947).

92. Chen Boda, *Renmin gongdi Jiang Jieshi* (The enemy of the people, Chiang Kai-shek; Beijing: Renmin chuban she,1954).

93. The Economic Information Service, Hong Kong, "How Chinese Officials Amass Millions." New York: Committee for a Democratic Far Eastern Policy, 1948. For a full discussion of this issue see Dai Hongzhao, "Song Ziwen de siren caichan yu shifou gong wubi zhi pingxi" (An examination of whether or not T. V. Soong private property involved corruption), in Wu Jingping, *Song Ziwen shengping yu ziliao wenxian yanjiu*, pp. 393–399.

94. Arthur Young, *Cycle of Cathay*, p. 236.

95. Harry S. Truman, *Memoirs: Vol. 1: Year of Decisions* (Garden City: Doubleday, 1955), p. 267.

96. For additional information on this point see Hsiao-ting Lin, *Accidental State: Chiang Kai-shek, The United States and the Making of Taiwan* (Cambridge, MA: Harvard University Press, 2016), *passim.*

97. Wu Song, Jiang Renmin, and Rao Fanghu, *Da caifa Kong Xiangxi zhuan* (A biography of the big tycoon H. H. Kung; Wuhan: Wuhan chuban she, 1995).

98. Chen Feng, *Sida jiazu miwen* (Secrets of the four great families; Beijing: Tuanjie chuban she, 2008).

99. For an example of how the new sources have led to a revised view of T. V. Soong and the issue of his wealth, see Dai Hongchao, "Song Ziwen de xiren caichan," pp. 393–399. An early article by Wu Jingping on the importance of studying T. V. Soong is "Song Ziwen lungang" (A brief discussion of T. V. Soong), *Lishi yanjiu* 6 (1991), pp. 106–121.

100. Sterling Seagrave, *The Soong Dynasty* (New York: Harper and Row, 1985). For a summary of arguments by Seagrave, see Dai Hongchao, "Song Ziwen de xiren caichan," pp. 394–396.

101. Laura Tyson Li, *Madame Chiang Kai-shek: China's Eternal First Lady* (New York: Atlantic Monthly Press, 2006).

102. See, for example, Pakula's treatment of Madame Chiang's relationship with Wendell Wilkie. Hannah Pakula, *The Last Empress: Madame Chiang Kai-shek and the Birth of Modern China* (New York: Simon and Schuster, 2009), pp. 432–434.

103. Jung Chang, *Big Sister, Little Sister, Red Sister: Three Women at the Heart of Twentieth-Century China* (New York: Alfred A. Knopf, 2019), p. 100; Edward McCord, *The Power of the Gun: The Emergence of Modern Chinese Warlordism* (Berkeley: University of California Press, 1993).

104. Jung Chang, *Big Sister, Little Sister, Red Sister*, p. 139.

105. *Beijing Review*, July 19, 2001, documents supplement, p. v.

106. Arthur N. Young, *China's Wartime Finance and Inflation*, pp. 107–108; Zheng Huixing, *Cong touzi gongsi*, pp. 102–119.

107. T. V. Soong Papers, Hoover Institution Archives, box 29, folder 2, China Development Finance Corporation, letter from D. S. Yuan to T. V. Soong, October 5, 1945, and October 31, 1945; letter of T. V. Soong to D. S. Yuan, October 27, 1945.

108. Theodore H. White and Analee Jacoby, *Thunder Out of China* (New York: William Sloan Associates, 1946), pp. 114–115.

109. Roger J. Sandilands, *The Life and Political Economy of Lauchlin Currie: New Dealer, Presidential Adviser, and Development Economist* (Durham, NC: Duke University Press, 1990), pp. 107–109. Sandilands states that Currie assumed his mission would be concerned with technical issues regarding finances and currency but quickly realized that his visit was being used for broader political purposes. Roosevelt had asked him to convey a personal message to Chiang Kai-shek that he hoped that civil war between the Nationalists and Communists would not break out.

110. Lauchlin Currie Papers, Hoover Institution Archives, Stanford University, box 4, folder "Currie first trip to China," p. 38.

111. Lauchlin Currie Papers, Hoover Institution Archives, box 4, folder "Currie first trip to China," p. 20.

112. Lauchlin Currie Papers, Hoover Institution Archives, box 4, folder "Currie first trip to China," p. 39.

113. Lauchlin Currie Papers, Hoover Institution Archives, box 4, folder "Currie first trip to China," pp. 39–40.

114. Zheng Huixin, "Meijin gongzhai wubi an de fasheng ji chuli jingguo" (The US dollar bond embezzlement scandal and its handling), *Lishi yanjiu* 4 (2009) pp. 99–123 (pp. 103–104); Arthur N. Young, *China and the Helping Hand, 1937–1945* (Cambridge, MA: Harvard University Press, 1963), pp. 234–237.

115. Zheng Huixin, "Meijin gongzhai wubi an," pp. 103–104; Arthur Young, *China and the Helping Hand*, pp. 235–238.

116. Chen Gengya, "Kong Xiangxi jingtun meijin gongzhai de neimu zhenxiang" (The true inside story of H. H. Kung devouring the American dollar loan), *Wenshi ziliao xuanji* 50 (1986) pp. 246–252; *Jiang Zhongzheng zongtong dang'an: Shilue gaoben* (The Chiang Kai-shek collections: the chronological events; Taipei: Guoshi guan, 2011), vol. 61, pp. 514–517; Yang Tianshi, *Zhaoxun zhenshi de Jiang Jieshi: Jiang Jieshi riji jiedu* (Seeking the real Chiang Kai-shek: Reading the Chiang Kai-shek diary; Taiyuan: Shanxi renmin chuban she, 2008), vol. 2, p. 449.

117. Wu Song, Jiang Renmin, and Rao Fanghu, *Da caifa Kong Xiangxi zhuan*, pp. 239–40; Zheng Huixin, "Meijin gongzhai wubi an," pp. 105–106.

118. Arthur Young, *China and the Helping Hand*, p. 239.

119. Paul Preston and Michael Partridge, eds., *British Documents on Foreign Affairs: Reports and Papers from the Foreign Office Confidential Print* (Bethesda, MD: University Press of America, 1997), vol. 7, p. 289; Zheng Huixin, "Meijin gongzhai wubi an," p. 106.

120. Zheng Huixin, "Meijin gongzhai wubi an," p. 113.

121. *Foreign Relations of the United States: Diplomatic Papers: 1944*, vol. 6, *China*, pp. 319–322.

122. *Amerasia* 9, no. 4 (February 23, 1945), p. 51. The article also attacked General He Yingqin saying that he had "the biggest bank balance in New York of any Chinese."

123. Preston and Partridge, *British Documents on Foreign Affairs*, vol. 7, p. 476.

124. Preston and Partridge, *British Documents on Foreign Affairs*, vol. 7, p. 403.

125. Zheng Huixin, "Meijin gongzhai wubi an," pp. 108–112; Yang Tianshi, *Zhaoxun zhenshi de Jiang Jieshi*, vol. 2, pp. 452–453.

126. Xu Bingsheng, "Guomin dang xingzheng yuan yuanhui jianwen" (Information on the meetings of the Guomindang Executive Yuan), *Shanghai wenshi ziliao xuanji* 43 (1983), pp. 122–132 (p. 128).

127. Preston and Partridge, *British Documents on Foreign Affairs*, vol. 8, p. 23.

128. Preston and Partridge, *British Documents on Foreign Affairs*, vol. 8, p. 257.

129. Preston and Partridge, *British Documents on Foreign Affairs*, vol. 8, pp. 256–267.

130. *Jiang Zhongzheng zongtong dang'an: Shilue gaoben*, vol. 61, pp. 521–563.

131. Zheng Huixin, "Meijin gongzhai wubi an," pp. 118–119; *Jiang Zhongzheng zongtong dang'an: Shilue gaoben*, vol. 61, pp. 588–592; Yang Tianshi, *Zhaoxun zhenshi de Jiang Jieshi*, pp. 459–460; Yang Tianshi, *Yang Tianshi wenji* (The collected works of Yang Tianshi; Shanghai: Shanghai Cishu chuban she, 2005), pp, 579–582; Wang Fan-sen, *Fu Ssu-nien: A Life in Chinese History and Politics* (New York: Cambridge University Press, 2000), pp. 168–170.

132. *Foreign Relations of the United States: Diplomatic Papers: 1944*, vol. 7, *The Far East*, pp. 1095–1097, 1101; Zheng Huixin, "Meijin gongzhai wubi an," p. 113.

133. Arthur Young, *Cycle of Cathay*, p. 244.

134. Wang Chaoguang, "Jianbuduan libuluan – kangzhan zhonghou," in Wu Jingping, *Song Ziwen shengping yu ziliao wenxian yanjiu*, pp. 218–221.

135. Wu Jingping, "Kangzhan shiqi Song Ziwen yu Kong Xiangxi guanxi zhi shuping" (A review of the relationship between T. V. Soong and H. H. Kung during the war period), in Wu Jingping, *Song Ziwen shengping yu ziliao wenxian yanjiu*, pp. 205–206.

136. Zheng Huixin, "Meijin gongzhai wubi an," pp. 115–122; *Jiang Zhongzheng zongtong dang'an: Shilue gaoben*, vol. 61, pp. 514, 600–608, vol. 62, pp. 19, 45, 57, 63; Yang Tianshi, *Zhaoxun zhenshi de Jiang Jieshi*, vol. 2, pp. 458–459; Yang Tianshi, "Jiang Kong guanxi tanwei" (An exploration of the Chiang–Kung relationship), *Mingguo dang'an* 4 (1992), pp. 119–120.

CHAPTER 3 SUDDEN SURRENDER AND BOTCHED LIBERATION

1. Paul Preston and Michael Partridge, eds., *British Documents on Foreign Affairs: Reports and Papers from the Foreign Office Confidential Print* (Bethesda, MD: University Press of America, 1997), part II from 1940 through 1945, Series E Asia, vol. 8, pp. 217, 252.

2. Clayton Mishler, *Sampan Sailor: A Navy Man's Adventures in WWII China* (Washington, DC: Brassey's, 1994), pp. 161–164. SACO was the Sino-American Cooperative Organization, a mutual intelligence service.

3. Arthur N. Young, *Cycle of Cathay: An Historical Perspective* (Vista, CA: Ibis Publishing, 1997), pp. 1–4.

4. Chang Kia-ngau, *The Inflationary Spiral: The Experience in China, 1939–1950* (Cambridge, MA: MIT Press, 1958), p. 49.

5. Arthur N. Young Papers, Hoover Institution Archives, Stanford University, box 97, folder "Currency from August 15, 1945 to December 31, 1945," confidential memo, August 20, 1945; Arthur Young, *China's Wartime Finance and Inflation* (Cambridge, MA: Harvard University Press, 1965), pp. 12, 15. In her study, Lin Meili gives slightly different figures: for 1943, the deficit was 41,943,703,152; for 1944, 138,726,128,798; and for 1945, 1,202,205,543,309. See Lin Meili, *Kangzhan shiqi de huobi zhanzheng* (The currency war during the war of resistance period; Taibei: Guoshi guan, 1996), p. 38.

6. Arthur Young Papers, Hoover Institution Archives, box 84, folder "Planning for Postwar, 1945.

7. Arthur Young, *Cycle of Cathay*, pp. 210–211.

8. Arthur Young Papers, Hoover Institution Archives, box 97, folder "Currency August 15–December 31, 1945," memo of August 20, 1945.

9. Arthur Young Papers, Hoover Institution Archives, box 97, folder "August 15–December 31, 1945," memo dated September 6, 1945.

10. Wanyan Shaoyuan, *Da jieshou* (The great takeover; Shanghai: Shanghai yuandong chuban she, 1995), p. 57.

11. Cited in the Chinese Press Review, US Consulate, Shanghai, November 2, 1945.

12. Arthur Young Papers, Hoover Institution Archives, box 97, folder "August 15–December 31, 1945," memo of September 6, 1945.

13. Chou Shun-hsin, *The Chinese Inflation, 1937–1949* (New York: Columbia University Press, 1963), pp. 23–24.

14. Adapted from Chang Kia-ngau, *The Inflationary Spiral*, p. 372; see also United States, Department of State. Office of the HIstorian, *Foreign Relations of the United States: Diplomatic Papers, 1945: The Far East*, vol. 7, pp. 1129–1130.

15. T. V. Soong Papers, Hoover Institution Archives, box 25, folder 1, "Report on Money and Banking," unpublished draft by Frank M. Tamagna, October 10, 1946, p. 28.

16. Chihyun Chang, *Government, Imperialism and Nationalism in China: The Maritime Customs Service and Its Chinese Staff* (London: Routledge, 2013), p. 149.

17. Adapted from Chang Kia-ngau, *The Inflationary Spiral*, p. 372.

18. Ho Lien (He Lian), "The Reminiscences of Ho Lien (Franklin L. Ho)," Chinese Oral History Project, East Asian Institute, Columbia University, pp. 499–500.

19. Chang Kia-ngau, *The Inflationary Spiral*, p. 71.

20. *Wenhui bao*, April 3, 1946, cited in Chinese Press Review, US Consulate, Shanghai, April 3, 1946. Translation by the consulate.

21. Arthur Young Papers, Hoover Institution Archives, box 113, folder "China Diary," entry for May 8, 1946.

22. Arthur Young Papers, Hoover Institution Archives, box 113, folder "China Diary," entry for February 18, 1946.

23. Arthur Young Papers, Hoover Institution Archives, box 113, folder "China Diary," entry of July 13, 1946.

24. United States, Department of State, Office of Intelligence Research, "Themes in the Chinese National Budget," July 15, 1947, pp. 6–7.

25. United States, Department of State, Office of Intelligence Research, "Themes in the Chinese National Budget," July 15, 1947, p. 8.

26. United States, Department of State, Office of Intelligence Research, "Themes in the Chinese National Budget," July 15, 1947, pp. 13–14.

27. Philip Thai, *China's War on Smuggling: Law, Economic Life, and the Making of the Modern State, 1842–1965* (New York: Columbia University Press, 2018), p. 218.

28. United States, Department of State, Office of Intelligence Research, "Themes in the Chinese National Budget," July 15, 1947, pp. 14–16.

29. United States, Department of State, Office of Intelligence Research, "Themes in the Chinese National Budget," July 15, 1947, pp. 16–17.

30. Diana Lary, *China's Civil War: A Social History, 1945–1949* (Cambridge: Cambridge University Press, 2015), p. 46.

31. Quoted in Frank H. H. King, *The Hongkong Bank in the Period of Development and Nationalism: From Regional Bank to Multinational Group*, vol. 4 of *The History of the Hongkong and Shanghai Banking Corporation* (Cambridge: Cambridge University Press, 1991) p. 89.

32. Arthur Young, *Cycle of Cathay*, p. 206.

33. Preston and Partridge, *British Documents on Foreign Affairs*, vol. 8, p. 330.

34. Isabella Jackson, *Shaping Modern Shanghai: Colonialism in China's Global City* (Cambridge: Cambridge University Press, 2018), p. 239.

35. Isabella Jackson, *Shaping Modern Shanghai*, pp. 239–241.

36. Preston and Partridge, *British Documents on Foreign Affairs*, vol. 8, p. 353.

37. Arthur Young Papers, Hoover Institution Archives, box 113, folder "China Diary," entry for November 23, 1945.

38. Arthur Young Papers, Hoover Institution Archives, box 97, folder "Currency from August 15, 1945–December 31, 1945.

39. *China Weekly Review*, August 10, 1946, p. 243.

40. Peng Xiaoliang, ed. *Zhou Zuomin riji shuxin ji* (Zhou Zuomin diary and letters; Shanghai: Shanghai yuandong chuban she, 2014), pp. 45, 49, 55–58; Parks M. Coble, "Zhou Zuomin and the Jincheng Bank," in Sherman Cochran, ed., *The Capitalist Dilemma in China's Communist Revolution* (Ithaca, NY: East Asia Program, Cornell University, 2014), pp. 151–174 (pp. 162–165).

41. Peng Xiaoliang, *Zhou Zuomin riji shuxin ji*, pp. 63–64, 68–69; Parks M. Coble, "Zhou Zuomin and the Jincheng Bank," p. 165.

42. Peng Xiaoliang, *Zhou Zuomin riji shuxin ji*, p. 123.

43. Chinese Press Review, US Consulate, Shanghai, November 20, 1945; Yun Xia, *Down with Traitors: Justice and Nationalism in Wartime China* (Seattle: University of Washington Press, 2017), p. 85.

44. *Dagong bao*, December 3, 1945, quoted in Chinese Press Review, US Consulate, Shanghai, December 3, 1945, p. 2; Cui Meiming, "Song Ziwen zhuchi xia de Shanghai qu diwei chanye chuli ju" (The management of enemy and puppet property in the Shanghai area under T. V. Soong's direction), *Jindai shi yanjiu* (Research into modern history) 1 (1988), pp. 267–268.

45. *North China Daily News,* February 14, 1946, p. 1; Suzanne Pepper, *Civil War in China: The Political Struggle 1945–1949* (Lanham, MD: Rowman and Littlefield, 1999), pp. 23–29.

46. *China Weekly Review,* July 12, 1947, p. 168.

47. Parks M. Coble, *Chinese Capitalists in Japan's New Order: The Occupied Lower Yangzi, 1937–1945* (Berkeley: University of California Press, 2003), pp. 136–137, Qian Keting, "Rong Desheng de jizhe zhaodai hui" (Rong's Desheng's press conference), *Shanghai wenshi ziliao xuanji* (A collection of Shanghai literary and historical materials) 73 (1993), pp 201–204; *Shen bao,* June 26, 1946, p. 1; Zhongguo di'erh lishi dang'an guan, ed., "1946 nian Rong Desheng bei bangjia an shiliao erjian" (Two documents of historical materials on the 1946 kidnapping of Rong Dengshe" *Minguo dang'an* (Republican archives) 1 (2001), pp. 31–33.

48. Yun Xia, *Down with Traitors,* p. 72.

49. Yun Xia, *Down with Traitors,* p. 100.

50. Frederic Wakeman, Jr., *Spymaster: Dai Li and the Chinese Secret Service* (Berkeley: University of California Press, 2003), pp. 353–356; Yun Xia, *Down with Traitors,* p. 33.

51. Feng Bing and Wang Qiang, "A Study of Postwar Nationalist Government's Policies on Traitors' Properties, 1945 to 1949," *Chinese Studies in History* 49, no. 4 (2016), pp. 218–236 (pp. 218–219).

52. Feng Bing and Wang Qiang, "A Study of Postwar," pp. 225–226.

53. Yun Xia, *Down with Traitors,* pp. 80–82.

54. *Dagong bao,* September 9, 1946, Chinese Press Review, US Consulate, Shanghai, September 9, 1946.

55. Ding Zhijin, "Taobei Xianggang de nichan wenti" (Problems of traitors' properties hidden in Hong Kong), *Jingji zhoubao* (Economics weekly) 9 (1946), p. 8, quoted in Feng Bing and Wang Qiang, "A Study of Postwar," p. 236.

56. Feng Bing and Wang Qiang, "A Study of Postwar," pp. 227–228.

57. Arthur Young Papers, Hoover Institution Archives, box 84, folder "Planning for postwar, general 1944."

58. For a discussion of this issue, see Wu Qiyuan, *You zhanshi jingji dao pingshi jingji* (From a wartime economy to a peace time economy; Shanghai: Dadong shuju, 1946), pp. 308–310.

59. Arthur Young, *Cycle of Cathay,* pp. 209–210.

60. Arthur Young, *Cycle of Cathay,* pp. 209–210; Arthur Young, *China's Wartime Finance and Inflation, 1937–1945,* p. 182.

61. Diana Lary, *China's Civil War,* p. 48; see also Ho Lien (He Lian), "The Reminiscences of Ho Lien (Franklin L. Ho)," Chinese Oral History Project, East Asian Institute of Columbia University, p. 384.

62. Chang Kia-ngau, *The Inflationary Spiral,* pp. 69–70; Wu Qiyuan, *You zhanshi jingji,* pp. 339–340.

63. Suzanne Pepper, *Civil War in China,* p. 21.

64. Mi Qingyun, "Cong Chongqing dao Shanghai di jieshou jianwen," (From Chongqing to Shanghai, impressions of the takeover), in *Wenshi ziliao cungao xuanbian* (An edited collection of selections from literary and historical materials; Beijing: Zhongguo wen

chuban she, 2002), vol. 7, pp. 736–740. See also Tao Juyin, *Gudao jianwen: Kangzhan shiqi de Shanghai* (Experiences in the solitary island: Shanghai during the war of resistance; Shanghai; Shanghai renmin chuban she, 1979), pp. 325–326, 332, and Wanyan Shaoyuan, *Da jieshou*, pp. 41–45.

65. Chou Shun-hsin, *The Chinese Inflation*, p. 24; Tao Juyin, *Gudao jianwen*, p. 332.
66. T. V. Soong Papers, Hoover Institution Archives, box 25, folder 1, "Report on Money and Banking," unpublished draft, by Frank M. Tamagna, October 10, 1946, p. 4.
67. Suzanne Pepper, *Civil War in China*, p. 35.
68. Preston and Partridge, *British Documents on Foreign Affairs*, vol. 8, p. 367.
69. Arthur Young Papers, Hoover Institution Archives, box 97, folder, "Currency, August 15–December 31, 1945," memo of October 16, 1945.
70. Chihyun Chang, *Government, Imperialism and Nationalism in China*, pp. 148–149; Arthur Young Papers, Hoover Institution Archives, box 97, folder, "Currency, August 15–December 31, 1945," memo of October 16, 1945. See also Wu Qiyuan, *You zhanshi jingji*, pp. 343–344.
71. Most observers noted that as soon as the government raised the exchange rate as in August 1946, merchants took this as a signal to raise prices. See for instance, Roger B. Jeans, ed., *The Marshall Mission to China, 1945–1947: The Letters and Diary of Colonel John Hart Caughey* (Lanham, MD: Rowman and Littlefield, 2011), pp. 149–150, entry for August 23, 1946.
72. Wu Qiyuan, *You zhanshi jingji dao pingshi jingji*, pp. 343–344; Yang Peixin, *Jiu Zhongguo de tonghuo pengzhang* (Currency inflation in old China; Beijing: Renmin chuban she, 1985), pp. 86–87; *Shenbao*, March 4, 1946; *Zaisheng* 139 (November 16, 1946), p. 7.
73. Arthur Young Papers, Hoover Institution Archives, box 77, folder "Press clippings, currency, 1946," box 113, folder "China Diary," entry for December 13, 1945; J. Franklin Ray, Jr. Papers, Hoover Institution Archives, box 2, folder "China Office," monthly reports, February 1946; Shun-hsin Chou, *The Chinese Inflation, 1937–1949*, p. 131.
74. Yang Peixin, *Jiu Zhongguo de tonghuo pengzhang*, pp. 88–89.
75. Arthur Young, *Cycle of Cathay*, p. 213.
76. *China Weekly Review*, September 28, 1946, p. 116.
77. *Dagong bao*, June 25, 26, 27, 1946, Chinese Press Review, US Consulate, Shanghai, June 28, 1946; *Shen bao*, November 24, 1946, p. 7.
78. *Dagong bao* editorial of April 29, 1946, Chinese Press Review, US Consulate, Shanghai, no. 37, April 29, 1946, p. 1.
79. *Xinwen bao*, May 14, 1946, Chinese Press Review, US Consulate, Shanghai, May 14, 1946, p. 10.
80. *Shen bao*, June 4, 1946, Chinese Press Review, US Consulate, Shanghai, June 4, 1946, p. 1.
81. Sheng Mo-chieh, "Shanghai's International Trade," September 12, 1946, Chinese Press Review, US Consulate, Shanghai, October 22, 1946, pp. 1–2.
82. *Shen bao*, November 18, 1946, Chinese Press Review, US Consulate, Shanghai, November 18, 1946, p. 1; *Xinwen bao*, November 18, 1946, Chinese Press Review.

83. T. V. Soong Papers, Hoover Institution Archives, box 36, folder 10, "China, foreign exchange," "Exchange Rate Policy," January 20, 1947, p. 8; Arthur Young Papers, Hoover Institution Archives, box 98, folder "Exchange equalization fund."

84. "Trends in the Chinese National Budget," confidential report by the Division of Research for Far East, Office of Intelligence Research, Department of State, July 15, 1947, p. 13.

85. United Kingdom, Foreign Office Files for China, 1918–1980, Adam Mathew, Archives Direct, FO 371/69559, British shipping in China, folder 1, 1948, March 1, 1948.

86. Ann Reinhardt, *Navigating Semi-Colonialism: Shipping, Sovereignty, and Nation-Building in China, 1860–1937* (Cambridge, MA: Harvard University Asia Center, 2018), pp. 304–305.

87. Arthur Young Papers, Hoover Institution Archives, box 94, folder "Water transport 1944–1946," memo, December 21, 1945. Great Britain by contrast allowed foreign-flag vessels to call at domestic ports in Britain provided that the privileges were reciprocal.

88. "An Analysis of the Problem of Restoring and Expanding Chinese Merchant Shipping in the Postwar Period," Office of Intelligence Coordination and Liaison," Department of State (United States), July 22, 1946, pp. 1–30.

89. Chen Junren, "Kangzhan hou guomin zhengfu chuanye zhengce yu zhaoshang ju de fazhan" (Postwar shipping policies of the National Government and the development of the China Merchants Steam Navigation Company), *Guojia hanghai* (National shipping) 19 (Shanghai: Shanghai guji chuban she, 2017), pp. 89–103 (p. 95).

90. *Shenbao*, November 22, 1945, Chinese Press Review, US Consulate, Shanghai, November 23, 1945, p. 8; Chen Junren, "Kangzhan hou guomin zhengfu chuanye," pp. 94–95.

91. T. V. Soong Papers, Hoover Institution Archives, box 3, folder 8, telegram from T. V. Soong to Dr. C. C. Wang, China Purchasing Agency, London, January 31, 1946; the agency had been negotiating for older Canadian vessels engaged in coastal trade, but Soong opted for newer ships. Telegram of January 10, 1946.

92. See for example the telegram of March 2, 1946, from the China Purchasing Agency, London, to T. V. Soong. T. V. Soong Papers, Hoover Institution Archives, box 3, folder 8.

93. Chen Junren, "Kangzhan hou guomin zhengfu chuanye," pp. 93–100.

94. Arthur Young, Hoover Institution Archives, box 93, folder "Cotton Credit, 1946," memo of July 2, 1946.

95. UNRRA China Office Papers, Hoover Institution Archives, box 1, folder "Office of the Director, staff meeting minutes," August 8, 1946.

96. Arthur Young Papers, Hoover Institution Archives, box 113, folder "China Diary," January 29, 1946.

97. *Dagong bao*, June 7, 1946, Chinese Press Review, US Consulate, Shanghai, June 7, 1946.

98. *North China Daily News*, July 15, 1946, p. 2; UNRRA China Office Papers, Hoover Institution Archives, box 9, folder "Special Reports," CNRRA/UNRRA Supply Program for Communist Areas, July 5, 1947, pp. 16–17.

99. *North China Daily News*, August 10, 1946, p. 2; UNRRA China Office Papers, Hoover Institution Archives, box 1, folder "UNRRA Council, Program and Estimated

Requirements for Relief and Rehabilitation in China"; folder "Office of the Director, Staff Meeting Minutes," August 6, 1946; August 8, 1946; box 9, folder "Special Reports CNRRA/UNRR Supply Program for Communist Areas, July 5, 1947, p. 15.

100. George Woodbridge, compiler, *UNRRA: The History of the United Nations Relief and Rehabilitation Administration* (New York: Columbia University Press, 1950), vol. 2, pp. 373–376.

101. Arthur Young Papers, Hoover Institution Archives, box 74, folder "Trade 6/1/1946 to 12/31/1946."

102. *Li bao*, June 10, 1946, Chinese Press Review, US Consulate, Shanghai, June 10, 1946.

103. *Shang bao*, June 13, 1946, Chinese Press Review, US Consulate, Shanghai, June 13, 1946, p. 1.

104. Frank H. H. King, *The Hongkong Bank in the Period of Development and Nationalism*, pp. 157–158.

105. T. V. Soong Papers, Hoover Institution Archives, box 36, folder 7, letter from S. F. Soh, China Textile Industries, Shanghai, to T. V. Soong, February 9, 1946.

106. T. V. Soong Papers, Hoover Institution Archives, box 25, folder 1, "Report on Money and Banking," unpublished draft, Frank M. Tamagna, October 10, 1946, pp. 6–7.

107. H. H. Kung Papers, Hoover Institution Archives, box 8, folder 9, "Aviation," report on Proposed Chinese Air Transport Co. with British Assistance, January 10, 1944.

108. H. H. Kung Papers, Hoover Institution Archives, box 8, folder 9, "Aviation," confidential report of W. L. Bond, November 25, 1943.

109. "Trends Toward State Control of Industry in China," confidential report of the Office of Intelligence Coordination and Liaison of the Department of State, August 20, 1946, p. 37.

CHAPTER 4 1946: FAILURE TO REVIVE THE ECONOMY
IN THE AFTERMATH OF WAR

1. Chihyun Chang, ed., *The Chinese Journals of L. K. Little, 1943–1954: An Eyewitness to War and Revolution*, vol. 2, *The Last Foreign Inspector General, 1946–1949* (London: Routledge, 2018), vol. 2, p. 34.

2. Arthur Young papers, Hoover Institution Archives, box 97, folder "Currency, 1/1/46 to 9/1/46," confidential memo to Chiang Kai-shek, August 31, 1946.

3. Compiled from Chang Kia-ngau, *The Inflationary Spiral: The Experience of China, 1939–1950* (Cambridge, MA: MIT Press, 1958), pp. 371–373.

4. Arthur Young Papers, Hoover Institution Archives, box 94, folder "US aid, post war."

5. *China Weekly Review*, January 4, 1947, p. 149.

6. Arthur Young Papers, Hoover Institution Archives, Box 113, folder "China Diary," entries for May 18, 1946, and June 26, 1946.

7. Arthur Young Papers, Hoover Institution Archives, box 92, folder 6, memo of April 3, 1946, Arthur Young for Bei Zuyi, Central Bank of China.

8. Arthur Young Papers, Hoover Institution Archives, box 92, folder 6, memo of April 3, 1946, Arthur Young for Bei Zuyi, Central Bank of China.

9. Wang Ju, *Jindai Shanghai mianfang ye de zuihou huihuang, 1945–1949* (The final flourishing of the modern Shanghai cotton textile industry; Shanghai: Shanghai shehui kexue yuan, 2003). Wang labels the immediate postwar period as a "golden age" for cotton textiles. See pp. 76–153, *passim*.

10. Arthur Young Papers, Hoover Institution Archives, box 113, folder "China Diary," entry of January 23, 1946.

11. Arthur Young Papers, Hoover Institution Archives, box 112, folder "China Diary," entry of March 28, 1946.

12. Arthur Young Papers, Hoover Institution Archives, box 94, folder 3, "Surplus Property, 1946," June 24, 1946.

13. Daniel Kurtz-Phelan, *The China Mission: George Marshall's Unfinished War, 1945–1947* (New York: W. W. Norton, 2018), p. 187.

14. Arthur Young Papers, Hoover Institution Archives, box 26, folder 7, "U.S. Economic Assistance, 1946–1947," letter from Shou Chin Wang, Washington DC to H. C. Kiang, Office of the President, Executive Yuan, Nanking [Nanjing], November 29, 1946; Shou Ching Wang, Washington, DC to T. V. Soong, President of the Executive Yuan, July 22, 1946.

15. Arthur Young Papers, Hoover Institution Archives, box 113, folder "China Diary," entries of January 19, 1946, January 23, 1946.

16. Arthur Young Papers, Hoover Institution Archives, box 113, folder "China Diary," entry for January 14–17, 1946.

17. "Wartime and Postwar Status of the Silk Industry in the Far East: China," report by the Office of Intelligence Research, Division of Research for Far East, US Department of State, March 15, 1947.

18. T. V. Soong Papers, Hoover Institution Archives, box 34, folder 1, letter from General A. C. Wedemeyer to T. V. Soong, February 3, 1946; "Wartime and Postwar Status of the Silk Industry in the Far East: China," pp. 13–14.

19. *Dagong bao*, December 3, 1945, China Press Review, US Consulate, Shanghai, December 3, 1945, p. 2; Cui Meiming, "Song Ziwen zhuchi xia de Shanghai qu di wei chanye chuli ju" (The management of enemy and puppet property in the Shanghai area under T. V. Soong's direction), *Jindai shi yanjiu* (Research on recent history) 1 (1988), pp. 267–268.

20. *Guancha* (The observer) 1, no. 20, January 11, 1947, pp. 12–14; Chou Shun-hsin, *The Chinese Inflation, 1937–1949* (New York: Columbia University Press, 1963), pp. 194–199.

21. Ho Lien, "The Reminiscences of Ho Lien (Franklin L. Ho)," Chinese Oral History Project, East Asian Institute, Columbia University, p. 401.

22. Peng Xiaoliang, ed., *Zhou Zuomin riji shuxin ji* (Zhou Zuomin diary and letters; Shanghai: Shanghai yuandong chuban she, 2014), pp. 68, 78, 89–92, 108, 117–118.

23. J. Franklin Ray Jr. Papers, Hoover Institution Archives, box 1, folder "China Office Monthly Report," January 1947, pp. 11–14. Ray was the head of the UNRRA office in China.

24. "Trends Toward State Control of Industry in China," Secret Intelligence Research Report, Office of Intelligence Coordination and Liaison, [US] Department of State, August 20, 1946.

25. Arthur Young Papers, Hoover Institution Archives, box 113, folder "China Diary," February 14, 1946.

26. C. X. George Wei, *Sino-American Economic Relations, 1944–1949* (Westport, CT: Greenwood Press, 1997), pp. 85–88.

27. *Dagong bao*, November 6, 1946, Chinese Press Review, US Consulate, Shanghai, November 6, 1945, pp. 1–2.

28. *Dagong bao*, November 6, 1946, Chinese Press Review, pp. 1–2.

29. C. X. George Wei, *Sino-American Economic Relations*, pp. 90–92.

30. Tao Juyin, *Gudao jianwen: Kangzhan shiqi de Shanghai* (Experiences in the solitary island: Shanghai during the war of resistance; Shanghai: Shanghai renmin chuban she, 1979), p. 334.

31. Wang Ju, *Jindai Shanghai mianfang*, chapter 2, *passim*; Christian Henriot, "Shanghai Industries in the Civil War (1945–1947)," *Journal of Urban History* 43 (2015), https://doi.org/10.1177/0096144214566977. Published online April 2, 2015.

32. Wang Ju, *Jindai Shanghai mianfang*, *passim*.

33. Chao Kang, *The Development of Cotton Textile Production in China* (Cambridge, MA: Harvard East Asian Monographs, 1977) p. 133; Shanghai shehui kexue yuan, Jingji yanjiu suo, ed., *Rongjia qiye shiliao* (Historical materials on the Rong family enterprises; Shanghai: Shanghai renmin chuban she, 1980), vol. 2, pp. 404–406.

34. T. V. Soong Papers, Hoover Institution Archives, box 45, folder 21; Liu Guoliang, *Zhongguo gongye shi xiandai juan* (A history of China's modern industry; Nanjing: Jiangsu kexue jichu chuban she, 2003), pp. 515, 542.

35. Wang Ju, *Jindai Shanghai mianfang*, *passim*.

36. Ho Lien, "The Reminiscences of Ho Lien," pp. 382–383.

37. Christian Henriot, "Shanghai Industries in the Civil War," p. 9.

38. Christian Henriot, "Shanghai Industries in the Civil War," p. 19.

39. Arthur Young Papers, Hoover Institution Archives, box 113, folder "China Diary," January 25, 1946.

40. Arthur Young Papers, Hoover Institution Archives, box 93, folder "Cotton Credit, 1947," memo of December 11, 1947.

41. Arthur Young Papers, Hoover Institution Archives, box 113, folder "China Diary," February 21, 1946.

42. *Dagong bao*, June 24, 1946, Chinese Press Review, US Consulate, Shanghai, June 24, 1946, p. 2.

43. For a discussion of this issue see Parks M. Coble, *Chinese Capitalists in Japan's New Order: The Occupied Lower Yangzi, 1937–1945* (Berkeley: University of California Press, 2003), pp. 16–19.

44. Juanjuan Peng, *The Yudahua Business Group in China's Early Industrialization* (Lanham, MD: Lexington Books, 2020), p. 105.

45. Juanjuan Peng, *The Yudahua Business Group*, pp. 105–107.

46. "Wartime and Postwar Status of the Silk Industry in the Far East: China," Office of Intelligence Research, US Department of State, March 15, 1947, pp. 5–6.

47. "Wartime and Postwar Status of the Silk Industry," p. 10.

48. "Wartime and Postwar Status of the Silk Industry," p. 11.

49. Arthur Young Papers, Hoover Institution Archives, box 94, folder "Shanghai Power Company;" Wei, *Sino-American Economic Relations, 1944–1949*, pp. 128–129.

50. J. Franklin Ray, Jr. Papers, Hoover Institution Archives, box 2, folder "UNRRA Monthly Report."

51. Arthur Young Papers, Hoover Institution Archives, box 94, folder "Shanghai Power Company."

52. Wei, *Sino-American Economic Relations, 1944–1949*, pp. 129–133.

53. Arthur Young Papers, Hoover Institution Archives, box 113, "China Diary," January 31, 1946; April 9, 1946.

54. "Resume of Postwar Labor Developments in Nationalist China," Department of State, Intelligence Research Report, November 1, 1946, pp. 6–7; Wei, *Sino-American Economic Relations*, p. 130.

55. "Resume of Postwar Labor Developments," pp. 7–9.

56. "Developments in the State Control of Chinese Industries," Confidential Intelligence Memorandum by the Office of Intelligence Coordination and Liaison, US Department of State, July 17, 1946, p. 5.

57. "Developments in the State Control of Chinese Industries," pp. 5–11.

58. Suzanne Pepper, *Civil War in China: The Political Struggle, 1945–1949* (Lanham, MD: Rowman and Littlefield, 1999), pp. 100–101.

59. T. V. Soong Papers, Hoover Institution Archives, box 26, folder 7, letter of August 26, 1946.

60. T. V. Soong Papers, Hoover Institution Archives, box 28, folder 6, "Proposed Extension Program of Electrification for Nanking, Changchow and Wusih," July 1947.

61. T. V. Soong Papers, Hoover Institution Archives, box 28, folder 6, "Proposed Extension Program of Electrification for Nanking, Changchow and Wusih," July 1947.

62. *Economic Bulletin*, no. 24, Hong Kong, June 12, 1947, Chinese Press Review, US Consulate, Shanghai, July 5, 1947, p. 1.

63. *Wenhui bao*, May 27, 1946, Chinese Press Review, US Consulate, Shanghai, May 27, 1946, p. 10.

CHAPTER 5 1947: SPEEDING TOWARD DISASTER

1. United States, Department of State, Office of Intelligence Research, "The Trend of Inflation in China, 1946–47," secret report, March 18, 1947, p. iii, p. 4.

2. "The Trend of Inflation in China," pp. 2–3.

3. Frank H. H. King, *The Hongkong Bank in the Period of Development and Nationalism: From Regional Bank to Multinational Group*, vol. 4 of *The History of the Hongkong and Shanghai Banking Corporation* (Cambridge: Cambridge University Press, 1991), p. 163.

4. Arthur Young Papers, Hoover Institution Archives, box 92, folder "Revenues and Expenditures, 1947," memo of December 22, 1947.

5. Chihyun Chang, ed., *The Chinese Journals of L. K. Little, 1943–1954: An Eyewitness to War and Revolution*, vol. 2, *The Last Foreign Inspector General, 1946–1954* (London: Routledge, 2018), p. 49.

6. "The Trend of Inflation in China," p. 9; United Kingdom, Foreign Office Files for China, 1918–1980, Adam Mathew, Archives Direct, FO 371/63339, "Currency and Exchange Problems and Financial Situation in China," folder 1, 1946; see also *Guancha* (The observer) 2, no. 1 (March 1, 1947), pp. 8–11; Chihyun Chang, *The Chinese Journals of L. K. Little*, vol. 2, p. 46.

7. Chihyun Chang, *The Chinese Journals of L. K. Little*, vol. 2, pp. 51–53.

8. *Shidai pinglun* (Contemporary critique), vol. 4, no. 96 (December 16, 1947), p. 21.

9. Odd Arne Westad, *Decisive Encounters: The Chinese Civil War, 1946–1950* (Stanford, CA: Stanford University Press), p. 75.

10. *Dagong bao*, Chinese Press Review, US Consulate, Shanghai, February 18, 1947, p. 2; United States, Department of State, Division of Research for Far East, Office of Intelligence Research, "Trends in the Chinese National Budget," confidential report, July 15, 1947, p. 27.

11. T. V. Soong Papers, Hoover Institution Archives, box 25, folder 10, "China, foreign exchange," "Foreign Exchange Regulations Supplement to Economic Emergency Measures," February 16, 1947; Yang Tianshi, *Yang Tianshi wenji* (Collected works of Yang Tianshi; Shanghai: Shanghai cishu chubanshe, 2005), pp. 584–585.

12. *Shenbao*, February 12, 1947, Chinese Press Review, US Consulate, Shanghai, p. 3.

13. United Kingdom, Foreign Office Files for China, 1918–1980, FO 371/69567, "Currency and Exchange Problems and Financial Structure in China, 1947," folder 2, from the Shanghai Consulate to the Foreign Office, February 18, 1947, private conversation with Mayor Wu Guozhen.

14. *The China Weekly Review*, Shanghai, March 22, 1947, p. 87.

15. Arthur Young Papers, Hoover Institution Archives, box 95, folder "Currency 9/1/46 to 1947."

16. *Dagong bao*, Feb. 8, 1947, Chinese Press Review, US Consulate, Shanghai, p. 1. At the time 3,350 yuan to US$1 was the official exchange rate.

17. *The North-China Daily News*, Shanghai, February 11, 1947, p. 1.

18. *Dagong bao*, Chinese Press Review, US Consulate, Shanghai, February 18, 1947, p. 1.

19. *The North-China Daily News*, February 20, 1947, p. 1.

20. *The North-China Daily News*, July 4, 1947, p. 2.

21. *Dagong bao*, Chinese Press Review, US Consulate, Shanghai, February 18, 1947, p. 2.

22. *Wenhui bao*, Chinese Press Review, US Consulate, Shanghai, February 18, 1947, p. 3.

23. *Dagong bao*, Chinese Press Review, US Consulate, Shanghai, April 25, 1947, p. 9.

24. Suzanne Pepper, *Civil War in China: The Political Struggle, 1945–1949* (Lanham, MD: Rowman and Littlefield, 1999), p. 112.

25. A. Doak Barnett, *China on the Eve of Communist Takeover* (London: Thames & Hudson, 1963), p. 20.

26. *Zhongyang ribao*, Chinese Press Review, US Consulate, Shanghai, May 2, 1947.

27. *Shen bao*, Chinese Press Review, US Consulate, Shanghai, June 28, 1947.

28. Barnett, *China on the Eve of Communist Takeover*, p. 20.

29. J. Franklin Roy Jr. Papers, Hoover Institution Archives, box 1, folder "China Office [of UNRAA] Monthly Report, January 1947," p. 2; Wang Chaoguang, "Sheng yu moshi

yunbian xiao: Song Ziwen churen xingzheng yuan qianhou jingwei zhi yanjiu"
(Fading away in the final years: Research on T. V. Soong before and after heading
the Executive Yuan), in Wu Jingping, ed., *Song Ziwen yu zhanshi Zhongguo* (T. V. Soong
and wartime China; Shanghai: Fudan daxue chuban she, 2008), pp. 284–300 (pp. 290,
296); Wang Chaoguang, "Guanyu 'guanliao ziben' de zhenglun yu guomin dang
zhizheng de weiji" (Regarding the bureaucratic capitalism controversy and the crisis
of governing by the Guomindang), *Minguo dang'an* (Republican archives) 2 (2008),
pp. 105–111 (p. 110).

30. *The North-China Daily News*, January 31, 1947, p. 1.

31. Fan-sen Wang, *Fu Ssu-nien: A Life in Chinese History and Politics* (Cambridge: Cambridge
University Press, 2000), p. 181.

32. Lloyd E. Eastman, *Seeds of Destruction: Nationalist China in War and Revolution, 1937–1949*
(Stanford, CA: Stanford University Press, 1984), pp. 109, 123–124; Gregory Scott Lewis,
"Shades of Red and White: The Life and Political Career of Ji Chaoding, 1903–1963,"
unpublished PhD dissertation, Arizona State University, 1999.

33. J. Franklin Ray, Jr. Papers, Hoover Institution Archives, box 1, China Office Monthly
Report, February 1947; *Shen bao*, March 2, 1947, p. 1.

34. *The North-China Daily News*, February 15, 1947, p. 1.

35. *Dagong bao*, February 21, 1947, Chinese Press Review, US Consulate, Shanghai, pp. 10–
11; *The Century Review*, February 22, 1947, Chinese Press Review, March 6, 1947, p. 9; Xu
Bingsheng, "Guomindang xingzheng yuan yuanhui jianwen" (Information on the
meetings of the Guomindang Executive Yuan), *Shanghai wenshi ziliao xuanji*
(Selections from literary and historical material, Shanghai) 43 (1983), pp. 122–132
(pp. 127–128).

36. T. V. Soong Papers, Hoover Institution Archives, box 62, folder 22, Youngman letters,
T. V. Soong to William S. Youngman, December 31, 1946. After the resignation of
Soong, the China Defense Supplies was closed and turned its assets over to the
Universal Trading Corporation.

37. United Kingdom, Foreign Office Files for China, 1918–1980, FO 371/63340, "Currency
and Exchange Problems and Financial Situation in China, 1947," folder 2, T. V. Soong
Address to the Legislative Yuan, March 1, 1947. Soong still had some supporters among
the Westerners who worked in China. L. K. Little, inspector general of the Maritime
Customs Service wrote in his diary on January 24, 1947, "If China had 50 men like
Soong, it could be a different country! He is really a great administrator, and one of the
very few Chinese who gets things done. I believe him to be thoroughly patriotic."
Chihyun Chang, *The Chinese Journals of L. K. Little*, vol. 2, p. 51.

38. United Kingdom, Foreign Office Files for China, 1918–1980, FO 371/63340, "Currency
and Exchange Problems and Financial Situation in China, 1947," folder 2, T. V. Soong
Address to the Legislative Yuan, March 1, 1947.

39. Chang Kia-ngau (Zhang Jia'ao) Papers, Hoover Institution Archives, box 27, folder 1,
Correspondence 1962; *Jiang Zhongzheng zontgong dang'an: Shilue gaoben* (The Chiang
Kai-shek collections: chronological events; Taibei: Guoshi guan, 2013), vol. 69, pp.
5–132. This source lists a few meetings about the financial crisis but many more about

the fighting with the communists and the tense situation in Taiwan. Chiang spared little time to deal with financial issues.

40. *Wenhui bao*, May 16, 1947, Chinese Press Review, US Consulate, Shanghai, June 4, 1947, pp. 1–2; United Kingdom, Foreign Office Files for China, 1918–1980, FO 371/ 63344, "Currency and Exchange Problems and Financial Situation in China, 1947," folder 6.

41. The Economic Information Service, Hong Kong, *How Chinese Officials Amass Millions: An Analytical Study of the Financial Basis of the Chinese Kuomintang "CC" Clique* (New York: Committee for a Democratic Far Eastern Policy, 1948), pp. 4–5, 20, 26.

42. *Shen bao*, March 2, 1947, Chinese Press Review, US Consulate, Shanghai, March 3, 1947, p. 2.

43. *Wenhui bao*, March 2, 1947, Chinese Press Review, US Consulate, Shanghai, March 3, 1947, pp. 3–4.

44. *Wenhui bao*, May 16, 1947, Chinese Press Review, US Consulate, Shanghai, June 4, 1947, p. 1.

45. *Dagong bao*, March 2, 1947, Chinese Press Review, US Consulate in Shanghai, March 3, 1947, p. 4.

46. *The North-China Daily News*, May 6, 1947, p. 3; Chihyun Chang, *The Chinese Journals of L. K. Little*, vol. 2, p. 66.

47. *The North-China Daily News*, May 10, 1947, p. 1.

48. *The North-China Daily News*, June 1, 1947, p. 1.

49. Sherman Cochran, ed., *The Capitalist Dilemma in China's Communist Revolution* (Ithaca, NY: East Asia Program, Cornell University, 2014).

50. Zheng Huixin, "Zhanhou zhongguo de 'guanban shanghang' (Bureaucratic capitalism after the war), *Minguo dang'an* (Republican archive) 1 (2014), pp. 134–143; Zheng Huixin, "Zhanhou guanban shangxing de xingqi; yi zhongguo fuzhong shiye gongsi de chuangli weili" (The emergence of state enterprises after World War II, the establishment of the Fuzhong Corporation), *Zhongguo jingji shi yanjiu* (Research on Chinese economic history) 4 (2009), pp. 119–122.

51. Zheng Huixin, "Zhanhou zhongguo de 'guanban shanghang,'" pp. 136–139.

52. Central China News English Service, "Report of the Control Yuan on Foreign Exchange," found in Arthur Young Papers, Hoover Institution Archives, box 95, folder "Currency, 1947," October 6, 1947; Zheng Huixin, "Zhanhou zhongguo de 'guanban shanghang,'" p. 135; Wu Guozhen, *Cong Shanghai shichang zhi "Taiwan sheng zhuxi"* (From mayor of Shanghai to chairman of Taiwan province; Shanghai: Shanghai renmin chuban she, 1999), pp. 232–233.

53. Fu Sinian, *The Century Review*, February 22, 1947, Chinese Press Review, American Consulate, Shanghai, March 6, 1947, p. 10.

54. T. V. Soong Papers, Hoover Institution Archives, box 29, folder 2, "China Development Finance Corporation," "Memorandum on the Business Activities of the China Development Finance Corporation," August 31, 1947.

55. T. V. Soong Papers, Hoover Institution Archives, box 29, folder 2, "China Development Finance Corporation," August 31, 1947.

56. Zheng Huixin, *Cong touzi gongsi dao "Guanban shangxing"; Zhongguo jiangshe yin gongsi de chuangli ji qi jingying huodong* (From private investment company to state enterprise: The development and operation of the China Development Finance Corporation; Hong Kong: Zhongwen daxue chuban she, 2001), pp. 223–232.

57. Arthur Young Papers, Hoover Institution Archives, box 113, folder "China Diary," May 11, 1946.

58. Arthur Young Papers, Hoover Institution Archives, box 113, folder "China Diary," October 5, 1947; box 93, folder "Trade control, 1945," clipping from the *Shanghai Evening Post*, April 30, 1946.

59. Zheng Huixin, "Zhanhou zhongguo de 'guanban shanghang,'" pp. 140–141.

60. Zheng Huixin, "Zhanhou zhongguo de 'guanban shanghang,'" pp. 136–140.

61. Zheng Huixin, "Zhanhou zhongguo de 'guanban shanghang,'" p. 141; *Jiang Zhongzheng zongtong dang'an: Shilue gaoben*, vol. 70, pp. 489–490; 511–512.

62. Zheng Huixin, "Zhanhou zhongguo de 'guanban shanghang,'" p. 141.

63. United Kingdom, Foreign Office Files for China, 1918–1980, FO 371/63342, "Currency and Exchange Problems and Financial Situation in China, 1947," folder 4, memo of April 9, 1947, disposal of state-owned enterprise.

64. *The North-China Daily News*, July 10, 1947, p. 6.

65. Arthur Young Papers, Hoover Institution Archives, box 113, folder "China Diary," October 4, 1947.

66. United States Department of State, Office of the Historian, *Foreign Relations of the United States, 1947*, vol. 7, *The Far East*, p. 661.

67. Report contained in the *Shanghai Evening Post and Mercury*, October 18, 1947, p. 6, found in the Arthur N. Young Papers, Hoover Institution Archives, box 93, folder "Trade and Trade Control 1947."

68. Report contained in the *Shanghai Evening Post and Mercury*, p. 6.

69. *The North-China Daily News*, July 26, 1947, p. 1.

70. *The North-China Daily News*, August 14, 1947, p. 1.

71. T. V. Soong Papers, Hoover Institution Archives, box 5, folder 10, telegram from Wellington Koo to T. V. Soong, August 13, 1947, T. V. Soong to Wellington Koo, August 14, 1947.

72. *Dagong bao*, July 15, 1947, Chinese Press Review, US Consulate, Shanghai, July 15, 1947.

73. Bruce Smith Papers, Hoover Institution Archives, box 1, letter of July 24, 1947.

74. Bruce Smith Papers, Hoover Institution Archives, box 1, memo of January 14, 1948.

75. Arthur Young Papers, Hoover Institution Archives, box 93, folder 1, "Trade and Trade Control, 1947," Liddell Brothers memo, 27 November 1947.

76. Edwin Chester Allan Papers, Hoover Institution Archives, box 2, folder "C. P. Ling," "Letter from Allan to wife Dolly from Shanghai, April 8, 1947; letter from Allan to Li Zhi Tang, Shanghai."

77. Albert C. Wedemeyer Papers, Hoover Institution Archives, box 92, folder "Claire Chennault," letter of July 27, 1947.

78. Albert C. Wedemeyer Papers, Hoover Institution Archives, box 92, folder "Claire Chennault," letter of July 27, 1947.

79. Albert C. Wedemeyer Papers, Hoovers Institution Archives, box 92, folder "Chiang Kai-shek and Mei-ling Soong Chiang," memo to the Generalissimo from Alfred Wedemeyer, August 20, 1947.

80. Arthur Young Papers, Hoover Institution Archives, box 94, folder "U.S. aid post-war."

81. Arthur Young Papers, Hoover Institution Archives, box 96, folder "Unauthorized imports."

82. C. X. George Wei, *Sino-American Economic Relations, 1944–1949* (Westport, CT: Greenwood Press, 1997), pp. 160–163.

83. Arthur Young Papers, Hoover Institution Archives, box 94, folder "U.S. aid postwar"; C. X. George Wei, *Sino-American Economic Relations*, pp. 160–163.

84. Lloyd E. Eastman, "Nationalist China during the Nanking Decade, 1927–1937," in Lloyd E. Eastman, Jerome Ch'en, Suzanne Pepper, and Lyman P. Van Slyke, eds., *The Nationalist Era in China, 1927–1949* (Cambridge: Cambridge University Press, 1991), pp. 115–176 (pp. 120–121).

85. Westad, *Decisive Encounters*, p. 75.

86. Ho Lien, "The Reminiscences of Ho Lien (Franklin L. Ho)," Chinese Oral History Project, East Asian Institute of Columbia University, 1975, pp. 358–360.

87. *Jiang Zhongzheng zongtong dang'an: Shilue gaoben*, 2003 and continuing; for a discussion of this source see Grace C. Huang, "Creating a Public Face for Posterity: The Making of Chiang Kai-shek's Shilue Manuscripts," *Modern China* 36, no. 6 (2010), pp. 617–643. The twentieth wedding anniversary of Chiang and Soong Meiling was in December 1947. Madame Chiang's fiftieth birthday was on March 22, 1948. See *Jiang Zhongzheng zongtong dang'an: Shilue gaoben*, vol 71, p. 540; vol. 73, p. 429.

88. *Jiang Zhongzheng zongtong dang'an: Shilue gaoben*, vol. 69, vol. 70, *passim*; vol. 71, p. 345.

89. *Jiang Zhongzheng zongtong dang'an: Shilue gaoben*, vol. 69, pp. 28, 131, 132, 213.

90. *Jiang Zhongzheng zongtong dang'an: Shilue gaoben*, vol. 70, pp. 183, 225; Yao Songling, "Jingdao Zhang gongquan xiansheng (In memory of Zhang Jia'ao), *Zhuanji wenxue* (Biographical literature) 211 (December 1979), pp. 64–68 (p. 67).

91. *Jiang Zhongzheng zongtong dang'an: Shilue gaoben*, vol. 70, pp. 489–490; 553.

92. *The North-China Daily News*, July 20, 1947, p. 9.

93. *The China Weekly Review*, August 23, 1947, p. 344.

94. Philip Thai, *China's War on Smuggling: Law, Economic Life, and the Making of the Modern State, 1842–1965* (New York: Columbia University Press, 2018), p. 211.

95. Thai, *China's War on Smuggling*, p. 212.

96. *Dagong bao*, June 24, 1947, Chinese Press Review, US Consulate, Shanghai, June 24, 1947.

97. King, *The Hongkong Bank in the Period of Development and Nationalism*, vol. 4, p. 156.

98. *The North-China Daily News*, August 19, 1947, p. 1; *Dagong bao*, August 23, 1947, Chinese Press Review, US Consulate, Shanghai, August 23, 1947, p. 3.

99. Arthur Young Papers, Hoover Institution Archives, box 95, folder "Foreign Exchange 8/17/47."

100. Arthur Young Papers, Hoover Institution Archives, box 94, folder 1, "U.S. aid post-war," secret memo of November 27, 1947; box 95, folder "Currency 1947," letter from

H. J. Shen, Cyril Rogers, and Arthur Young to Chen Guangfu in Nanjing, November 25, 1947; memo by Arthur Young, October 3, 1947.

101. Arthur Young Papers, Hoover Institution Archives, box 95, folder "Currency, 1947."

102. Arthur Young Papers, Hoover Institution Archives, box 94, folder "U.S. aid postwar."

103. Arthur Young Papers, Hoover Institution Archives, box 95, folder "Currency, 1947." No date is given on the memo, but it would have dated from 1947.

104. *Shen bao*, October 20, 1947, Chinese Press Review, US Consulate, Shanghai, October 20, 1947.

105. *Shen bao*, October 25, 1947, Chinese Press Review, US Consulate, Shanghai, October 25, 1947.

106. *Dagong bao*, editorial, November 10, 1947, Chinese Press Review, US Consulate, Shanghai, November 10, 1947.

107. *Jiang Zhongzheng zongtong dang'an: Shilue gaoben*, vol. 71, pp. 350–530, *passim*.

108. *Jiang Zhongzheng zongtong dang'an: Shilue gaoben*, vol. 71, pp. 580, 584, 616, 627, 651–652, 655, 711.

109. Westad, *Decisive Encounters*, p. 168.

CHAPTER 6 1948: THE COLLAPSE OF FABI AND THE GOLD YUAN REFORM DISASTER

1. United Kingdom, Foreign Office Files for China, 1918–1980, Adam Mathew, Archives Direct, FO 371/69559, "Shipping in China," folder 2, 1948, secret report of March 26, 1948.

2. *Xinwen bao*, January 13, 1948, *Dagong bao*, January 15, 1948, Chinese Press Review, US Consulate, Shanghai, January 15, 1948, pp. 2–3.

3. Chihyun Chang, ed., *The Chinese Journals of L. K. Little, 1943–1954: An Eyewitness Account of War and Revolution*, vol. 2, *The Last Foreign Inspector General, 1946–1949* (London: Routledge, 2018), vol. 2, pp. 90–95.

4. United Kingdom, Foreign Office Files for China, 1918–1980, Adam Mathew, Archives Direct, FO 371/69564, "Currency and Exchange Problems and Financial Structure in China," folder 1, 1948.

5. United Kingdom, Foreign Office Files for China, 1918–1980, Adam Mathew, Archives Direct, FO 371/69566, "Currency and Exchange Problems and Financial Structure in China," folder 13, 1948.

6. United Kingdom, Foreign Office Files for China, 1918–1980, Adam Mathew, Archives Direct, FO 371/69567, "Currency and Exchange Problems and Financial Structure in China," folder 14, 1948.

7. *China Weekly Review*, July 10, 1048, p. 173; *Jiang Zhongzheng zongtong dang'an: Shilue gaoben* (Taibei: Guoshi guan, 2013), vol. 75, pp. 275, 308.

8. *China Weekly Review*, July 10, 1948, July 17, 1948, August 7, 1948, August 21, 1948, cover price.

9. T. V. Soong Papers, Hoover Institution Archives, box 25, folder 10, China, foreign exchange, "Notes on the Exchange Certificate System," June 2, 1948.

10. *Dagong bao*, July 20, 1948, Chinese Press Review, US Consulate, Shanghai, July 20, 1948, p. 1.

11. *Xinwen bao*, March 8, 1948, Chinese Press Review, US Consulate, Shanghai, March 8, 1948, p. 1; Chihyun Chang, *The Chinese Journals of L. K. Little*, vol. 2, p. 97.

12. *Xinwen bao*, April 9, 1948, *Shen bao*, April 9, 1948, both found in Chinese Press Review, US Consulate, Shanghai, April 9, 1948, p. 1.

13. *Dagong bao*, April 20, 1948, Chinese Press Review, US Consulate, Shanghai, April 20, 1948, p. 10.

14. *Shen bao*, January 20, 1948, Chinese Press Review, US Consulate, Shanghai, January 20, 1948, p. 1; Chang Kia-ngau, *The Inflationary Spiral: The Experience in China, 1939–1950* (Cambridge, MA: MIT Press, 1958), p. 82.

15. Chao Hsiang-ke and Lin Hsiao-ting, "Beyond the Carrot and the Stick: The Political Economy of US Military Aid to China, 1945–1951," *Journal of Modern Chinese History* 5, no. 2 (2011), pp. 199–216 (p. 211); Odd Arne Westad, *Decisive Encounters: The Chinese Civil War, 1946–1950* (Stanford, CA: Stanford University Press, 2003), p. 161.

16. *Shen bao*, May 12, 1948, Chinese Press Review, US Consulate, Shanghai, May 12, 1948, p. 1.

17. *Shidai gonglun* (Contemporary public opinion) 5, no. 101 (May 15, 1948), p. 12.

18. *China Weekly Review*, July 3, 1948, p. 150. The cover price for this issue was 300,000 yuan.

19. Wu Xiangxiang, "Wang Yunwu yu jinyuan quan de faxing" (Wang Yunwu and the issuance of the gold yuan notes), *Zhuanji wenxue* (Biographical literature) 213 (February 1980), pp. 44–50 (p. 44); Heng Dafeng, *Wang Yunwu pingzhuan* (A critical biography of Wang Yunwu; Shanghai: Shanghai shudian chuban she, 1999), pp. 310–321.

20. *Xinwen bao*, June 16, 1948, Chinese Press Review, US Consulate, Shanghai, June 16, 1948, p. 1.

21. Chihyun Chang, *The Chinese Journals of L. K. Little*, vol. 2, p. 113.

22. *Xinwen bao*, June 27, 1948, Chinese Press Review, US Consulate, Shanghai, June 27, 1948.

23. *Shen bao*, June 25, 1948, Chinese Press Review, US Consulate, Shanghai, June 25, 1948, p. 8.

24. *Zhongyang ribao*, June 30, 1948, Chinese Press Review, US Consulate, Shanghai, June 30, 1948,

25. *Foreign Relations of the United States, 1948*, vol. 8, *The Far East* (1973), p. 377; Lloyd E. Eastman, *Seeds of Destruction: Nationalist China in War and Revolution, 1937–1949* (Stanford, CA: Stanford University Press, 1984), pp. 177–178; Chihyun Chang, *The Chinese Journals of L. K. Little*, vol. 2, p. 116.

26. Wu Xiangxiang, "Wang Yunwu yu jinyuan quan de faxing," p. 46.

27. Cited in *Qunzhong* (The masses), Hong Kong, December 7, 1947, China Press Review, US Consulate, Shanghai, January 7, 1948, pp. 8–9.

28. T. V. Soong Papers, Hoover Institution Archives, box 3, folder 11, "Chinese National Relief and Rehabilitation Administration, 1947–48" reveals extensive plans for development projects. For instance, in December 1947, Soong had directed the Fishery Rehabilitation Administration to develop a plan for reviving the fishing industry and

constructing piers in Swatow (Shantou). See also C. X. George Wei, *Sino-American Economic Relations, 1944–1949* (Westport, CT: Greenwood Press, 1997), pp. 154–155.

29. *Zaisheng* (The national renaissance) 184 (November 4, 1947), p. 2, Chinese Press Review, US Consulate, Shanghai, October 4, 1947, p. 8.

30. *Dagong bao*, June 24, 1948, Chinese Press Review, US Consulate, Shanghai, June 24, 1948, p. 6.

31. *Heping ribao*, Shanghai, October 22, 1948, Chinese Press Review, US Consulate, October 22, 1948, p. 5.

32. *The Century Critique Weekly*, Nanjing, 2, no. 14 (October 4, 1947), Chinese Press Review, US Consulate, Shanghai, p. 8.

33. T. V. Soong Papers, Hoover Institution Archives, box 8, folder 19, correspondence, Ralph Stevenson.

34. Chou Shun-hsin, *The Chinese Inflation, 1937–1949* (New York: Columbia University Press, 1963), p. 150.

35. United Kingdom, Foreign Office Files for China, 1918–1980, Adam Mathew, Archives Direct, FO 371/69569, "Currency and Exchange Problems and Financial Structure in China," folder 16, September 27, 1948.

36. T. V. Soong Papers, Hoover Institution Archives, box 27, folder 6, "China – National Resources Commission," "Ammonium Sulfate Plant for Canton, April 12, 1948."

37. T. V. Soong Papers, Hoover Institution Archives, box 29, folder 19, "Hainan Island," letters, April 15, 1948, April 19, 1948.

38. T. V. Soong Papers, Hoover Institution Archives, box 8, folder 20, "Leighton Stuart," letter of August 16, 1948, from Stuart in Nanjing to Soong in Guangzhou.

39. T. V. Soong Papers, Hoover Institution Archives, box 34, folder 31, "Correspondences, F. Chang," letter of June 28, 1948, from the Customs Building, Shanghai to Soong in Guangzhou.

40. Frank H. H. King, *The Hongkong Bank in the Period of Development and Nationalism: From Regional Bank to Multinational Group*, vol. 4 of *The History of the Hongkong and Shanghai Banking Corporation* (Cambridge: Cambridge University Press, 1991), p. 153.

41. Eastman, *Seeds of Destruction*, p. 177; Tso Shun-sheng, "The Reminiscences of Tso Shun-sheng," Chinese Oral History Project, East Asian Institute of Columbia University, 1975, p. 262.

42. Chou Shun-hsin, *The Chinese Inflation, 1937–1949*, p. 25.

43. Eastman, *Seeds of Destruction*, p. 185.

44. *Jiang Zhongzheng zongtong dang'an: Shilue gaoben*, vol. 75, pp. 287–603, *passim*. Meetings between Chiang Kai-shek and Jiang Jingguo occurred on June 28, 1948, July 2, July 11, July 17, July 20, July 22, July 23, July 25, July 26, July 28, and July 31; vol. 76, August 3, p. 41. These meetings did not focus solely on the economic situation. Many were labeled as training meetings where the elder Chiang instructed his son on Chinese culture and values.

45. Wu Guozhen, *Cong Shanghai shichang zhi "Taiwan sheng zhuxi"* (From mayor of Shanghai to chairman of Taiwan province; Shanghai: Shanghai renmin chuban she, 1999), p. 54; Wang Chaoguang, *Zhongguo mingyun de juezhan, 1945–1949* (The decisive war for

China's fate, 1945–1949), vol. 10, p. 312; Wang Feng, *Jiang Jieshi fuzi 1949 weiji dang'an* (Archives on the crisis of 1949: Chiang Kai-shek, father and son; Taibei: Shangzhou chuban she, 2008), pp. 94–95.

46. *Dagong bao*, August 21, 1948, Chinese Press Review, US Consulate, Shanghai, August 21–23, 1948, p. 1; Wang Yunwu, *1948 dafeng dalang: Wang Yunwu congzheng huiyi lu* (The great wind and waves of 1948: Wang Yunwu's record of his memories in government; Taipei: Taiwan shangwu, 2010), pp. 148–50.

47. *Shen bao*, August 23, 1948, Chinese Press Review, US Consulate, Shanghai, August 21–23, 1948, p. 3.

48. Quoted in Wu Xiangxiang, "Wang Yunwu yu jinyuan quan de faxing," p. 48.

49. *Shidai gonglun* 5, no. 98 (February 15, 1948), pp. 19–20.

50. Ho Lien, "The Reminiscences of Ho Lien (Franklin L. Ho), Chinese Oral History Project, East Asian Institute of Columbia University, 1975, p. 426.

51. Wu Guozhen, *Cong Shanghai shichang*, p. 55.

52. United Kingdom, Foreign Office Files for China, 1918–1980, Adam Mathew, Archives Direct, FO 371/69568, "Currency and Exchange Problems and Financial Structure in China," folder 15, confidential report, September 25, 1948.

53. *Foreign Relations of the United States: Diplomatic Papers, 1948*, vol, 8, *The Far East, China* (1973), p. 405; Eastman, *Seeds of Destruction*, p. 199.

54. Wang Yunwu, *1948 dafeng dalang*, pp. 129–131.

55. Chou Shun-hsin, *The Chinese Inflation, 1937–1949*, pp. 144–147.

56. *Dagong bao*, September 8, 1948, Chinese Press Review, US Consulate in Shanghai, September 8, 1948, p. 9.

57. Eastman, *Seeds of Destruction*, pp. 186–187.

58. Chou Shun-hsin, *The Chinese Inflation*, p. 149.

59. *Dagong bao*, September 15, 1948, Chinese Press Review, US Consulate, Shanghai, September 15, 1948.

60. *Shang bao*, August 20, 1948, Chinese Press Review, US Consulate, Shanghai, August 20, 1948, p. 4.

61. Wang Yunwu. *1948 dafeng dalang*, pp. 202–206. Price controls were not as effective outside of Nanjing and Shanghai, especially in the southwest.

62. Chang Kia-ngau, *The Inflationary Spiral*, p. 80.

63. Wu Guozheng, *Cong Shanghai shichang*, pp. 65–66; Jay Taylor, *The Generalissimo's Son: Chiang Ching-kuo and the Revolutions in China and Taiwan* (Cambridge, MA: Harvard University Press, 2000), pp. 154–155; Wang Feng, *Jiang Jieshi fuzi 1949 weiji dang'an*, pp. 94–98; *Fabi jinyuan quan yu huangjin fengchao* (Legal tender, the gold yuan note, and the gold unrest; Beijing: Wenshi ziliao chuban she, 1985), p. 88.

64. Eastman, *Seeds of Destruction*, p. 184; Thomas A. Marks, *Counterrevolution in China: Wang Sheng and the Kuomintang* (London: Frank Cass, 1998), pp. 103–106, 109.

65. A. Doak Barnett, *China on the Eve of Communist Takeover* (London: Thames & Hudson, 1963), p. 73.

66. Eastman, *Seeds of Destruction*, pp. 182–83.

67. Shou Chongyi, "Jiang Jingguo Shanghai 'Daohu' ji" (A record of Jiang Jingguo striking big tigers in Shanghai), in *Fabi jinyuan quan yu huangjin fengchao* (Legal tender, the gold yuan notes, and the gold unrest; Beijing: Wenshi ziliao chuban she, 1985), p. 79; Wu Xiangxiang, "Wang Yunwu yu jinyuan quan," p. 48.

68. Eastman, *Seeds of Destruction*, p. 183.

69. *Shen bao*, September 13, 1948, Chinese Press Review, US Consulate, Shanghai, September 11–13, 1948, p. 1; *Dagong bao*, September 14, 1948, Chinese Press Review, US Consulate, Shanghai, September 14, 1948, p. 8; *Fabi jinyuan quan yu huangjin fengchao*, pp. 70–71.

70. Wang Chaoguang, *Zhongguo mingyun de juezhan: 1945–1949*, vol. 10, pp. 313–317; Wang Feng, *Jiang Jieshi fuzi 1949*, p. 113.

71. Wu Guozhen, *Cong Shanghai shichang*, pp. 64–65.

72. Wu Guozhen, *Cong Shanghai shichang*, pp. 58–59; *Xinwen tiandi*, October 16, 1948, Chinese Press Review, US Consulate, Shanghai, October 20, 1948, p. 10.

73. Juanjuan Peng, *The Yudahua Business Group in China's Early Industrialization* (Lanham, MD: Lexington Books, 2020), p. 107.

74. Ji Zhaojin, *A History of Modern Shanghai Banking: The Rise and Decline of China's Finance Capitalism* (Armonk, NY: M. E. Sharpe, 2003), p. 230; Wang Feng, *Jiang Jieshi fuzi 1949*, p. 103, Ho Lien, "The Reminiscences of Ho Lien," p. 428.

75. Taylor, *The Generalissimo's Son*, p. 155; Wang Feng, *Jiang Jieshi fuzi*, pp. 113–120.

76. United Kingdom, Foreign Office Files for China, 1918–1980, Adam Mathew, Archives Direct, FO 371/69566, "Currency and Exchange Problems, 1948," folder 16, October 13, 1948; Eastman, *Seeds of Destruction*, pp. 186–187; Yang Peixin, *Jiu Zhongguo de tonghuo pengzhang*, p. 106; Marks, *Counterrevolution in China*, pp. 108–109.

77. United Kingdom, Foreign Office Files for China, 1918–1980, Adam Mathew, Archives Direct, FO371/6956, "Currency and Exchange Problems, 1948," folder 16, October 13, 1948; Taylor, *The Generalissimo's Son*, p. 160; Marks, *Counterrevolution in China*, p. 109.

78. Wang Feng, *Jiang Jieshi fuzi, 1949*, pp. 116–120; Ho Lien, "The Reminiscences Ho Lien (Franklin L. Ho)," pp. 435–536; Tso, Shun-sheng, "The Reminiscences of Tso Shun-sheng," Chinese Oral History Project, East Asian Institute of Columbia University, 1975, pp. 261–262.

79. *Jiang Zhongzheng zongtong dang'an: Shilue gaoben*, vol. 77, pp. 49, 50, 55, 59, 60.

80. Wu Guozhen, *Cong Shanghai shichang*, pp. 69–71; Wang Chaoguang, *Zhongguo mingyun de juezhan*, vol. 10, pp. 317–18; Zheng Huixin, "Zhanhou zhongguo de 'guanban shanghang'" (Bureaucratic capitalism after the war), *Minguo dang'an* (Republican archives) 1 (2014), pp. 134–143 (p. 142); Wang Jeng, *Jiang Jieshi fuzi*, p. 104.

81. Zheng Huixin, "Zhanhou zhongguo de 'guanban shanghang,'" p. 142.

82. Wang Feng, *Jiang Jieshi fuzi*, p. 122.

83. *Dongnan ribao*, November 3, 1948, Chinese Press Review, US Consulate, Shanghai, November 3, 1948, p. 7.

84. Taylor, *The Generalissimo's Son*, p. 161; Wang Feng, *Jiang Jieshi fuzi*, pp. 266, 276.

85. *Zhongyang ribao*, September 9, 1948, Chinese Press Review, US Consulate, Shanghai, September 9, 1948.

86. The China Democratic League was part of the so-called "Third Force." *Shidai piping* 106 (October 15, 1948), pp. 12–14.

87. *Shang bao*, September 13, 1948, Chinese Press Review, US Consulate, Shanghai, September 11–13, 1948, pp. 2–3.

88. *Shang bao*, September 21, 1948, Chinese Press Review, US Consulate, Shanghai, September 21, 1948, p. 4.

89. *Shishi xin bao*, September 21, 1948, Chinese Press Review, US Consulate, Shanghai, September 21, 1948, p. 2.

90. Eastman, *Seeds of Destruction*, pp. 190–191.

91. *China Weekly Review*, October 30, 1948, p. 1; Shen Yunlong, "Dui jinyuan quan an yingjin yibu zhuizong yanjiu" (Advancing research on the matter of the gold yuan case), *Zhuanji wenxue* 214 (March 1980), pp. 40–42 (p. 41); Yang Peixin, *Jiu Zhongguo de tonghuo pengzhang*, p. 107.

92. *Dagong bao*, October 7, 1948, Chinese Press Review, US Consulate, Shanghai, October 7, 1948, p. 2.

93. Diary quoted in Wu Xiangxiang, "Wang Yunyu yu jinyuan quan," pp. 48–49; *Dagong bao*, October 15, 1948, Chinese Press Review, US Consulate, Shanghai, October 15, 1948, p. 10.

94. *Zhongyang ribao*, October 29, 1948, Chinese Press Review, US Consulate, Shanghai, October 20, 1948, p. 1.

95. Chang Kia-ngau, *The Inflationary Spiral*, pp. 80–81; Barnett, *China on the Eve*, pp. 71–72; *Dagong bao*, September 24, 1948, Chinese Press Review, US Consulate, Shanghai, September 24, 1948, p. 1.

96. *Shang bao*, October 6, 1948, Chinese Press Review, US Consulate, Shanghai, October 6, 1948, p. 4.

97. Wu Xiangxiang, "Wang Yunwu yu jinyuan quan," p. 49.

98. *Dagong bao*, October 28, 1948, Chinese Press Review, US Consulate, Shanghai, October 28, 1948, p. 1.

99. *Dagong bao*, October 28, 1948, Chinese Press Review, US Consulate, Shanghai, October 28, 1948, pp. 1–2.

100. Diary quoted in Wu Xiangxiang, "Wang Yunwu jinyuan quan," p. 49; Marks, *Counterrevolution in China*, p. 110.

101. *Foreign Relations of the United States: Diplomatic Papers, 1948*, vol. 8; *The Far East*, p. 428; United Kingdom. Foreign Office Files for China, 1918–1980, Adam Mathew, Archives Direct, FO 371/69569, "Currency and Exchange Problems," folder 16, Nanjing Embassy to the British Foreign Office in London, November 2, 1948; Wu Jingping, "Jinyuan quan zhengce de zai yanjiu" (On the study of the gold yuan policy), *Minguo dang'an* (Republican archives) 1 (2004), pp. 99–110 (pp. 107–108); Eastman, *Seeds of Destruction*, pp. 192–193; Yang Peixin, *Jiu Zhongguo de tonghuo pengzhang*, p. 108; *Jiang Zhongzheng zongtong dang'an: Shilue gao ben*, vol. 77, pp. 325, 333, 338, 354, 362, 419.

102. Eastman, *Seeds of Destruction*, pp. 193–94.

103. Chihyun Chang, *The Chinese Journals of L. K. Little*, vol. 2, p. 135.

104. Zhongguo renmin yinhang zonghang canshi shi, ed., *Zhonghua minguo huobi shi ziliao* (Historical materials on currency in the Republic of China; Shanghai: Shanghai renmin chuban she, 1991), vol. 2, p. 595.

105. Eastman, *Seeds of Destruction*, pp. 197–99.

106. *Shen bao*, November 9, 1948, Chinese Press Review, US Consulate, Shanghai, November 9, 1948, p. 3.

107. British Consulate in Shanghai to the Foreign Office, London, November 9, 1948, FO 371/69569, "Currency and Exchange Problems, 1948," folder 16.

108. *Dagong bao*, November 10, 1948, Chinese Press Review, US Consulate, Shanghai, November 10, 1948, p. 1.

109. Chang Kia-ngau, *The Inflationary Spiral*, p. 84; Huang Yuanbin, "Jinyuan quan de faxing he tade bengkui" (The introduction of the gold yuan notes and their collapse), in *Fabi jinyuan yuan yu huangjin fengchao* (Legal tender, the gold yuan notes, and the gold unrest; Beijing: Wenshi ziliao chuban she, 1985), pp. 51–62 (p. 61); British Embassy in Nanjing to the Foreign Office, London, November 5, 1948, FO 371/69569, "Currency and Exchange Problems, 1948," folder 16.

110. *China Weekly Review*, July 9, 1949, p. 124.

111. *Foreign Relations of the United States: Diplomatic Papers, 1948*, vol. 8; *The Far East*, p. 407.

112. *Foreign Relations of the United States*, vol. 8; *The Far East*, p. 428.

113. United Kingdom, Foreign Office Files for China, 1918–1980, Adam Mathew, Archives Direct, FO 371/69569, "Currency and Exchange Problems and Financial Structure in China," folder 16, telegram to London on October 19, 1948, reply October 28, 1948.

114. Paul Frillman Papers, Hoover Institution Archives, box 1, folder "Correspondence," L. Iverson from Fuzhou, December 1, 1948.

115. Wang Feng, *Jiang Jieshi fuzi 1949 weiji*, p. 123.

116. Wu Guozheng, *Cong Shanghai shichang*, pp. 67–68.

117. *Dagong bao*, December 10, 1948, Chinese Press Review, US Consulate, Shanghai, December 10, 1948, p. 3; Eastman, *Seeds of Destruction*, pp. 193–195.

118. Shou Chongyi, "Wang Yunwu yu jin yuan quan," p. 65; Wu Jingping, "Jinyuan quan zhengce de zai yanjiu," p. 108.

119. United Kingdom, Foreign Office Files for China, 1918–1980, Adam Mathew, Archives Direct, Commercial Report from the British Consulate in Shanghai, China, Reports of December 1948 and January 1949, FO 371/75840, "Economic Situation in China, Economics Reports, November 1948 to July 1949," folder 1.

120. Quoted in Eastman, *Seeds of Destruction*, p. 196.

121. United States, Department of State, Intelligence Section, "Economic Development in China, 1948," issued December 14, 1948, p. 1.

122. *Xinwen tiandi* 50 (October 16, 1948), Chinese Press Review, US Consulate, Shanghai, October 20, 1948, p. 11.

123. United States, Department of State, Intelligence Section, "Economic Development in China, 1948," issued December 14, 1948, p. 1.

124. United States, Department of State, Intelligence Section, "Economic Development in China, 1948," issued December 14, 1948, p. 1.

125. *Jiang Zhongzheng zongtong dang'an: Shilue gaoben*, vols. 69–74, *passim.*

126. *Jiang Zhongzheng zongtong dang'an: Shilue gaoben*, vol. 71, pp. 188; 208; 213; 289.

127. *Jiang Zhongzheng zongtong dang'an: Shilue gaoben*, vols. 72–73, *passim*, vol. 74, pp. 195, 377.

128. *Jiang Zhongzheng zongtong dang'an: Shilue gaoben*, vol. 74, pp. 59, 242, 247; vol. 75, p. 119.

129. *Jiang Zhongzheng zongtong dang'an: Shilue gaoben*, vol. 75, pp. 299, 388, 462, 477, 482, 595, 603; vol. 76, pp. 122, 123, 127, 181, 220.

130. *Jiang Zhongzheng zongtong dang'an: Shilue gaoben*, vol. 76, pp. 400, 419, 478; vol. 77, p. 59, 60, 147, 176, 443.

131. *Jiang Zhongzheng zongtong dang'an: Shilue gaoben*, vol. 77, pp. 357, 469, 451, 475, 506; Ho Lien, "The Reminiscences of Ho Lien, p, 433.

132. *Xinwen bao*, December 30, 1948, Chinese Press Review, US Consulate, Shanghai, December 30, 1948, p. 1.

133. British Embassy in Nanjing to Foreign Office, London, 13, February 1949; British Consulate in Shanghai to the Foreign Office, London, February 18, 1949, FO 371/75844, "Currency Exchange Problems, December 1948 to April 1949," folder 1.

134. Chihyun Chang, *The Chinese Journals of L. K. Little*, vol. 2, pp. 154–155.

135. Wu Jingping, "Jinyuan quan zhengce de zai yanjiu," pp. 109–110.

136. *Dagong bao*, March 8, 1949, Chinese Press Review, US Consulate, Shanghai, March 8, 1949, p. 4, March 10, 1949, p. 1.

137. *Jiefang ribao*, May 28, 1949, Chinese Press Review, US Consulate, Shanghai, May 28, 1949, p. 10.

138. *The China Daily Tribune*, Shanghai, May 16, 1949, Chinese Press Review, US Consulate, Shanghai, May 19, 1949, p. 10.

139. T. V. Soong Papers, Hoover Institution Archives, box 8, folder 1, *The Saturday Evening Post.*

140. T. V. Soong Papers, Hoover Institution Archives, box 61, folder 31, Madame Chiang Kai-shek, personal letters. See especially letters of August 14, 1950, July 14, 1956, and July 2, 1962. Madame Chiang (May) refers to Chiang Kai-shek as "Kai" in these letters. In terms of Chiang Kai-shek's treatment, the plan was to have an internal specialist come to Taiwan as a visiting professor at a medical school in Taiwan. The specialist's actual duties would primarily be to provide medical treatment for Chiang.

141. T. V. Soong Papers, Hoover Institution Archives, box 62, folder 19, "Personal financial ledger of T. V. Soong, 1965."

142. T. V. Soong Papers, Hoover Institution Archives, box 62, folder 16, "Will and lists of personal financial assets," decree settling final account of the executor, filed September 4, 1975, surrogate court of county of New York.

143. T. V. Soong Papers, Hoover Institution Archives, box 61, folder 31, Madame Chiang Kai-shek, letter of February 14, 1951.

144. Jung Chang, *Big Sister, Little Sister, Red Sister: Three Women at the Heart of Twentieth-Century China* (New York: Alfred A. Knopf, 2019), p. 304.

145. T. V. Soong Papers, Hoover Institution Archives, box 61, folder 31, Madame Chiang Kai-shek, personal letters. See especially letters of July 2, 1962, November 5, 1962, December 10, 1962, October 7, 1963, and letter from T. V. Soong to Madame Chiang Kai-shek, September 1, 1962.

146. T. V. Soong Papers, Hoover Institution Archives, box 62, folder 22, "Youngman letters," January 22, 1984.

147. Sterling Seagrave, *The Soong Dynasty* (New York: Harper and Row, 1985), p. 416. For a discussion of this issue, see Dai Hongchao, "Song Ziwen de siren caichan yu shifou gong wubi zhi Pingxi" (An examination of whether or not T. V. Soong's private property involved corruption), in Wu Jingping, ed., *Song Ziwen shengping yu ziliao wenxian yanjiu* (T. V. Soong: Personal wartime archive; Shanghai: Fudan daxue chuban she, 2010), pp. 393–399 (pp. 393–396).

148. Seagrave, *The Soong Dynasty*, p. 453.

149. T. V. Soong Papers, Hoover Institution Archives, box 62, folder 22, "Youngman letters," letter to Sterling Seagrave, March 18, 1985, sent care of Harper and Row.

150. T. V. Soong Papers, Hoover Institution Archives, box 62, folder 22, "Youngman letters," letter of March 18, 1985.

151. T. V. Soong Papers, Hoover Institution Archives, box 62, folder 22, "Youngman letters," Soong Mei-ling to Michael Feng, July 7, 1986; Donald G. Gillin, *Falsifying China's History: The Case of Sterling Seagrave's The Soong Dynasty* (Stanford, CA: Hoover Institution, 1986).

152. Albert Wedemeyer Papers, Hoover Institution Archives, box 46, folder 6, letters, Ling-kai (David) Kung.

153. Albert Wedemeyer Papers, Hoover Institution Archives, box 46, folder 6, letters, Ling-kai (David) Kung; *Independent,* April 21, 1962, p. 11.

154. Albert Wedemeyer Papers, Hoover Institution Archives, box 46, folder 6, letters, Ling-kai (David) Kung; *Houston Business Journal,* May 11, 2003, by Jennifer Dawson, "Bizarre Bomb Shelter Becoming Data Center."

155. Chihyun Chang, *The Chinese Journals of L. K. Little,* vol. 2, p. 50.

156. T. V. Soong Papers, Hoover Institution Archives, box 64, folder 7, letter from T. V. Soong to Soong Mei-ling, March 22, 1965. Also box 64, folder 31. See also Laura Tyson Li, *Madame Chiang Kai-shek: China's Eternal First Lady* (New York: Atlantic Monthly Press, 2006), pp. 399–400.

157. A recent is example is the commercial publication by Jung Chang, *Big Sister, Little Sister, Red Sister* (2019).

CONCLUSION

1. Lloyd E. Eastman, *Seeds of Destruction: Nationalist China in War and Revolution, 1937–1949* (Stanford, CA: Stanford University Press, 1984), pp. 216–217. Since Eastman wrote those words, a considerable literature has developed challenging this thesis or at least parts of it. See, for example, Julia Strauss, *Strong Institutions in Weak Polities: State Building in Republican China, 1927–1940* (Oxford: Oxford University Press, 1998).

2. Eastman, *Seeds of Destruction*, p. 221.

3. Stephen R. MacKinnon, *Wuhan, 1938: War, Refugees, and the Making of Modern China* (Berkeley: University of California Press, 2008).

4. Lloyd E. Eastman, *The Abortive Revolution: China under Nationalist Rule, 1927–1937* (Cambridge, MA: Harvard University Press, 1947), p. 10.

5. Yun Xia, *Down with Traitors: Justice and Nationalism in Wartime China* (Seattle: University of Washington Press, 2017), p. 100.

6. Parks M. Coble, *The Shanghai Capitalists and the Nationalist Government, 1927–1937* (Cambridge, MA: Harvard East Asian Monographs, 1986), pp. 129–132.

Bibliography

Allan, Edwin Chester. Papers. Hoover Institution on War, Revolution, and Peace, Stanford University, Archives.

Alman, Norman. Papers. Hoover Institution on War, Revolution, and Peace, Stanford University, Archives.

Amerasia: A Review of America and the Far East. New York, 1946–1947.

Barnett, A. Doak. *China on the Eve of Communist Takeover.* London: Thames & Hudson, 1963.

Barnett, Robert W. *Economic Shanghai: Hostage to Politics, 1937–1941.* New York: Institute of Pacific Relations, 1941.

Beijing Review. Beijing.

Bernstein, Richard. *China 1945: Mao's Revolution and America's Fateful Choice.* New York: Alfred A. Knopf, 2014.

Blum, John Morton. *From the Morgenthau Diaries: Years of Crisis, 1928–1938.* Boston: Houghton Mifflin, 1959.

Roosevelt and Morgenthau: A Revision and Condensation from the Morgenthau Diaries. Boston: Houghton Mifflin, 1970.

Boorman, Howard L., ed. *Biographical Dictionary of Republican China.* 4 vols. New York: Columbia University Press, 1970.

Brooks, Charlotte. *American Exodus: Second-Generation Chinese Americans in China, 1901–1949.* Oakland: University of California Press, 2019.

Cao Juren. *Caifang waiji, caifang erji* (A record of covering the news, a second record of covering the news). Beijing: Sanlian shudian, 2007.

Chang, Chihyun, ed. *The Chinese Journals of L. K. Little, 1943–1954: An Eyewitness Account of War and Revolution;* vol. 1, *The Wartime Inspector General, 1943–1945;* vol. 2, *The Last Foreign Inspector General, 1946–1949.* London: Routledge, 2018.

Government, Imperialism and Nationalism in China: The Maritime Customs Service and Its Chinese Staff. London: Routledge, 2013.

Chang, Jung. *Big Sister, Little Sister, Red Sister: Three Women at the Heart of Twentieth-Century China.* New York: Alfred A. Knopf, 2019.

Chang Kia-ngau [Zhang Jia'ao]. *The Inflationary Spiral: The Experience in China, 1939–1950.* Cambridge: MIT Press, 1958.

Chao Hsiang-ke and Lin Hsiao-ting, "Beyond the Carrot and the Stick: The Political Economy of US Military Aid to China, 1945–1951," *Journal of Modern Chinese History,* vol. 5, no. 2, 2011, pp. 199–216.

Chao Kang. *The Development of Cotton Textile Production in China.* Cambridge: Harvard East Asian Monographs, 1977.

Chen Boda. *Renmin gongdi Jiang Jieshi* (The enemy of the people, Chiang Kai-shek). Beijing: Renmin chuban she, 1954.

Zhongguo sida jiazu (China's four great families). Hong Kong: Changjiang, 1947.

Chen Feng. *Sida jiazu miwen* (Secrets of the four great families). Beijing: Tuanjie chuban she, 2008.

Chen Gengya. "Kong Xiangxi jingtun meijin gongzhai de neimu zhenxiang" (The true inside story of H. H. Kung devouring the American dollar loan), *Wenshi ziliao xuanji* (Selections from literary and historical materials) 50 (1986), pp. 246–252.

Chen Junren. "Kangzhan hou guomin zhengfu chuanye zhengce yu zhaoshang ju de fazhan" (Postwar shipping policies of the National Government and the development of the China Merchants Steam Navigation Company). *Guojia hanghai* (National shipping), no. 19, Shanghai: Shanghai guji chuban she, 2017, pp. 89–103.

Ch'en Li-fu. *The Storm Clouds Clear over China: The Memoir of Ch'en Li-fu, 1900–1993.* Stanford: Hoover Institution Press, 1994.

Chen Yung-fa. "Chiang Kai-shek and the Japanese Ichigo Offensive, 1944." In Laura De Giorgi and Guido Samarani, eds., *Chiang Kai-shek and His Time: New Historical and Historiographical Perspectives.* Venice: Sinica venetiana (2017), pp. 37–74.

Cheng, Linsun. *Banking in Modern China: Entrepreneurs, Professional Managers, and the Development of Chinese Banks, 1897–1937.* New York: Cambridge University Press, 2003.

Ch'i, Hsi-sheng. *Nationalist China at War: Military Defeats and Political Collapse, 1937–1945.* Ann Arbor: University of Michigan Press, 1982.

China at War. Chongqing, 1939–1941.

The China Weekly Review. Shanghai, 1945–1950.

Chou Shun-hsin. *The Chinese Inflation, 1937–1949.* New York: Columbia University Press, 1963.

Coble, Parks M. *China's War Reporters: The Legacy of Resistance against Japan.* Cambridge, MA: Harvard University Press, 2015.

Chinese Capitalists in Japan's New Order: The Occupied Lower Yangzi, 1937–1945. Berkeley: University of California Press, 2003.

The Shanghai Capitalists and the Nationalist Government of China, 1927–1937. Cambridge: Harvard East Asian Monographs, 1986.

"Zhou Zuomin and the Jincheng Bank." In Sherman Cochran, ed., *The Capitalist Dilemma in China's Communist Revolution.* Ithaca: East Asia Program, Cornell University, 2014, pp. 151–174.

Cochran, Sherman, ed. *The Capitalist Dilemma in China's Communist Revolution.* Ithaca: East Asia Program, Cornell University, 2014.

Combs, Matthew T. "Chongqing 1943: People's Livelihood, Price Control, and State Legitimacy." In Joseph W. Esherick and Matthew T. Combs, eds., *1943: China at the Crossroads.* Ithaca: Cornell East Asian Series, 2015, pp. 282–322.

Cui Meiming. "Song Ziwen zhuchi xia de Shanghai qu diwei chanye chuli ju" (The management of enemy and puppet property in the Shanghai area under T. V. Soong's direction). *Jindai shi yanjiu* (Research on modern history), vol. 1, 1988, pp. 267–268.

Currie, Lauchlin. Papers. Hoover Institution on War, Revolution, and Peace, Stanford University, Archives.

Dagong bao ("L'Impartial"). Chongqing, 1941–1946; Shanghai, 1946–1952.

Dai Hongchao. "Song Ziwen de siren caichan yu shifou gong wubi zhi pingxi" (An examination of whether or not T. V. Soong's private property involved corruption). In Wu Jingping, ed., *Song Ziwen shengping yu ziliao wenxian yanjiu* (T. V. Soong: personal wartime archives). Shanghai: Fudan daxue chuban she, 2010, pp. 393–399.

Eastman, Lloyd E. *The Abortive Revolution: China under Nationalist Rule, 1927–1937.* Cambridge: Harvard University Press, 1974.

"Nationalist China during the Nanking Decade, 1927–1937." In Lloyd E. Eastman, Jerome Ch'en, Suzanne Pepper, and Lyman P. Van Slyke, eds., *The Nationalist Era in China, 1927–1949.* Cambridge: Cambridge University Press, 1991, pp. 115–176.

Seeds of Destruction: Nationalist China in War and Revolution, 1937–1949. Stanford: Stanford University Press, 1984.

The Economic Information Service, Hong Kong. *How Chinese Officials Amass Millions.* New York: Committee for a Democratic Far Eastern Policy, 1948.

Esherick, Joseph W. ed. *Lost Chance in China: The World War II Dispatches of John S. Service.* New York: Random House, 1974.

Feng Bing and Wang Qiang. "A Study of Postwar Nationalist Government's Policies on Traitors' Properties, 1945 to 1949." *Chinese Studies in History*, vol. 49, no. 4, 2016, pp. 218–236.

Gillin, Donald G. *Falsifying China's History: The Case of Sterling Seagrave's* The Soong Dynasty. Stanford, CA: Hoover Institution, 1986.

Guancha (The observer). Shanghai, 1945–1950.

Hara Takeshi. "The Ichigo Offensive." In Mark Peattie, Edward Drea, and Hans Van de Ven, eds., *The Battle for China: Essays on the Military History of the Sino-Japanese War of 1937–1945.* Stanford: Stanford University Press, 2011, pp. 392–402.

Heng Dafeng. *Wang Yunwu pingzhuan* (A critical biography of Wang Yunwu). Shanghai: Shanghai shudian chuban she, 1999.

Henriot, Christian. "Shanghai Industries in the Civil War (1945–1947)." *Journal of Urban History*, vol. 43 (2015), pp. 744–766. https://doi.org/10.1177/009614 4214566977

Hinder, Eleanor. *Life and Labour in Shanghai.* New York: International Secretariat, Institute of Pacific Relations, 1944.

Ho Lien (He Lian). "The Reminiscences of Ho Lien (Franklin L. Ho), Chinese Oral History Project, East Asian Institute, Columbia University, 1967.

Huang, Grace C. "Creating a Public Face for Posterity: The Making of Chiang Kai-shek's Shilue Manuscripts," *Modern China*, vol. 36, no. 6 (2010), pp. 617–643.

"Madame Chiang's Visit to America." In Joseph W. Esherick and Matthew T. Combs, eds., *1943: China at the Crossroads.* Ithaca: East Asia Program Cornell, 2015, pp. 41–74.

Huang Yuanbin. "Jinyuan quan de faxing he tade bengkui" (The introduction of the gold yuan notes and their collapse). In *Fabi jinyuan yuan yu huangjin fengchao* (Legal tender, the gold yuan notes, and the gold unrest). Beijing: Wenshi ziliao chuban she, 1985, pp. 51–62.

Jackson, Isabella. *Shaping Modern Shanghai: Colonialism in China's Global City.* Cambridge: Cambridge University Press, 2018.

Jeans, Roger B. *The Marshall Mission to China, 1945–1947: The Letters and Diary of Colonel John Hart Caughey.* Lanham, MD: Rowman and Littlefield, 2011.

Ji Zhaojin. *A History of Modern Shanghai Banking: The Rise and Decline of China's Finance Capitalism.* Armonk, NY: M. E. Sharpe, 2003.

Jiang Zhongzheng zongtong dang'an: Shilue gaoben. (The Chiang Kai-shek collections: the chronological events), 82 vols. General ed. Wang Zhenghua. Taibei: Guoshi guan, 2003–2013.

King, Frank H. H. *The Hongkong Bank in the Period of Development and Nationalism: From Regional Bank to Multinational Group.* Vol. 4 of *The History of the Hongkong and Shanghai Banking Corporation.* Cambridge: Cambridge University Press, 1991.

Koo, Wellington [Gu Weijun]. "Wellington Koo Memoir." New York Times Oral History Project. Columbia University Oral History Project, 1978.

Kung, H. H. Papers. Hoover Institution on War, Revolution and Peace, Stanford University, Archives.

Kurtz-Phelan, Daniel. *The China Mission: George Marshall's Unfinished War, 1945–1947.* New York: W. W. Norton, 2018.

Lary, Diana. *China's Civil War: A Social History, 1945–1949.* Cambridge: Cambridge University Press, 2015.

The Chinese People at War: Human Suffering and Social Transformation, 1937–1945. Cambridge: Cambridge University Press, 2010.

Lewis, Gregory Scott. "Shades of Red and White: The Life and Political Career of Ji Chaoding, 1903–1963." Unpublished PhD dissertation, Arizona State University, 1999.

Li Huang, "The Reminiscences of Li Huang," Chinese Oral History Project, East Asian Institute of Columbia University, 1975.

Li, Laura Tyson. *Madame Chiang Kai-shek: China's Eternal First Lady.* New York: Atlantic Monthly Press, 2006.

Li, Lincoln. "An Alternative View on Occupation Policy: China's Resistance Potential." In David Pong, ed., *Resisting Japan: Mobilizing for War in Modern China, 1935–1945.* Norwalk, CT: EastBridge, 2008, pp. 79–104.

The Japanese Army in North China, 1937–1941: Problems of Political and Economic Control. Tokyo: Oxford University Press, 1975.

Li, T. G. *A China Past: Military and Diplomatic Memoires.* Lanham: University Press of America, 1989.

Lin, Hsiao-ting. *Accidental State: Chiang Kai-shek, the United States and the Making of Taiwan.* Cambridge: Harvard University Press, 2016.

"Chiang Kai-shek and the Cairo Summit." In Joseph W. Esherick and Matthew T. Combs, eds., *1943: China at the Crossroads.* Ithaca: Cornell East Asian Series, 2015, pp. 426–458.

"Wartime Sino-U.S. Relations Revisited: American Aid, Persona and Power Politics, 1938–1949." In Wu Jingping, ed., *Song Ziwen shengping yu ziliao wenxian yanjiu* (T. V. Soong: personal wartime archives). Shanghai: Fudan daxue chuban she, 2010, pp. 260–285.

Lin Meili. *Kangzhan shiqi de huobi zhangzheng.* (The currency war during the war of resistance period). Taibei: Guoli shifan daxue lishi yangjiu so, 1996.

Lin Xiaoting [Lin Hsiao-ting] and Wu Jingping, eds., *Song Ziwen yu waiguo renshi wanglai handian gao* (T. V. Soong: important wartime correspondences, 1940–1942). Shanghai: Fudan daxue chuban she, 2009.

Lin Xiaoting and Wu Jingping, eds. *Zhanshi mengyue: Song Ziwen yu waiguo renshi lai handian gao xinbian, 1940–1943* (T. V. Soong: selected wartime correspondences). Shanghai: Shanghai Fudan daxue chuban she, 2010.

Liu, Guoliang. *Zhongguo gongye shi xiandai juan* (A history of China's modern industry). Nanjing: Jiangsu kexue jichu chuban she, 2003.

Ma Yinchu. *Zhanshi jingji lunwen ji* (A collection of essays on the wartime economy). Chongqing: Zuojia shushi, 1945.

Ma Zhendu. "Song Ziwen yu xibei kaifa'" (T. V. Soong and the development of the northwest). In Wu Jingping, ed., *Song Ziwen shengping yu ziliao wenxian yanjiu* (T. V. Soong: personal wartime archives). Shanghai: Fudan daxue chuban she, 2010, pp. 96–113.

MacKinnon, Stephen R. *Wuhan, 1938: War, Refugees, and the Making of Modern China.* Berkeley: University of California Press, 2008.

Marks, Thomas A. *Counterrevolution in China: Wang Sheng and the Kuomintang.* London: Frank Cass, 1998.

Masuda Yoneji. *Shina senso keizai no kenkyu* (Research on China's wartime economy). Tokyo: Daiyamonda sha, 1944.

McCord, Edward. *The Power of the Gun: The Emergence of Modern Chinese Warlordism.* Berkeley: University of California Press, 1993.

Mi Qingyun. "Cong Chongqing dao Shanghai de jieshou jianwen" (From Chongqing to Shanghai, impressions of the takeover). In *Wenshi ziliao cungao xuanbian* (An edited collection of selections from literary and historical materials). Beijing: Zhongguo wen chuban she, 2002, vol. 7, pp. 736–740.

Mishler, Clayton. *Sampan Sailor: A Navy Man's Adventures in World War II China.* Washington, DC: Brassey's, 1994.

Mitter, Rana. *China's Good War: How World War II Is Shaping a New Nationalism.* Cambridge: Harvard University Press, 2020.

Morgenthau, III, Henry. *Mostly Morgenthaus: A Family History.* New York: Ticknor and Fields, 1991.

Nakamura Takafusa. "The Yen Bloc, 1931–1941." In Peter Duus, Ramon H. Myers, and Mark Peattie, eds., *The Japanese Wartime Empire, 1931–1945.* Princeton: Princeton University Press, 1996, pp. 171–186.

North China Daily News. Shanghai, 1945–1949.

Obayashi jimusho, ed. *Dai Toa senso daiichi nendo ni okeru Shanhai keizai no hensen* (Economic changes in Shanghai during the first year of the Great East Asia War). Shanghai: Obayashi jimusho, 1943.

Pakula, Hannah. *The Last Empress: Madame Chiang Kai-shek and the Birth of Modern China.* New York: Simon and Schuster, 2009.

Peattie, Mark, Edward Drea, and Hans Van de Ven, eds. *The Battle for China: Essays on the Military History of the Sino-Japanese War of 1937–1945*. Stanford: Stanford University Press, 2011.

Peng, Juanjuan. *The Yudahua Business Group in China's Early Industrialization*. Lanham: Lexington Books, 2020.

Peng Xiaoliang, ed. *Zhou Zuomin riji shuxin ji* (Zhou Zuomin, diary, and letters). Shanghai: Shanghai yuandong chuban she, 2014.

Pepper, Suzanne. *Civil War in China: The Political Struggle, 1945–1949*. Lanham: Rowman and Littlefield, 1999.

Preston, Paul and Michael Partridge, eds. *British Documents on Foreign Affairs: Reports and Papers from the Foreign Office Confidential Print*. Part II from 1940 through 1945; Series E, Asia. Bethesda: University Press of America, 1997.

Qi Chunfeng. "Kangzhan shiqi da houfang yu lunxian qujian de huobi liudong" (The flow of Guomindang currency between Chinese-controlled and enemy-occupied areas during the Resistance War against Japan). *Jindai shi yanjiu* (Research on modern history), no. 5 (2003), pp. 137–169.

Qian Keting. "Rong Desheng de jizhe zhaodai hui" (Rong Desheng's press conference). In *Shanghai wenshi ziliao xuanji* (A collection of Shanghai literary and historical materials), no. 73 (1993), pp. 201–204.

Ray, Jr., J. Franklin. Papers. Hoover Institution on War Revolution and Peace, Stanford University, Archives.

Reinhardt, Ann. *Navigating Semi-Colonialism: Shipping, Sovereignty, and Nation-Building in China, 1860–1937*. Cambridge: Harvard University Asia Center, 2018.

Sandilands, Roger J. *The Life and Political Economy of Lauchlin Currie: New Dealer, Presidential Adviser, and Developmental Economist*. Durham: Duke University Press, 1990.

Seagrave, Sterling. *The Soong Dynasty*. New York: Harper and Row, 1985.

Shanghai shehui kexue yuan, Jingji yanjiu suo, ed., *Rongjia qiye shiliao* (Historical materials on the Rong family enterprises). Shanghai: Shanghai renmin chuban she, 1980.

Shen Yunlong. "Dui jinyuan quan an yingjin yibu zhuizong yanjiu" (Advancing research on the matter of the gold yuan case). *Zhuanji wenxue* (Biographical literature), vol. 214 (March 1980), pp. 40–42.

Shenbao (Shanghai newspaper). Shanghai, 1945–1949.

Sherwood, Robert E. *Roosevelt and Hopkins: An Intimate History*. New York: Harper and Row, 1950.

Shidai gonglun (Contemporary public opinion). Guangzhou. 1946–1947.

Shidai pinglun (Contemporary critique). Kunming. 1947.

Shou Chongyi. "Jiang Jingguo Shanghai 'Daohu' ji" (A record of Jiang Jingguo striking big tigers in Shanghai). In *Fabi jinyuan quan yu huangjin fengchao*. Beijing: Wenshi ziliao chuban she, 1985, pp. 77–84.

— *Kong Xiangxi qiren qishi* (H. H. Kung, the man, and his affairs). Beijing: Zhongguo wenshi chuban she, 1987.

Shou Jinhua. *Zhanshi Zhongguo de yinhang ye* (China's wartime banking industry). n.p., 1944.

Smith, Bruce. Papers. Hoover Institution on War, Revolution and Peace, Stanford University, Archives.

Song Shiqi and Yan Jingzheng, eds. *Jizhe bixia de kangri zhangzheng* (The writing of reporters in the war of resistance). Beijing: Renmin ribao chuban she, 1995.

Soong, T. V. Papers. Hoover Institution on War, Revolution and Peace, Stanford University, Archives.

Strauss, Julia. *Strong Institutions in Weak Polities: State Building in Republican China, 1927–1940.* Oxford: Oxford University Press, 1998.

Sze, Sao-ke Alfred. *Reminiscences of His Early Years, As Told to Anming Fu.* Washington, DC: n.p., 1962.

Tan, Ying Jia. *Recharging China in War and Revolution, 1882–1955.* Ithaca, NY: Cornell University Press, 2022.

Tanner, Harold M. *The Battle for Manchuria and the Fate of China: Siping, 1946.* Bloomington: Indiana University Press, 2013.

Tao Juyin. *Gudao jianwen: Kangzhan shiqi de Shanghai* (Experiences in the solitary island: Shanghai during the war of resistance). Shanghai: Shanghai renmin chuban she, 1979.

Taylor, Jay. *The Generalissimo's Son: Chiang Ching-kuo and the Revolutions in China and Taiwan.* Cambridge, MA: Harvard University Press, 2000.

Thai, Philip. *China's War on Smuggling: Law, Economic Life, and the Making of the Modern State, 1842–1965.* New York: Columbia University Press, 2018.

Tillman, Margaret Mih. *Raising China's Revolutionaries: Modernizing Childhood for Cosmopolitan Nationalists and Liberated Comrades, 1920s–1950s.* New York: Columbia University Press, 2018.

Truman, Harry S. *Memoirs: Vol. 1: Years of Decisions.* Garden City: Doubleday, 1955.

Tso Shun-sheng. "The Reminiscences of Tso Shun-sheng." Chinese Oral History Project, East Asian Institute of Columbia University, 1975.

United Kingdom. Foreign Office Files for China, 1918–1980. Adam Mathew, Archives Direct.

United Kingdom, Public Records Office.

United States. Consulate, Shanghai, China. Chinese Press Review. 1945–1949.

United States, Department of State. Office of the Historian. *Foreign Relations of the United States, Diplomatic Papers*: 1944, vol. 6, *China*; 1945, vol. 7, *The Far East*, vol. 8, *The Far East*, 1973.

United States, Department of State. Office of Intelligence Coordination and Liaison. "Developments in the State Control of Chinese Industries," July 17, 1946.

United States, Department of State. Office of Intelligence Coordination and Liaison. "Trends Towards State Control of Industry in China," August 20, 1946.

United States, Department of State. Office of Intelligence Research. "Themes in the Chinese National Budget." 1947.

United States, Department of State. Office of Intelligence Research. "The Trend of Inflation in China, 1946–1947." Secret Report. March 18, 1947.

United States: Department of State. Office of Intelligence Research, Division of Research for Far East. "Resume of Postwar Labor Developments in Nationalist China." November 1, 1946.

United States: Department of State. Office of Intelligence Research, Division of Research for Far East. "Wartime and Postwar Status of the Silk Industry in the Far East: China." 1947.

United States, Office of Strategic Services. *Programs of Japan in China with Biographies. Extracts from FCC Intercepts of Short Wave Broadcasts from Radio Tokyo and Affiliated Stations, December 1941–March 1, 1945.* Honolulu, 1945.

UNRRA China Office. Papers. Hoover Institution on War Revolution and Peace, Stanford University, Archives.

Van de Ven, Hans. *China at War: Triumph and Tragedy in the Emergence of New China.* Cambridge, MA: Harvard University Press, 2018.

Wakeman, Jr. Frederic. *Spymaster: Dai Li and the Chinese Secret Service.* Berkeley: University of California Press, 2003.

Wang Chaoguang. "Guanyu 'guanliao ziben' de zhenglun yu guomin zhizheng de weiji" (Regarding the bureaucratic capitalism controversy and the crisis of governing by the Guomindang). *Minguo dang'an* (Republican archives), vol. 2 (2008), pp. 105–111.

"Guanyu Guomindang zhengfu gaoji guanyuan ziren caichan de yili diaochao" (An investigation into one case of private wealth of high-level officials of the Guomingdang government). *Jindai shi yanjiu* (Research on modern history), vol. 3 (2000), pp. 297–305.

"Jianbuduan libuluan – kangzhan zhonghou qi de Jiang Kong Song guanxi" (Unending chaos: The relationship between Chiang Kai-shek, H. H. Kung, and T. V. Soong during and after the war of resistance). In Wu Jingping, ed., *Song Ziwen shengping yu ziliao wenxian yanjiu.* Shanghai: Fudan dauxue chuban she, 2010, pp. 209–232.

"Sheng yu moshi yunbian xiao: Song Ziwen churen xingzheng yuan qianhou jingwei zhi yanjiu" (Fading away in the final years: Research on T. V. Soong before and after heading the Executive Yuan), in Wu Jingping, ed., *Song Ziwen yu zhanshi Zhongguo.* Shanghai: Fudan daxue chuban she, 2008, pp. 284–300

Zhongguo mingyun de juezhan, 1945–1949 (The decisive war for China's fate, 1945–1949). Nanjing: Jiangsu renmin chuben she, 2006.

Wang, Fan-sen. *Fu Ssu-nien: A Life in Chinese History and Politics.* New York: Cambridge University Press, 2000.

Wang Feng. *Jiang Jieshi fuzi 1949 weiji dang'an* (Archives on the crisis of 1949: Chiang Kai-shek, father and son). Taibei: Shangzhou chuban she, 2008.

Wang Ju. *Jindai Shanghai mianfang ye de zuihou huihuang, 1945–1949* (The final flourishing of the modern Shanghai cotton textile industry). Shanghai: Shanghai shehui kexue yuan, 2003.

Wang, Ke-wen. "Collaborators and Capitalists: The Politics of 'Material Control' in Wartime Shanghai." *Chinese Studies in History,* vol. 26, no. 1 (Fall 1992), pp. 42–62.

Wang Qisheng. "The Battle of Hunan and the Chinese Military's Response to Operation Ichigo." In Mark Peattie, Edward J. Drea, and Hans Van de Ven, eds., *The Battle for China: Essays on the Military History of the Sino-Japanese War of 1937–1945.* Stanford: Stanford University Press, 2011, pp. 403–418.

Wang Yunwu. *1948 dafeng dalang: Wang Yunwu congzheng huiyi lu* (The great wind and waves of 1948: Wang Yunwu's memories of his record in government). Taibei: Taiwan shangwu, 2010.

Wanyan Shaoyuan. *Da jieshou* (The great takeover). Shanghai: Shanghai yuandong chuban she, 1995.

Wedemeyer, Albert C. Papers. Hoover Institution on War, Revolution and Peace, Stanford University, Archives.

Wei, C. X. George. *Sino-American Economic Relations, 1944–1949.* Westport: Greenwood Press, 1997.

Westad, Odd Arne. *Decisive Encounters: The Chinese Civil War, 1946–1950.* Stanford: Stanford University Press, 2003.

White, Theodore and Annalee Jacoby. *Thunder Out of China.* New York: William Sloane Associates, 1946.

Woodbridge, George, compiler. *UNRRA: The History of the United Nations Relief and Rehabilitation Administration.* New York: Columbia University Press, 1950.

Wu Guozhen. *Cong Shanghai shichang zhi "Taiwan sheng zhuxi"* (From mayor of Shanghai to chairman of Taiwan province). Shanghai: Shanghai renmin chuban she, 1999.

Wu Jingping. "Jinyuan quan zhengce de zai yanjiu" (On the study of the gold yuan policy). *Minguo dang'an* (Republican Archives). 2004, no. 1, pp. 99–110.

"Kangzhan shiqi Song Ziwen yu Kong Xiangxi zhi guanxi zhi shuping" (A review of the relationship between T. V. Soong and H. H. Kung during the war period). In Wu Jingping, ed., *Song Ziwen shengping yu ziliao wenxian yanjiu* (T. V. Soong: personal wartime archives). Shanghai: Fudan daxue chuban she, 2010, pp. 189–208.

Wu Jingping, ed. *Minguo renwu de zai yanjiu yu zai pingjie* (The restudy and revaluation of the Republic of China's leadership). Shanghai: Fudan daxue chuban she, 2013.

Wu Jingping. "Song Ziwen lungang" (A brief discussion of T. V. Soong). *Lishi yanjiu* (Historical research), vol. 6 (1991), pp. 106–121.

Wu Jingping, ed. *Song Ziwen shengping yu ziliao wenxian yanjiu* (T. V. Soong: personal wartime archives). Shanghai: Fudan daxue chuban she, 2010.

Wu Jingping, ed. *Song Ziwen yu zhanshi Zhongguo, 1937–1945* (T. V. Soong and wartime China). Shanghai: Fudan daxue chuban she, 2008.

Wu Jingping. *Song Ziwen zhengzhi shengya biannian* (A chronology of the political career of T. V. Soong). Fuzhou: Fujian renmin chuban she, 1998.

Wu Jingping and Guo Daijun [Kuo Tai-chun], eds. *Song Ziwen zhu Mei shiqi dianbao xuan, 1940–1943* (Select telegrams between Chiang Kai-shek and T. V. Soong, 1940–1943). Shanghai: Fudan daxue chuban she, 2008.

Wu Qiyuan. *You zhanshi jingji dao pingshi jingji* (From a wartime economy to a peacetime economy). Shanghai: Dadong shuju, 1946.

Wu Song, Jiang Shimin, and Rao Fanghu. *Dai caifa Kong Xiangxi zhuan* (A biography of the big tycoon H. H. Kung). Wuhan: Wuhan chuban she, 1995.

Wu Xiangxiang. "Wang Yunwu yu jinyuan quan de faxing" (Wang Yunwu and the issuance of gold yuan notes). *Zhuanji wenxue* (Biographical literature), vol. 213 (February 1980), pp. 44–50.

Xia, Yun. *Down with Traitors: Justice and Nationalism in Wartime China.* Seattle: University of Washington Press, 2017.

Xiao Ruping. "Kangzhan shengli hou Zhejiang de shanhou jiuji" (Relief aid in Zhejiang after the victory in the war of resistance). *Kangri zhanzheng yanjiu* (Journal of research on the war of resistance against Japan), vol. 1 (2013), pp. 126–128.

Xu Bingsheng. "Guomindang xingzheng yuan yuanhui jianwen" (Information on the meetings of the Guomindang Executive Yuan). *Shanghai wenshi ziliao xuanji* (Selections from literary and historical material, Shanghai), vol. 43 (1983), pp. 122–132.

Yang Peixin. *Jiu Zhongguo de tonghuo pengzhang* (Currency inflation in old China). Beijing: Renmin chuban she chuban, 1985.

Yang Tianshi. "Jiang Kong guanxi tanwei" (An exploration of the Chiang–Kung relationship). *Minguo dang'an* (Republican archives), vol. 4 (1992), pp. 115–120.

Kangzhan yu zhanhou Zhongguo (Wartime and postwar China). Beijing: Zhongguo renmin daxue chuban she, 2007.

Yang Tianshi wenji (The collected works of Yang Tianshi). Shanghai: Shanghai Cishu chuban she, 2005.

Zhaoxun zhenshi de Jiang Jieshi: Jiang Jieshi riji jiedu (Seeking the real Chiang Kai-shek: Reading the Chiang Kai-shek diary), 2 vols. Taiyuan: Shanxi renmin chuban she, 2008.

Yao Songling. "Jingdao Zhang Gongquan xiansheng" (In memory of Zhang Jia'ao). *Zhuanji wenxue* (Biographical literature), vol. 211 (December 1979), pp. 64–68.

Yin Xiqi. "Waihui tongzhi xin zhengce zhi jiantao" (An examination of the new policy to control foreign exchange). *Dongfang zazhi* (The eastern miscellany), vol. 36, no. 2 (February 1, 1938), p. 19.

Yinhang zhoubao (Bankers' weekly). Shanghai. 1917–1948.

Young, Arthur N. *China's Wartime Finance and Inflation*. Cambridge: Harvard University Press, 1965.

China and the Helping Hand, 1937–1945. Cambridge: Harvard University Press, 1963.

Cycle of Cathay: An Historical Perspective. Vista: Ibis Publishing Company, 1997.

Young, Arthur N. Papers. Hoover Institution on War, Revolution and Peace, Stanford University, Archives.

Zaisheng (The national renaissance). Shanghai and Guangzhou, 1946–1949.

Zheng Huixin. "Cong Song Ziwen fumei qijian dianbao kan zhanshi Chongqing guanchang yidong" (Telegrams from T. V. Soong during the period when he was in America observing the war situation in Chongqing). In Wu Jingping, ed., *Song Ziwen shengping yu ziliao wenxian yanjiu* (T. V. Soong: personal wartime archives). Shanghai: Fudan daxue chuban she, 2010, pp. 233–259.

Cong touzi gongsi dao "Guanban shangxing"; Zhongguo jiangshe yin gongsi de chuangli ji qi jingying huodong (From private investment company to state enterprise: The development and operation of the China Development Finance Corporation). Hong Kong: Zhongwen daxue chuban she, 2001.

"Meijin gongzhai wubi an de fasheng ji chuli jingguo" (The US dollar bond embezzlement scandal and its handling). *Lishi yanjiu* (Historical research), vol. 4 (2009), pp. 99–123.

Minguo zhengfu zhanshi tongzhi jingji yu maoyi yanjiu, 1937–1945 (Research into economic control and trade during wartime period of the Nationalist Government 1937–1945). Shanghai: Shanghai shehui kexue yuan chuban she, 2009.

"Zhanhou zhongguo de 'guanban shanghang'" (Bureaucratic capitalism after the war). *Minguo dang'an* (Republican archives), vol. 1 (2014), pp. 134–143.

"Zhanhou guanban shangxing de xingqi: yi zhongguo fuzhong shiye gongsi de chuangli weili" (The emergence of state enterprises after the war: The establishment of the Fuzhong Corporation). *Zhongguo jingji shi yanjiu* (Research on Chinese economic history), vol. 4 (2009), pp. 119–122.

Zhongguo di'erh lishi dang'an guan, ed. "1946 nian Rong Desheng bei bangjia an shiliao erjian" (Two documents of historical materials on the 1946 kidnapping of Rong Deshen). *Minguo dang'an* (Republican archives), vol. 1 (2001), pp. 31–33.

Zhongguo renmin kangri zhanzheng jinian guan, ed. *Kangzhan jishi* (Memoranda of the war of resistance). Bejing: Zhongguo youyi chuban she, 1989.

Zhongguo renmin yinhang zonghang canshi shi, ed. *Zhonghua minguo huobi shi ziliao* (Historical materials on the currency of Republican China). Shanghai: Shanghai renmin chuban she, 1991.

Zhongguo renmin zhengzhi xieshang huiyi, Quanguo weiyuan hui, wenshi ziliao yanjiu wenyuan hui. *Fabi jinyuan quan yu huangjin fengchao* (Legal tender, the gold yuan note, and the gold unrest). Beijing: Wenshi ziliao chuban she, 1985.

Zhu Chuxin. "Sannian lai de women de huobe zhan" (The war of the enemy against our currency in the last three years). *Dushu yuebao* (Readers monthly), vol. 1, no. 11 (January 1, 1940), pp. 485–488.

Index